Cost-Effective
Risk Assessment
for Process Design

Other McGraw-Hill Chemical Engineering Books of Interest

BRUNNER • *Hazardous Waste Incineration*

COOK, DUMONT • *Process Drying Practice*

CHOPEY • *Environmental Engineering in the Process Plant*

CHOPEY • *Handbook of Chemical Engineering Calculations*

CROOM • *Filter Dust Collectors*

DEAN • *Analytical Chemistry Handbook*

DEAN • *Lange's Handbook of Chemistry*

DILLON • *Materials Selection for the Chemical Process Industries*

FREEMAN • *Hazardous Waste Minimization*

FREEMAN • *Industrial Pollution Prevention Handbook*

FREEMAN • *Standard Handbook of Hazardous Waste Treatment and Disposal*

KISTER • *Distillation Design*

KISTER • *Distillation Operation*

KOLLURU • *Environmental Strategies Handbook*

LEVIN, GEALT • *Biotreatment of Industrial Hazardous Waste*

McGEE • *Molecular Engineering*

MANSFIELD • *Engineering Design for Process Facilities*

MILLER • *Flow Measurement Handbook*

PALLUZI • *Pilot Plant and Laboratory Safety*

PALLUZI • *Pilot Plant Design, Construction and Operation*

PERRY, GREEN • *Perry's Chemical Engineers' Handbook*

POWER • *Steam Jet Ejectors for the Process Industries*

REID ET AL. • *Properties of Gases and Liquids*

REIST • *Introduction to Aerosol Science*

SATTERFIELD • *Heterogenous Catalysis in Practice*

SHINSKEY • *Feedback Controllers for the Process Industries*

SHINSKEY • *Process Control Systems*

SHUGAR, DEAN • *The Chemist's Ready Reference Handbook*

SHUGAR, BALLINGER • *The Chemical Technicians' Ready Reference Handbook*

SMITH, VAN LAAN • *Piping and Pipe Support Systems*

STOCK • *AI in Process Control*

TATTERSON • *Fluid Mixing and Gas Dispersion in Agitate Tanks*

TATTERSON • *Scale-up of Industrial Mixing Processes*

WILLIG • *Environmental TQM*

YOKELL • *A Working Guide to Shell-and-Tube Heat Exchangers*

Cost-Effective Risk Assessment for Process Design

Robert D. Deshotels

Robert Zimmerman
Editors

McGraw-Hill, Inc.
New York   San Francisco   Washington, D.C.   Auckland   Bogotá
Caracas   Lisbon   London   Madrid   Mexico City   Milan
Montreal   New Delhi   San Juan   Singapore
Sydney   Tokyo   Toronto

Library of Congress Cataloging-in-Publication Data

Cost-effective risk assessment for process design / Robert L.
  Deshotels, Robert D. Zimmerman, editors.
        p.   cm.
  Includes index.
  ISBN 0-07-006463-6
  1. Factories—Design and construction.   2. Risk assessment.
  I. Deshotels, Robert L.   II. Zimmerman, Robert D. (Robert Dale).
  TS177.C67 1995
  725'.4'0289—dc20   94-43007
                                                            CIP

1 2 3 4 5 6 7 8 9 0   DOC/DOC   9 0 0 9 8 7 6 5

ISBN 0-07-006463-6

*The sponsoring editor for this book was Gail Nalven, the editing supervi-
sor was Ruth W. Mannino, and the production supervisor was Suzanne
W. S. Rapcavage. It was set in New Century Schoolbook by Ron Painter
of McGraw-Hill's Professional Book Group composition unit.*

Printed and bound by R. R. Donnelley & Sons Company.

This book is printed on recycled, acid-free paper containing
a minimum of 50% recycled, de-inked fiber.

McGraw-Hill books are available at special quantity discounts to use
as premiums and sales promotions, or for use in corporate training programs. For more information, please write to the Director of Special
Sales, McGraw-Hill, Inc., 11 West 19th Street, New York, NY 10011.
Or contact your local bookstore.

Contents

Contributors

Lisa M. Bendixen *Director, Safety and Risk, Arthur D. Little, Inc., Cambridge, Massachusetts* (CHAP. 8)

Evaristo J. Bonano, Ph.D. *President, Beta Corporation International, Albuquerque, New Mexico* (CHAP. 1)

Robert Deshotels *Principal Process Engineer, Fluor Daniel, Inc., Irvine, California* (PREF., CHAP. 4)

Charles E. Fryman *Manager, Health, Safety, and Environmental, BP Oil Company, Cleveland, Ohio* (INTRO.)

Michael Kalfopoulos *Risk and Safety Consultant, Arthur D. Little, Inc., Cambridge, Massachusetts* (CHAP. 8)

Mardy Kazarians, Ph.D. *Principal, Kazarians & Associates, Glendale, California* (CHAP. 5)

Peter LeRoy *Engineering Supervisor, Duke Engineering & Services, Inc., Charlotte, North Carolina* (CHAP. 11, IN PART)

Thomas C. McKelvey *Principal Engineer, Four Elements, Columbus, Ohio* (CHAPS. 4, 9)

Najmedin Meshkati, Ph.D., C.E.P. *Associate Professor and Associate Executive Director for Professional Programs, Institute of Safety and Systems Management, University of Southern California, Los Angeles, California* (CHAP. 6)

Krishna S. Mudan, Ph.D. *President, U.S. Operations, Four Elements, Columbus, Ohio* (CHAP. 7)

Philip M. Myers *Senior Engineer, Four Elements, Columbus, Ohio* (CHAP. 9)

Gareth W. Parry, Ph.D. *Senior Executive Consultant, NUS, Gaithersburg, Maryland* (CHAP. 9)

Jatin N. Shah *Senior Engineer, Four Elements, Columbus, Ohio* (CHAP. 7)

R. Peter Stickles *Director, Safety and Risk, Arthur D. Little, Inc., Cambridge, Massachusetts* (CHAP. 3)

Robert D. Zimmerman *Nuclear Process Principal Engineer, Fluor Daniel, Inc., Irvine, California* (CHAPS. 2, 11)

Preface

Cost-effectiveness distinguishes engineering from pure science and puttering. The cost and effectiveness of a risk-analysis effort depend on the methods chosen, the degree of quantification, the level of detail, and the extent of independent review. Overall, the analysis must remain focused on providing only that information needed for making risk-reduction decisions concerning the design or operation of the facility. The final independent review of these decisions is usually voiced by the members of the public who feel they could be affected by the facility and who have their own objectives and values.

A cost-effective approach is advocated in this book; however, to be fair, some reasons for not attempting cost-effective analysis should be stated: A standard "cookbook" approach to analysis requires less expertise and judgment for both the producer of the analysis and the reviewers. When all companies or individuals analyze with the same method, no single company or individual will be blamed if the method does not yield good results. Although the money wasted on unneeded analysis in one area could have reduced serious problems elsewhere, "elsewhere" is someone else's problem.

This book is intended for a consultant or professor in the field of risk analysis, an engineer designing part of a facility, an engineering supervisor or manager responsible for choice of design methods and budgets, a client representative reviewing the design or analysis, a safety manager of an operating company, those who influence or contribute to government regulations, and technically inclined concerned citizens. The book applies to the design of facilities in the fuel, chemical, environmental remediation, and nuclear (nonreactor) industries.

By using this book, the reader can control the risk-assessment effort (even though there is uncertainty concerning the outcome) by choosing the analysis method and depth of analysis, evaluating the effectiveness of the analysis as it proceeds, and anticipating public concern.

This book demonstrates that cost-effectiveness can be achieved without placing a monetary value on human life. This book's answer to the question, "How much safety study is enough?" fills the gap left by other resources that address the related topics of designing for process safety, hazard-evaluation methods, decision making under uncertainty, and risk management. Each author in this book refers to many excellent publications concerning the various related topics.

The authors are experts from academia, engineering, and consulting who share the belief that facility owners and the public deserve cost-effective risk management. The authors collectively demonstrate a variety of good approaches. The choice of analysis method and depth of analysis goes beyond two levels (quantitative and qualitative). So-called qualitative methods can yield quantitative results, but with a greater degree of uncertainty than so-called quantitative methods. The authors explore many quantitative levels, determined by the analysis methods, modeling assumptions, and data sources. The best analysis approach is the one that uses the least effort to reduce uncertainty to the level needed for deciding between specific design options.

The chapter on human factors is different because it presents concepts rather than methods. Methods have been developed in the nuclear power industry for incorporating human factors into the user interface in control rooms. Without any increase in hardware cost, human factors improvements have been shown to greatly increase operator effectiveness. Unfortunately, human factors expertise is rarely applied to field operations. Given the importance of human error as a contributor to past catastrophes and the fact that design features can vary the rate of error by several multiples, experts should be encouraged to develop approaches suitable for field operations. Human factors improvement seems especially likely for intensive field operations such as chemical loading or refinery decoking.

Robert Deshotels

Introduction

Faced with ever-increasing costs and the need to remain competitive in the marketplace, private industry is almost constantly looking for less expensive and smarter ways to get the job done. This book is unique among those currently available on the market in that it addresses the cost-effective aspects of conducting traditional risk-assessment activities. It seeks to educate private industry, risk-assessment consultants, and regulatory agencies on getting the most out of risk-assessment activities with the least amount of cost.

Audiences for This Book

This book advises the consumer on the cost-conscious application of the various risk-assessment tools available. Some third-party consultants provide risk-assessment services that are matched to the willingness of their customers to pay and not the minimum amount of work needed to complete the job. Since their fees are based on the amount of work performed, third-party consultants lack some incentives to meet their customers' needs in a truly cost-effective manner. In a similarly wasteful manner, some internal company consultants in private industry provide overly sophisticated risk-assessment services, where less costly and less time-consuming services would be appropriate.

Risk-assessment consultants, both third-party and private industry's internal consultants, can learn about more cost-effective approaches and thus be in a better position to serve their customers. As customers become more educated about risk-assessment services, they will be able to demand more cost control. It would be more profitable for consultants to suggest these cost-effective approaches before being asked by their customers or losing work to competitors who have adopted these approaches.

It also can be hoped that regulators will be moved toward more application of risk-based regulations that use both cost-effective risk-assessment methodologies and cost-effective mitigating or control actions. Given their limited resources and heavy responsibilities, regulators should view cost-effective approaches as a way to help reduce risks working in partnership with industry. Risk assessment and cost control are two dominant themes currently operating at the federal legislative and regulatory levels, as well as in many state agencies and legislatures. It is hoped that this book may provide regulators insight into less expensive methods of risk-assessment that accomplish the same end result.

Risk versus Hazard

Although I have been practicing risk assessment in the health, safety, and environmental (HSE) areas within the petrochemical process industry for more than 20 years, I am constantly surprised at the number of HSE professionals who do not understand the difference between the terms *risk* and *hazard*. An important point to note is that this book focuses on risk assessment, not hazard analysis.

According to the Center for Chemical Process Safety, "hazard is a chemical or physical condition that has the potential for causing damage to people, property or the environment," and "risk is a measure of economic loss or human injury in terms of both the incident likelihood and the magnitude of the loss or injury." More simply stated, hazard is a measure of the potential to cause harm, whereas risk is a measure of the harm actually occurring. In my view, the significance of the difference between risk and hazard lies in the ability to more effectively manage risk, whereas hazards must be either tolerated or eliminated completely.

What Is Enough?

In the area of risk assessment, we are almost constantly asking ourselves the question, "What and how much is enough?" For example, we must determine what risk-assessment tools to use to study a particular problem. We must decide where to draw the boundaries for the risk assessment, which hazards are important, and which will not be included in our study. We must decide on the use of either a qualitative or a quantitative approach, recognizing and accepting the limitations of the different methods. And we must decide initially how much study is really needed to address the customer's concerns properly; often one study leads to another and sometimes yet another.

All the aforementioned questions and concerns are valid and need to be answered. But they should be answered in a cost-conscious context that does not result in wasted efforts or an overkill approach. Also, the extent of the risk assessment and analysis should be proportional to the risks being analyzed; $40,000 should not be spent for a risk assessment to study ways to mitigate a consequence of, say, $80,000.

Let me offer an example using a real-life situation we faced at our petroleum refineries within BP. Under OSHA's Process Safety Management Standard, we are required to evaluate the siting of process buildings. The greatest hazard to occupants of process buildings is from explosions, and we chose to use a risk-based approach to screen all the process buildings. A workbook was assembled for use by site safety professionals; the workbook contained refinery-specific information on hazards, frequencies, consequences, and mitigations presented in a step-by-step procedural format. The output of the workbook exercise included personnel and economic risk exposures and was an inexpensive screening tool that avoided the need for expensive studies of all buildings. The workbook exercise for an entire refinery could be completed within about 40 employee-hours using only site professionals. Thus, there was a significant cost savings over alternative approaches that would have relied on more sophisticated risk assessments using experts external to the site.

I suggest that readers of this book try to identify how they would actually apply the information presented to achieve cost savings in their operations and technical support activities.

Hazard Surveys

In the U.S. petrochemical process industry, the OSHA *Process Safety Management (PSM) Standard* requires that process hazards analyses (PHAs) be conducted for all covered processes. Covered processes include virtually every processing unit in a petroleum refinery or a large petrochemical plant. However, the PHA is a bit of a misnomer because it really results in the identification of hazards, using such tools as hazard and operability (HAZOP) studies, what-if reviews, checklists, and the like to identify the major hazards of concern; there is actually very little hazards analysis done in a PHA. When properly done, the PHA should identify all the major hazards as the starting point for conducting further studies of these hazards and deciding whether they need to be mitigated.

Again, considering cost savings applications, PHAs—or any hazards survey—can be done more cost-effectively by sharing information among similar process operations, thus saving time and expense in "reinventing the wheel" and providing assurances that all the hazards have been considered. For example, most crude distillation units are very similar, and it follows that the hazards associated with one will be similar to the hazards associated with another. However, this is not to say that one should not examine the specific process unit, because each process unit will be somewhat unique. Databases of these hazards are often available within a company or through other sources; for example, BP maintains a comprehensive collection of refinery and petrochemical plant incident reports covering the period beginning in 1971 through to the present.

PSM then requires that the identified hazards be addressed. In addressing the hazards, one needs to determine whether to tolerate, terminate, or mitigate the consequences of the hazard. This can best be done by a risk-analysis approach that considers the frequency of the event and the consequences.

Frequency of the Event and Consequence Evaluation

Since these two steps—frequency of the event and consequence evaluation—usually require the majority of risk-assessment resources, it is appropriate that considerable attention be directed at accomplishing this activity in the most cost-effective manner.

Following the hazard survey, the next major step in assessing risks is the evaluation of event frequencies. This can be done in either a qualitative manner (e.g., once in the lifetime of the plant) or in a quantitative manner (e.g., 5.4×10^{-3} times per year). The same sort of cost savings strategies can be applied to frequency evaluations as to the hazard survey discussed above, that is, sharing of data among similar process operations. Lacking specific failure frequencies for the process unit being evaluated, most consultants will use generic information (e.g., pump and piping failures).

Although it is necessary to determine the failure frequencies for all the events identified in the hazards survey, many of the events will produce consequences (damaged equipment, production losses, etc.) of a magnitude that is acceptable to the company. Rather than include those events in the detailed study, a more cost-effective approach would be to drop them entirely from the risk-assessment study.

Cost-Benefit Analysis of Mitigation Measures

Risk-reduction or risk-mitigation measures should be implemented based on their effectiveness. Thus, the estimated reduction in risk attributable to each measure should be determined and then compared with the installation and operating costs. Seeking to spend their money wisely, most managers in private industry would agree that the more cost-beneficial risk-reduction measures should be implemented first.

In order to perform a cost-benefit analysis, the costs associated with the various consequential losses and the risk-mitigation measures must be established. Consequential losses include those for equipment, business interruption, and human life and health. We have used this cost-benefit approach successfully in BP for many years now and look forward to using it even more in the future.

In some very few cases, public or employee outrage will be present such that it is difficult to argue for cost-benefit analysis. We must then rely on our ability to involve our publics and to openly communicate with them. BP uses an approach where internal company standards are only the starting point in controlling both on-site and off-site risks; the ultimate risk mitigations are based on open dialogue with and involvement of the stakeholders, in a manner that seeks to understand and address their concerns.

Closing Comments

I hope you find this book useful. It should result in the more cost-effective use of risk-assessment techniques, thus freeing up money to reduce more risks and allowing industry to become more successful in this competitive environment. As I mentioned earlier, I think you should challenge yourselves to identify how you would actually apply in your operations the cost-effective ideas presented in this book.

Charles E. Fryman

Decision Making under Uncertainty and Risk Assessment

Evaristo J. Bonano
Beta Corporation International

1.1 Introduction

Everyone faces the challenge at one time or another of having to select an alternative course of action from among a set of plausible ones. The decision could be as simple as whether or not to take an umbrella to work because the weather forecaster predicted a 50 percent chance of rain or as complicated as deciding whether a major overhaul is needed at a chemical plant to comply with new environmental regulations or where to site and construct a waste-disposal facility.

Many decisions are not easy to make for reasons such as (1) one cannot forecast the "right" solution and (2) the information available is not uniform across all alternatives or is incomplete; i.e., there is more information about some alternatives than about others. The factors that influence a decision in many instances are beyond one's control. These difficulties notwithstanding, a decision must be made, for the "no action" alternative is often not acceptable. The senior executive who is responsible for the management and operation of a chemical plant cannot ignore environmental regulations, for doing so will most likely result in civil and/or criminal penalties. Likewise, ignoring the need for the siting and construction of a waste-disposal facility may be unacceptable because the storage of wastes at present may be posing intolerably high risks to human health and safety and to the environment.

Finally, vacillating over whether to take an umbrella to work for too long could cause one to arrive late at the office, a situation that many bosses will not look upon favorably.

All decisions have associated consequences; however, such consequences are not known a priori. If one decides not to take an umbrella to work and it does not rain, then it was the "right" decision; on the other hand, if it rains, then it was the "wrong" decision. Obviously, the consequences of making the wrong decision in this particular example are minimal because it affects only one individual. Chances are that one would "play it safe" (i.e., be conservative) and take the umbrella to work because the associated cost is also minimal. For more complex decisions, such as the siting of a waste-disposal facility or the overhaul of a chemical plant, the consequences of the decision could be of major proportions and affect a large segment of society, and being conservative could be prohibitively expensive. Obviously, in this case, the decision needs to be made more carefully and involves more than one individual or groups of individuals as well as the use of a more formal process for making the decision.

This chapter presents a decision-making process as a generic framework that is applicable to a wide variety of situations from simple decisions to more complex ones. The level of rigor and formalism with which the process is applied needs to be commensurate with the scope and nature of decision. Uncertainties affecting the decision need to be considered explicitly, and risk assessment provides the template for considering the uncertainties and estimating the potential consequences of a decision. Risk management weighs the impacts from various alternatives and is the underpinning for arriving at a decision. It is not the purpose of this chapter to provide a complete treatise on the subject of decision analysis, risk assessment, uncertainty analysis, or risk management, for the literature abounds with treatises that address this subject in far more depth and breadth than is possible here. Rather, the intent is to provide a general snapshot of how these four topics are interrelated and to set the stage for the more detailed chapters that follow in this book. In preparing this chapter, material has been used from numerous references in the literature and careful attention has been paid to ensure that these references are duly noted as guidance for the reader who may want to examine any of the subjects or issues herein discussed in more detail.

1.2 Decision-Making Process

The issue is not whether decisions will or will not be made, but rather how one should go about making those decisions in light of the afore-

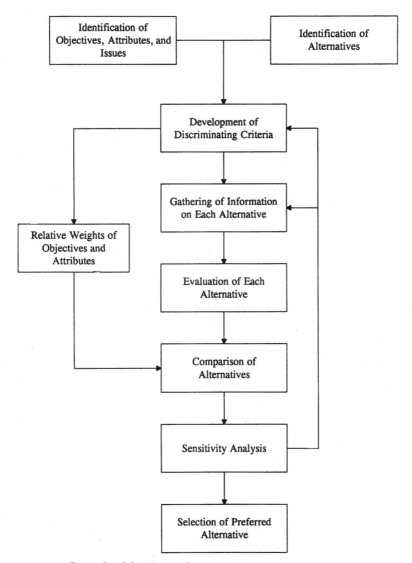

Figure 1.1 Generalized decision-making process.

mentioned difficulties. One approach is to use a systematic and transparent process for arriving at a decision; another is to rely on a more ad hoc process. Regardless of the level of rigor with which it is implemented, the decision-making process consists of five basic steps (Fig. 1.1):

1. Identification of objectives, attributes, and issues
2. Identification of alternative courses of actions (alternatives)

3. Assessment of impact of alternatives

4. Analysis of alternatives

5. Selection of preferred alternative

Each of these steps is briefly discussed in the following subsection.

1.2.1   Steps in decision-making process

Identification of objectives, attributes, issues, and discriminating criteria. The decision-making process starts by identifying the objectives, attributes, and issues that could affect the decision, e.g., cost, regulatory requirements, social acceptance, and political infrastructure. In reality, seldom is a decision driven by a single objective or influenced by a single issue. Realistic decisions often seek to maximize multiple objectives simultaneously and are influenced by several, often conflicting, issues. The decision to acquire a new car illustrates this point. The overall decision, in this case, is composed of several underlying decisions, such as buying versus leasing, the selection of the make and model of the car, and the selection of a car dealer. Each of these underlying decisions is affected by several issues. Whether to buy or lease the car depends on the expected use of the car, the length of time one expects to keep the car, the budget for monthly payments, etc. The selection of a specific make and model will be affected by the original price and expected resale value, quality, warranty, amenities and equipment, expected use of the car, etc. Finally, the selection of the car dealer depends on price, service, reputation, inventory, location, etc. One therefore can appreciate why many individuals spend months pondering and often agonizing about the decision to acquire a new car. Selection of the objectives to be maximized and the issues that can affect the decision is a critical step in the decision-making process and thus deserves careful attention, for it lays the foundation for implementation of the process. Failure to clearly identify and articulate the objectives and attributes in the implementation of the decision-making process is tantamount to building an edifice on quicksand.

Objectives are defined as general directions in which one wants to move when making a decision. Examples of common objectives are "maximize the health and safety of the public" and "minimize costs." Associated with objectives are *attributes,* which are used to measure how well a given alternative fares in relation to an objective.[1] Attributes associated with the two aforementioned objectives could be risks posed by an alternative to the health and safety of the public and the actual cost of implementing an alternative, respectively.

Decisions are often affected by issues or constraints beyond the control of the decision makers. Issues can affect a decision in a variety of ways, the most common one being restriction of the number of alternatives that can be considered. For example, when planning the construction of a new highway between two cities, the route with the lowest absolute cost is preferable. However, such a route might cross through a historical site, the protection of which is guaranteed by law. This would restrict the number of alternative routes considered to those which would avoid the historical site, and the preferred route would be the one with the lowest cost from among the group that could be considered.

Following identification of the attendant objectives, attributes, issues, and the set of plausible alternatives, one proceeds to the formulation of discriminating criteria. The quality of the decision will depend to a large extent on the decision maker's ability to identify and clearly articulate the objectives, attributes, issues, and "truly" discriminating criteria. If minimizing cost is one of the objectives, a specific dollar value can be set below which an alternative would be acceptable and above which it would not. Similarly, regulatory requirements may already contain specific quantitative criteria and associated threshold values for the criteria that determine whether or not the requirements are met. Arriving at discriminating criteria is not a trivial task. For some issues, such as cost, regulatory requirements, and time available for implementation of an alternative, it could be relatively straightforward; however, gauging acceptability for social issues could be difficult.

Identification of alternatives. The set of plausible alternatives is then developed, with the initial emphasis being on developing an exhaustive list of alternatives. It is better to be conservative and include all plausible alternatives—good and bad—than to be restrictive and increase the likelihood that some potentially good alternatives are unintentionally excluded. It should be noted that one does not know a priori which is a good or bad alternative; otherwise, there would be no need for applying this process. If the process is applied in a systematic fashion, the likelihood of bad alternatives being eliminated is high. In addition to being an exhaustive list, these alternatives should be mutually exclusive. Individuals with substantive knowledge about the problem of interest should be involved in the identification of alternatives. This should be a creative process with sufficient diversity of opinion.

Assessment of the alternatives. The next step in the process is assessment of the alternatives, and within this step, the first activity is the gathering and interpretation of information about each alternative. The key point here is to ensure, to the extent practicable, that the quantity and level of detail of the information base are both uniform and equitable across all the alternatives. It is preferable that the available information be assembled and arranged according to the discriminating criteria selected. Following assemblage of the information base, one proceeds to analysis of each alternative. It is here that, as will be discussed later, risk assessment comes into play. By and large, there will be uncertainties associated with the available information for each alternative, and also, the selection of one alternative over another will have some consequences—either good or bad—that are best expressed in terms of risk. Thus it follows that it would be advantageous to estimate the risk associated with each alternative—the risk can be financial, environmental, programmatic, or social. This will serve as the basis for comparisons among the alternatives, the next step in the decision-making process.

Analysis and comparison of alternatives.   Once the available information on all the alternatives has been assembled, the method, tools, and techniques for the analysis have been selected, and each alternative has been evaluated to assess its performance with respect to each of the discriminating criteria, it is customary to numerically "score" each alternative for each criterion as the means to make comparisons among them and to rank the alternatives in terms of relative value.

Because of the uncertainties that permeate most decisions, as will be discussed below, decision theory offers the framework for analyzing and comparing alternatives in light of the uncertainties. The foundations of decision theory lie in uncertainty analysis, risk assessment, and risk management.[2] Decision theory uses a variety of tools, methods, and procedures to compare alternatives, several of which are influence diagrams, game theory, and utility functions.[2] Herein the discussion concentrates on the construction of utility functions.

The basic tenet in the application of utility functions is that a numerical value can be associated with the degree to which an uncertainty maximizes the objective(s) of the decision. Thus fundamental assumptions when constructing utility functions are (1) the consequence(s) of each alternative can be mapped into a scale representing the numerical values from the least to most desirable with respect to the objective(s) of the decision, and (2) the different alternatives can be ranked in order of preference based on their assigned utility function. The values of the utility function are assigned based on an arbitrary scale and, therefore, are only meaningful for purposes of a relative comparison among the alternatives; i.e., whether the scale is from 1 to 10 or 1 to

100 is irrelevant as long as the value of the utility function increases monotonically with the desirability of an alternative.[2]

The utility function of a consequence can be combined with the probability of occurrence of the associated event to arrive at an estimate of the utility of a given decision. I shall borrow an example presented by Lindley[3] to illustrate this point. Suppose a manufacturer of a material for making curtains is faced with deciding whether or not to inspect the material before shipping it to a client because he or she is uncertain regarding the likelihood of defects in the material. The manufacturer's choices are two: inspect the material before shipping (denoted as alternative a_1) or not inspect the material (denoted as alternative a_2). There are two uncertain events that affect the decision: the material has no defect [denoted as event e_1 with probability of occurrence $p(e_1)$], and the material has at least one defect [denoted as event e_2 with probability of occurrence $p(e_2)$]. The taxonomy of alternatives, events, and consequences for this decision is presented in Table 1.1.

The consequence associated with the selection of alternative a_1 and the occurrence of event e_1 is c_{11}; the other three possible consequences can be related with a specific alternative and event. One can readily deduce that c_{21} would be the most desirable consequence or outcome, followed by c_{11}, c_{12}, and c_{22} in order from most to least desirable. The utility of alternative a_1—inspection—is given as

$$u(a_1) = u(c_{11})p(e_1) + u(c_{12})p(e_2)$$

where $u(c_{ij})$ is the utility of consequence c_{ij}. Likewise, the utility of alternative a_2—no inspection—is given by

$$u(a_2) = u(c_{21})p(e_1) + u(c_{22})p(e_2)$$

TABLE 1.1   Taxonomy of Decision for Inspection of Curtain Material

	Uncertain event	
Alternative	e_1 (no defects)	e_2 (at least one defect)
a_1 (inspection)	c_{11} (cost of inspection and satisfied customer)	c_{12} (cost of inspection, manufacture new material, and satisfied customer)
a_2 (no inspection)	c_{21} (satisfied customer)	c_{22} (unsatisfied customer, replace defective material)

Note: The consequences c that result from event e depend on alternative a.

To calculate the utility of an alternative, the probability of the uncertain events affecting the decision is needed. These two equations can be generalized to estimate the utility of an alternative a_i affected by the occurrence of n uncertain events as follows:

$$u(a_i) = \sum_{j=1}^{n} u(c_{ij}) p(e_j)$$

Although not strictly necessary, it is always useful to perform a sensitivity analysis to examine the possible impact of the uncertainties on the comparison among the alternatives. In some cases, the results of the sensitivity analysis will suggest the collection of new and/or additional data that will reduce the important sources of uncertainties and will contribute to further discrimination of the alternatives. The results of the sensitivity analysis also could assist in a reevaluation of the decision variables; it is quite likely that several iterations of the process would be necessary before a sufficiently high level of confidence is reached to proceed with the ratification of the decision.

Selection of preferred alternative.   The last step in the process is ratification of the selection of the preferred alternative by the decision makers following the weighing of all available evidence. A key point to consider here is that the decision must be sufficiently robust to withstand a critical review.

1.2.2   Advantages and disadvantages of the decision-making process

The framework for the decision-making process that has been presented so far puts the emphasis on the process itself rather than on the actual decision. Because, as stated earlier, it is not possible to predict the decision, how one goes about reaching the decision is more important than the decision itself.[1,3–5] While application of this process offers some clear advantages in ensuring the soundness of a decision, it also has some disadvantages. Among the latter are the cost and time required to implement the process and the reduced flexibility to modify the process once its implementation has commenced. As stated earlier, a key consideration before undertaking implementation of the process is deciding how rigorously it needs to be implemented. The rigor and formalism need to be commensurate with the importance of the decision and the severity of its potential consequence(s). Obviously, deciding whether to redesign a chemical plant or where to site a waste-disposal facility deserves by far more careful consideration than deciding whether to take an umbrella to work in case it rains.

1.2.3 Decision making under uncertainty

The fact that an individual faces the dilemma of having to choose one from two or more alternatives implies that he or she does not have a complete base of information. Otherwise, there would be no dilemma, and one alternative would be selected outright without the need to consider others. For example, if one knows that it will definitely rain, then there is no need to consider any other alternative but to take an umbrella to work. Likewise, if one has a sum of money that could be invested in the stock market and it is known with complete certainty that a particular stock will appreciate in value, then the only rational choice—unless the purpose is to lose money—is to invest the money in that stock. However, real situations are not quite this simple, and often one is faced with having to make a decision relying on less than 100 percent certain information. The issue is not whether uncertainties will permeate decision making, but rather whether or not decision makers recognize these uncertainties and deal with them explicitly.[1,3–6] Finkel[4] quotes the physicist Richard Wilson who once said "...a decision made without taking uncertainty into account is barely worth calling a decision."

Humans make decisions in the presence of uncertainty on a daily basis[5]; however, few recognize this. By and large, humans have learned how to make decisions in the presence of uncertainty even though they may not necessarily recognize the uncertainties, and more important, they have learned how to take appropriate measures to protect themselves against the consequences of their decisions. For example, when a bank decides whether or not to lend money to an individual for the purchase of an automobile, the bank managers base the decision on a number of factors about the prospective buyer, such as past credit record, current financial situation and the ability to repay the loan, and driving records. While the bank attempts to minimize the risk of the buyer forfeiting on the loan, there are no guarantees. Therefore, the bank takes appropriate measures to protect its interests against the possible adverse consequences of its decision to approve the financing, such as putting a lien on the car or any other tangible property of value that the buyer may own or requiring the buyer to purchase comprehensive automobile insurance. The buyer seeks to protect his or her investment by obtaining automobile insurance. Without this insurance, if the owner is involved in an accident that destroys the automobile, legally, he or she is still obligated to repay the loan. The insurance, depending on the coverage, should allow the owner to recover all or most of his or her investment and replace the automobile. An important point to note here is that actions designed to mitigate risks do not come without a price.

It has been argued[1,3–5] that by explicitly considering uncertainties in decision making one is indeed factoring in more information than if uncertainty is ignored. The probability distribution function that may be used to describe the uncertainty in a variable contains more information than a single deterministic value of the variable, be it the mean, median, highest value, etc. Furthermore, and perhaps more important, these researchers all argue—some more strongly than others—that failure to consider the uncertainties is not facing up to reality and that, in the end, the quality and robustness of the decision will suffer. To illustrate this point, Morgan and Henrion[5] introduced the concept of the "expected value of including uncertainty" (EVIU) as a means to determine when considering uncertainties enhances the value of the decision. Other authors present the same topic in a slightly different manner by discussing the "value of imperfect information."

1.2.4 Value judgments in decision making

As discussed earlier, one should obtain information about the different alternatives and conduct a sound analysis of each alternative, and this analysis will be used to support the selection of one of the alternatives. It also was mentioned in that discussion that a key ingredient in the decision-making process was the ranking—in order of relative importance—of the different issues that will have an impact on the decision and the assignment of relative weights representing such ranking. This ranking and the assignment of the relative weights are based on value judgments on the part of the decision makers. Value judgments, as opposed to factual judgments, cannot be proved to be right or wrong.[7–9]

Decision makers are often confronted with issues such as whether the value of a worker's life is more important than the value of the life of a member of the general public when considering health and safety hazards associated with the operation of a given manufacturing facility. Some may say that both lives are equal in value, whereas others may be inclined to state that the life of a member of the general public is more valuable than the life of a worker at the facility because the latter is exposing himself or herself to the hazard voluntarily and is reaping some benefits from such exposure (i.e., salary). A similar issue is the establishment of *de minimis* levels, below which specific hazards pose minute risks and therefore should go unregulated. Some argue that regulating these types of hazards will not contribute positively to minimizing risks and, more important, diverts limited resources from being devoted to the reduction of other more potentially problematic risks[10]; others have a different point of view.

Value judgments in decision making present an interesting challenge, for different individuals or groups may have different agendas or motives regarding a given decision and will most likely attempt to advance such agendas or motives through their value judgments. Let's consider the siting and construction of a waste-disposal facility. There are a number of individuals or groups—commonly referred to as *stakeholders*—that have an interest in the outcome of such a decision. The stakeholders may include proponents as well as opponents of the facility, regulatory authorities, technical oversight groups, politicians, and general public interest groups, to name a few. Each of these stakeholders may view the decision differently from the others and will attempt to influence the decision to maximize its objectives.[11] One way they can achieve such a goal is by articulating value judgments that tend to favor or enhance their particular objectives. The challenge for the decision maker lies in how to reconcile such disparity of views so that the value judgments contribute in a constructive manner to the decision and the solution of the problem in a timely and cost-effective manner. This is a difficult task, and—in the case of waste-disposal facility siting—it has been a major obstacle to the timely resolution of issues.

One more factor complicates the consideration of value judgments: They can change with both time and circumstances. Let's continue with the example of the siting of a waste-disposal facility to illustrate this point. Colglazier[12] discusses how politicians from the state of Washington changed their view regarding the siting of the first repository for high-level radioactive waste in the United States. When, according to the Nuclear Waste Policy Act (NWPA) of 1982, three different sites throughout the country were candidates for extensive site characterization to decide on the best repository location based on technical characteristics, the state of Washington was willing to accept the repository at Hanford, Washington, if it proved to be the best of the three sites. However, when in 1987 the U.S. Congress decided to amend the NWPA to reduce the number of sites to be characterized from three to one, the congressional delegation from Washington voted for Yucca Mountain, Nevada, to be the site. According to Colglazier, one of Washington's representatives stated that the change in his vote was driven primarily by protection of his interests as opposed to the available evidence.

1.2.5 Role of expert judgments

Bonano[9] states that "...the quality of the decision-making process will largely depend on its foundation of expert judgments." Von Winterfeldt and Edwards,[8] Keeney and von Winterfeldt,[13] Hora,[14] and more recently Cooke[15] present very strong arguments as to why failing to recognize that expert judgments are an integral part of the decision-making process is shying away from reality. According to Cooke, the elicitation, representation, and use of expert judgments are becoming increasingly important because the nature and complexity of the problems that are being tackled nowadays do not afford using other approaches, whether the problem is one of scientific inquiry or of policy analysis.

Expert judgments will permeate every aspect of the decision-making process. Such judgments will be used to (1) identify the issues that affect the decision, (2) identify the different alternatives, (3) interpret the information pertaining to each alternative, (4) make tradeoffs among the identified issues (i.e., express value judgments), (5) provide input into the analysis of the alternatives, (6) interpret the results of the analysis, and (7) ratify and communicate the decision.

The elicitation and use of expert judgments in the decision-making process need to be at the same level of detail, rigor, and formalism as the process itself. The more important the decision and the more severe its possible consequences, the more formal and structured should the elicitation and use of expert judgments be. There are many treatises in the literature regarding the methods, techniques, and procedures for elicitation of expert judgments, and the reader is encouraged to examine this literature. The most recent and comprehensive treatment of the subject is given by Cooke.[15] He surveys the wide range of applications for the use of expert judgments, from the more traditional risk-assessment applications to military intelligence, artificial intelligence, and policy analysis.

1.3 Consideration of Uncertainty

It has been established already that, by and large, decisions have to be made relying on less than perfect information. It has been submitted that if the information is 100 percent certain and the objectives of the choice are clearly stated and understood, then there is only one course of action, and implementing even an ad hoc decision-making process is a waste of resources. In other words, decision making is a challenge when the information base is incomplete or uncertain. The uncertainties are caused by different factors, such as cognitive limitations, poor understanding of the situation, and uncertainty about the future, among others.[2] Therefore, the fundamental premise in this discussion is that uncertainties will have an impact on the decision and that the relevant ones need to be considered explicitly and systematically.

The consideration of uncertainties in decision making consists of three parts:

1. Recognition of the sources of uncertainty

2. Quantification of the uncertainties

3. Documenting the handling and propagation of those uncertainties which affect the decision

It is critical that the sources of uncertainties that could affect the decision be identified and understood up front. Nothing can undermine the credibility of a decision and of the process used to arrive at that decision more than the discovery of a new uncertainty that changes the nature of the decision. The robustness of a decision relies on having identified and considered all potentially important uncertainties in a systematic and logical manner. This does not mean that one should delay making a decision until each and every uncertainty has been dealt with[11]; rather, it means that given the information available at the time the decision had to be made, all uncertainties that could reasonably have an impact on the decision were considered. It is not reasonable nor advisable to speculate about future actions or situations beyond the control of the decision makers that could change the decision.

As will be discussed later, consideration of the uncertainties does not mean that all uncertainties need to be quantified and factored into the analysis of alternatives. It means that the uncertainties have been considered in a systematic manner and that those which do not have an impact on the decision are eliminated from further consideration based on a set of sound screening criteria. Every practically possible effort should be made to quantify those uncertainties which will affect the decision. However, in practice, there are always some uncertainties that cannot be quantified, and in such cases, appropriate measures need to be taken to ensure that their impact on the decision is accounted for, at least qualitatively. The manner in which the important sources of uncertainty are propagated to the point of decision needs to be documented. Conventionally, this is accomplished in the risk assessment, as will be discussed below.

One final point is worth making before we embark on a discussion of uncertainty, and that is that the explicit consideration of uncertainties enhances the decision-making process in at least three ways[11]:

1. It assists in identification of the most relevant uncertainties.

2. It assists in the design of information-gathering strategies.

3. It enhances the defensibility of the decision.

Focusing on the most relevant sources of uncertainty accomplishes two goals: (1) It ensures that limited resources are expended dealing with issues that have a bearing on the decision, and (2) it discourages detractors of the process from derailing it by introducing issues that have little or no impact on the decision. It assists in determining the type of new or additional data that will help resolve the key uncertainties. Lastly, it enhances the credibility and the defensibility of the process and of the decision because, by dealing with the uncertainties explicitly, biases tend to be easier to discover and to neutralize.[4,5]

1.3.1 Sources of uncertainty in decision making

There are two major sources of uncertainty[11]: (1) technical uncertainty and (2) uncertainty in decision variables. The former are uncertainties that permeate through the analysis of different alternatives and the estimation of their potential consequence(s), whereas the latter refer to uncertainty in those variables which will be used to assess the "goodness" of the alternatives given the decision at hand. In principle, it is relatively easier to handle technical uncertainties than uncertainty in decision variables.

Technical uncertainties. Conventionally, technical uncertainties are divided into three categories[11]: (1) uncertainty in the future, (2) uncertainty in models, and (3) uncertainty in data and parameters needed to execute the models. Figure 1.2, after Gallegos and Bonano,[16] illustrates the hierarchy of these three categories of technical uncertainty. This categorization is purely out of convenience, and there is no scientific basis that supports it.[11,16,17] Others (e.g., Finkel[4]) use similar categorizations.

In reality, these uncertainties do not represent distinct or discrete domains, and there has been and continues to be much debate about where one category ends and the other begins.[18] However, this categorization offers some practical advantages in risk assessment.[11,16] First, the categorization allows the decomposition of a very complex problem into manageable components. Second, it facilitates the propagation and traceability of the uncertainties to the results of the risk assessment and eventually to the decision in a more transparent and explicit way. Third, it simplifies identification of the most significant uncertainties. Fourth, it makes it easier to incorporate new advances in the treatment of specific uncertainties into the process.

The following subsections summarize these sources of uncertainty and some of the methods that either are being employed or are recommended to reduce the uncertainties.

Uncertainty in the future. One of the most difficult aspects of the decision-making process is estimating the consequences of the decision because of one's inability to forecast the future. Making a decision on whether to take an umbrella to work is hampered by the fact that one cannot predict rain or not rain even a few hours into the future. As the time frame of interest increases, it becomes harder to forecast the future. For example, decision makers in the electric power industry

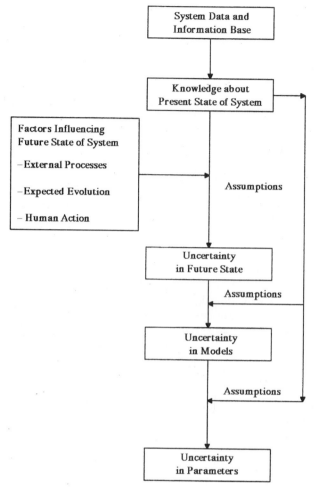

Figure 1.2 Hierarchy and relationship of sources of uncertainty. (*After Gallegos and Bonano.*[16])

need to forecast future electricity demands, and these forecasts need to consider factors that influence the future, such as (1) economics, (2) market assessments, (3) technological developments, (4) environmental issues and regulations, and (5) sociopolitical issues, among others,[6] all of which are highly uncertain. Another example is the siting of deep geologic radioactive waste repositories, which must consider the evolution of the system and human actions thousands of years into the future, a daunting task indeed.

A systematic approach that postulates likely realizations of the future (scenarios) is the tool needed to handle this uncertainty. Much work has been done in the reactor safety arena,[19] the radioactive waste-disposal area,[20] and other engineered systems to develop, apply, and evaluate methodologies for postulating scenarios. These methodologies generally consist of five major steps: (1) initial identification of a comprehensive, exhaustive, and exclusive list of events that could affect the behavior of the system of interest, (2) classification of the events into classes based on their origin, characteristics, or potential effect(s) or consequence(s), (3) initial screening of the events based on their reasonableness, probability of occurrence, and potential consequence(s), (4) combination of surviving events into scenarios, and (5) screening of the scenarios to arrive at a final set for the risk-assessment analysis.

Three issues need to be considered carefully when applying a scenario-selection methodology. First, it is impossible to ascertain that the initial list of events and the final set of scenarios include all the possible realizations of the future state of the system that can lead to high-risk situations. This issue is commonly referred to as the *completeness issue*.[17] Second is the development of meaningful screening criteria. The third issue relates to estimation of the probability of occurrence of the individual events and the scenarios. The resolution of these issues relies almost exclusively on the use of expert judgments.[9] When these issues are carefully addressed, the likelihood that one will end up with an exhaustive and comprehensive set of mutually exclusive scenarios is considerably enhanced.

Uncertainty in models. Models are typically divided into three classes[11,16,17]: (1) conceptual, (2) mathematical, and (3) computer codes. The distinction between conceptual models and mathematical models is not a strict one and, again, is more out of convenience.

Conceptual models generally provide a qualitative description of the real system that one is attempting to simulate. This description includes the attendant processes (physicochemical, economic, sociopolitical, etc.) that are taking or can take place, the initial and boundary conditions that define the domain over which the processes take place, and the parameters that govern the spatial and/or temporal evolution of the processes. A conceptual model is formulated by invoking a set of assumptions that represent simplifications of reality—a set of such assumptions is said to define a conceptual model. Often the paucity of available data makes it possible for more than one set of assumptions to be plausible, and herein lies the uncertainty in conceptual models, for the validity of each set of assumptions cannot be determined a priori. Conceptual model uncertainty is receiving a great deal of attention in the radioactive waste-disposal arena.[16] However, decision making in other fields also considers this uncertainty; in the chemical industry, uncertainty in conceptual models apparently is included in what-if analyses.[21] Other applications include uncertainty in conceptual models as part of uncertainty in the future state of the system,[6] an indication that, as stated earlier, the classification of uncertainties used here is merely out of convenience and that other classifications are equally reasonable and valid. As will be mentioned below, uncertainty in conceptual models also affects uncertainty in parameters.

In order to conduct a quantitative analysis of the alternatives, the conceptual model needs to be translated into a set of mathematical equations, i.e., a mathematical model. Uncertainty in mathematical models arises from various sources.[4,6,16] The solution of the mathematical equations must be tractable; otherwise, the model is of little value. Thus the complexity of the equations must be commensurate with existing solution capabilities. This requires simplifying assumptions, which inherently are uncertain. Uncertainty also can be introduced through the structure of the model. Different types of equations can be used, e.g., deterministic equations versus stochastic equations. Gutjahr et al.[22] have demonstrated that the propagation of parameter uncertainty using Monte Carlo simulation with a model based on deterministic equations is not equivalent to the use of a model of stochastic equations for the same processes.

Finally, the mathematical model has to be solved and the solution evaluated by supplying numerical values for the governing parameters. Depending on the complexity of the mathematical model, the solution can be obtained using analytical methods, numerical methods, or a combination thereof. One should endeavor to keep the models as parsimonious as possible[5]; however, for complex technological systems, even the simplest models require convoluted numerical solutions. More often than not, these solutions are implemented in computer codes. The development and application of computer codes can introduce uncertainties stemming from (1) programming errors, (2) computer truncation errors, and (3) user errors. Computer-code uncertainty can have an impact on the results of an analysis, and needs to be addressed. This uncertainty is far easier to reduce than uncertainty in conceptual and mathematical models[16,17] using a strict computer code quality-assurance program, such as the one discussed by Wilkinson and Runkle.[23]

Uncertainty in models (i.e., combination of conceptual model, mathematical model, and associated computer codes) might be reduced through data collection, model validation, and consistency checks for the assumptions in each model. Data collection provides information about the static and dynamic components of the models, while validation addresses the dynamic component.[16] Validation, which provides a measure of the adequacy of a model by comparing results from its application to measured values of one or more specific dependent variables, is the most accepted method for reducing uncertainty in the combination conceptual model–mathematical model–computer code. However, validation exercises require a great deal of interpretation by technical experts[9] because of (1) transferability of results from one experiment to another or from a spatially and temporally controlled experiment to the real situation and (2) because, due to the complexity of the models, not all their components can be validated, thus leaving some components untested. Model-verification exercises, where the results of models, the solution of which rely on numerical techniques, are compared with known analytical solutions, provide a means for reducing uncertainty in the mathematical models and the associated computer codes. Benchmarking, where, in principle, several different computer codes are used to simulate the same problem, is another mechanism for increasing confidence in the accuracy of the codes. A more subtle approach to test the adequacy of conceptual models is to test the consistency between the suite of assumptions in each model to ensure that each model is internally consistent and coherent.[16]

Uncertainty in data and parameters.   As stated earlier, to analyze the different alternatives being considered in a decision-making exercise, the models are executed to estimate potential consequences for each of the alternatives. In order to execute the models, the governing parameters need to be assigned numerical values. Model parameters are rarely measured directly; rather, they are usually inferred directly or indirectly from measured data.[11,16]

The data are themselves uncertain due to (1) limited accuracy and precision of measuring instruments, (2) inability to fully characterize spatial and/or temporal variability in the data, (3) human error, and (4) extrapolation of the data beyond the domain of applicability, among others.[4,6,11,16] Uncertainty in parameters arises from the uncertainty in the data from which the parameters are inferred and from assumptions involved in interpretation of the data, the latter being, in reality, a conceptual model uncertainty.

Reducing the uncertainty introduced by instrument and measurement error is by far the easiest to deal with. Every day more advanced measurement techniques and instruments are becoming available. These advances have a direct effect on reducing this uncertainty. Also, through better training, personnel using these instruments tend to minimize human error. The uncertainty associated with poor understanding and characterization of parameter variability is more difficult to reduce. However, in recent years, the use of stochastic models and techniques has allowed researchers to examine parameter variability and help reduce that uncertainty.[16] Most recently, the application of geographic information systems (GIS) has allowed investigators to display spatially distributed information in visual forms that facilitate the identification of patterns in the information.[11] By incorporating GIS technology into decision support systems, decision makers are in a better position to make more intelligent and judicious decisions on data collection—the most defensible means of reducing data and parameter uncertainty. Also, the use of GIS technology makes it easier to display and explain decisions to nonexperts.

Uncertainty in decision variables. Section 1.2 indicated that the key to any decision making was selection of attribute and discriminating criteria—often referred to as *decision variables*—that allow measurement of the performance of each alternative against the desired objectives. Selection of the discriminating criteria and attributes is not straightforward and relies almost exclusively on value judgments.[9] Further, although not strictly necessary, it is customary to rank the criteria and attributes in order of relative importance.[1,3] In doing so, tradeoffs are made among the criteria and attributes. The validity of the value judgments involved in the tradeoffs cannot be determined,[7–9] and as a result, these will be uncertain. This uncertainty has been referred to as *decision-rule uncertainty*[4] or *uncertainty in decision variables*.[5]

Uncertainty in decision variables is difficult to deal with because the value judgments involved tend to be influenced by a gamut of social, political, and economic factors that cannot be treated in the same vein as scientific queries.[4] In a decision-making process involving multiple stakeholders, each with perhaps a different set of objectives or agendas, reconciliation of the value judgments can be a tremendous undertaking. However, there are methods that can be used to analyze value judgments in a systematic and logical manner.[8]

1.3.2 Treatment of uncertainties

The treatment of uncertainties in decision making can be divided into three components: (1) quantification of the uncertainties, (2) propagation of the uncertainties to the decision variables, and (3) reduction of those uncertainties with the most influence on the decision. Earlier we discussed methods for reducing different sources of uncertainty; now the discussion focuses on the quantification and propagation of the uncertainties.

Quantification of uncertainty. To the extent practicable, uncertainties affecting a decision should be quantified conventionally in terms of a probability. The open literature abounds with discussions on this sub-

ject, and the reader is encouraged to examine it for more in-depth treatises; some suggested readings are Goodwin and Wright,[1] Kim,[2]
Lindley,[3] Finkel,[4] Morgan and Henrion,[5] de Finnetti,[24] and
Apostolakis.[25] Probabilities are typically classified into two major categories: (1) classic or frequentist probabilities and (2) subjective or
bayesian probabilities.

Classic or frequentist probability. Classic or frequentist probabilities get
their name because the probability is the frequency with which a given
outcome or result occurs during many identical repetitions of an experiment.[26] The numerical value of the probability is the "limiting frequency" for a specific outcome, which can be expressed mathematically as

$$P(E) = \lim_{n \to \infty} \frac{S^n(E)}{n}$$

where $P(E)$ is the probability of event E occurring, $S^n(E)$ is the number
of times the event E actually occurs, and n is the number of times the
experiment is repeated.

The most common example of classic or frequentist probability is the
so-called coin-toss experiment. In this experiment, tossing a "fair" coin a
large number of times shows that nearly half the times either heads or
tails comes up. As the number of tosses or repetitions of the experiment
increases, the frequency of heads or tails asymptotically approaches 0.5;
thus the probability of heads or tails is 0.5.

Frequentist or classic probabilities are widely used in the insurance
industry. Actuarial data are the primary basis for the determination of
insurance premiums. For example, in the United States, the cost of
automobile insurance is higher for unmarried males under age 25 than
for any other segment of the population because actuarial data clearly
indicate that a higher number of automobile accidents involve this
group. Insurance underwriters cannot predict that a specific member
of this group will be involved in an accident, but they can predict with
incredible accuracy the number of accidents involving members of this
group occurring on an annual basis. Similarly, the extensive data available uncontroversially show that the likelihood of perishing in an automobile accident is far higher than that of perishing in a commercial
airliner crash. Hence insurance premiums covering the latter are relatively inexpensive compared with the former.

While it is clear from these two examples that classic or frequentist
probabilities can be estimated quite reliably, Lindley[3] argues that truly
classic or frequentist probabilities do not exist because no two experiments are ever identical. One could say that no two automobile accidents involving unmarried males under age 25 are identical in the

strictest sense of the word; however, it would be foolish to argue against the strong correlation that exists between the two. Lindley's position, perhaps, is more applicable in the health sciences, where correlation between certain chemicals and adverse health effects in humans is not straightforward. Such correlations are often derived from results of short-term laboratory experiments with animals under conditions that seldom resemble those under which humans are likely to be exposed to the chemical.[27] The extrapolation of the data from such experiments leaves much room for subjective interpretation.

Subjective or bayesian probability.   A subjective or bayesian probability represents an individual's "degree of belief" that a given statement is true.[3,5,24,25] This type of probability depends on two factors: (1) the information available to the individual and (2) the individual's interpretation of that information. Conventionally, subjective or bayesian probabilities are denoted as $P(e \mid E)$, where e denotes the event and E the available information or "body of evidence." $P(e \mid E)$ is read as "the probability of e, given E." As the available information E changes, so should the probability of e, and Bayes' theorem provides the framework for updating the probability in light of the new information:

$$P_1(e \mid E_1) = L(E_1)P_0(e \mid E_0)$$

where $P_0(e \mid E_0)$ is the probability of event e prior to the incorporation of the new information or evidence (also called the *prior probability*), $L(E_1)$ is the likelihood that the new evidence is of relevance to the problem at hand, and $P_1(e \mid E_1)$ is the updated probability of the event after considering the new body of information (also called the *posterior probability*).

Subjective or bayesian probabilities are useful when establishing the likelihood of occurrence of one event relative to the likelihood of occurrence of another.[25] If event e is said to have a subjective probability of x, it means that e is more likely to occur than all other events with a probability less than x. As mentioned earlier, not only is this type of probability dependent on the current body of information, it also depends on an individual's interpretation of that information. Consequently, it is not only possible but very likely that different individuals can interpret the same information differently, leading to different estimates of the same probability. Subjective or bayesian probabilities cannot be assigned arbitrarily or capriciously because these are legitimate probabilities and as such must follow the axioms of probability theory.[5,25] If the probability of event e occurring is x, then the complement (i.e., the probability of event e not occurring) must be $1 - x$. For a set of mutually exclusive events, the sum of their respective subjective probabilities must be unity. Finally, when the probability of one event is updated, the probabilities of the other events in the set also must be updated.

Subjective or bayesian probabilities are useful in one-of-a-kind problems for which past data, if available, may not be sufficient to allow the estimation of a frequentist probability. Subjective or bayesian probabilities are more appropriate than classic or frequentist probabilities for quantifying the uncertainties that affect decisions for complex technological systems.[25] Subjective or bayesian probabilities can be used in quantification of the different sources of uncertainty discussed in Sec. 1.3.1. Finally, subjective or bayesian probabilities can be estimated using information from different sources such as experimental data, results from analyses, and expert judgments.

Propagation of uncertainty.   The purpose of quantifying the uncertainties is to be able to propagate them to the estimate of the decision variables. To date, the most common technique for propagating uncertainties through one or more models and/or computer codes simulating the behavior of a complex system is statistical sampling with Monte Carlo simulation.[5] By representing the uncertainties in terms of probability distribution functions, statistical samples are generated for all the quantified uncertainties. The samples are arranged in terms of vectors—a vector consisting of a sampled value for each of the uncertain variables. A simulation is performed for each of the vectors, in turn, resulting in a distribution of values that can be arranged in a probability distribution function or another type of distribution function to represent the uncertainty in the dependent variable(s) of interest. In this discussion, the dependent variables are the decision variables. The propagation of uncertainty using Monte Carlo simulation will be discussed in Sec. 1.4.2 (probabilistic risk assessment methodology). For more information on statistical sampling approaches, the reader is referred to Ahmed et al.[28]

1.4   Risk, Risk Assessment, and Risk Management

Risk is—in the simplest of terms—the product of the probability of occurrence of an event and the consequence or net effect of that event if it occurs.[29] Kaplan and Garrick[30] present the analysis of risk as consisting of three steps: (1) identification of events that can occur and have adverse consequences, (2) estimation of the likelihood of those events occurring, and (3) estimation of the potential consequences. *Risk assessment,* or *risk analysis,* is the formalism in which these three steps are carried out by (1) identifying the potential adverse events and combining them into scenarios, (2) quantifying the uncertainties associated with the occurrence of the events, the likelihood of the scenarios, and the simulation of the events and scenarios, (3) propagating the uncertainties to the dependent variable(s) of interest, and (4) calculating the risk and comparing it, if required, with specified target values.[29]

Risk management is concerned with the decision-making process that (1) ranks risks in terms of relative importance or level of unacceptability, (2) identifies practically achievable and tolerable levels of risk, and (3) selects measures to reduce the unacceptable risks to tolerable levels.[9,31] Many think that risk assessment and risk management are one and the same thing, although this is not the case. Risk assessment yields technical and quantitative information about the nature and extent of the hazards posing the risks to be utilized by risk-management decision makers; as such, risk assessment deals with technical and factual issues, whereas risk management considers policy and societal issues about risk as well as the cost, feasibility, and schedule to handle the risks.[10,32]

1.4.1   Risk, risk perception, and risk communication

Among the public, risk is a very poorly understood concept that seems to be dominated more by subjective opinion and alarmism than by objective reality.[27,33] Societal issues such as voluntary versus involuntary risk are at the forefront of the debate about risk. Individuals seem to accept higher risks if these are self-imposed and demand protection against much lower risks when these are caused by factors beyond their control.[34]

Understanding risk is further complicated because society, in general, seems to focus on the consequence of an event without considering its probability or likelihood of occurrence. Risk often is associated with events with extremely low probabilities and high consequences. The average person has difficulty appreciating low-probability events and therefore pays more attention to the consequences. It should come as no surprise that many people are afraid of traveling in a commercial airliner but do not give a second thought to riding in an automobile. Perhaps such fears are influenced by extensive media coverage of airliner accidents, in which several tens to hundreds of people can die in one accident, and little or no mention on the evening news of automobile accidents involving a handful of people at most. Statistical data are indisputable that travel in a commercial airliner is far safer than in an automobile, primarily because of the high frequency with which automobile accidents happen as opposed to airline accidents.

Key to a meaningful risk-assessment–risk-management system is an appreciation by decision makers of the public's attitudes and perceptions about risk.[35] People's perceptions about risk influence politicians, who in turn develop policies and regulations that affect—if not dictate—how risk-management programs are implemented. Nothing could be more detrimental to society in the long term than the unnecessary expenditure of limited resources attempting to eradicate hazards that pose only minute risks while other, more threatening, hazards go unattended.[10,11] Yet perceptions and attitudes about risks based on erroneous, misleading, or simply sensationalized information can have such an effect, as will be discussed below.

As stated earlier, the public's perceptions of risk tend to be dominated by known consequences, with little or no attention paid to the likelihood of occurrence of the associated events or hazards. Slovic[35] states: "... any factor that makes a hazard unusually memorable or imaginable, such as a recent disaster, heavy media coverage, or a vivid film, can seriously distort the public's perception of risks." Thus risks from dramatic causes, such as airliner crashes and AIDS, tend to be exaggerated, whereas risks from less dramatic causes, such as automobile accidents or diabetes, tend to be underestimated. Sensationalized reports about perceived risks can fuel the dissemination of false, exaggerated, or misleading information that becomes "truth" if repeated often enough. Such distortions seem to put science and technology at odds with basic human values.[27] Thus the public's preference for "zero" risks to accompany technological developments should surprise no one.

One of the most controversial subjects involving risk perception is the establishment of below regulatory concern (BRC) policies. The basic tenet of a BRC policy is the concept of *de minimis* risks; i.e., there are some hazards that pose such low risks to the health, safety, and welfare of the public that their regulation is difficult to justify.[36] The controversy arises because of differences in perception about what constitutes a negligibly low risk. Many factors influence the establishment of a BRC policy[36]; some are cost of risk reduction and of hazard mitigation, the evolution of scientific and technological developments, societal issues, and political issues. Technological innovation and maturation play a particularly important role in the determination of tolerable levels of risks, for these tend to allow ever-smaller hazards.[27] Consequently, the public becomes aware of lower levels of risks that it is willing to tolerate.[27]

The establishment of a BRC policy, for example, is essential for the decontamination and decommissioning of nuclear facilities.[37] However, until very recently,[38] the U.S. Nuclear Regulatory Commission had not published proposed radiologic criteria for the decommissioning of such facilities that utilize BRC-related criteria. As with radioactive wastes, a BRC policy is needed for chemical hazardous constituents[10] to determine "how clean is clean" in the environmental restoration of contaminated sites. Attempts to regulate concentrations of such constituents to levels below those found in nature constitute an effort in futility and a waste of valuable resources; nevertheless, some environmental regulations are aimed at doing exactly that.[27] Federal Focus, Inc. (FFI),[10] advocates a sound and balanced risk-assessment–risk-management system that will allow the explicit consideration of cost versus benefit in deciding those risks which should be the focus of risk-reduction efforts.

Slovic[35] points out that changing people's beliefs about risks is difficult. The paradigms that influence the public's perceptions about risks provide the framework for interpreting new evidence. Slovic states that "...new evidence will appear reliable...if it is consistent with one's initial beliefs, and conversely, contrary evidence will be dismissed as unreliable, erroneous, or unrepresentative." It is clear that overcoming the erroneous public perceptions about risk will be a difficult undertaking. Nonetheless—as discouraging as this picture may seem—concerted efforts to implement educational and communication programs are necessary. It is not my intention here to discuss such programs; the literature is quite abundant in such treatises, and some suggested readings are those by FFI,[10] Lowrance,[33] Ray,[27] Kemp,[34] Mayo and Hollander,[39] Morgan,[40] and Covello et al.[41] Covello et al., for example, offer guidelines for communicating the risks from chemical hazards.

Kemp[34] suggests five factors that are considered essential to the public's tolerance of managed risks; these factors are

1. *Knowledge.* The public deserves access to objective and authoritative information on the alternative solutions to problems that pose potential hazards so that risks are not simply accepted or rejected out of ignorance and emotion.

2. *Involvement.* Decisions on the solution of such problems that seek public participation and provide access to information about risk regulations, risk assessment, and risk management have a greater chance of success.

3. *Risk reduction.* Assurances should be provided that the most robust alternative is being used to reduce the risk to acceptable and practical levels.

4. *Comparisons.* Risks from unfamiliar problems may be tolerated if they can be shown to be less than risks that the public has already learned to tolerate and with which they are more familiar.

5. *Benefits.* The benefits reaped by the public that lead to the problems need to be clearly communicated; this may positively affect the acceptability of the solution of these problems.

1.4.2 Risk assessment

As stated earlier, risk assessment is the framework in which hazards are identified and analyzed and the risks that those hazards pose are estimated. While it is customary to think about hazards that present risks to human health and safety as the only ones addressed in risk assessments, the latter, in principle, can be used to evaluate all types of risks (e.g., economic and programmatic). Risk assessment is widely used by many agencies of the U.S. government in the analysis of engineered systems,[42] the chemical process industry,[43] the telecommunications industry,[44] the aviation industry,[45] and others. Risk assessment also has been suggested as the means for examining the feasibility and practicality of emerging environmental regulations and policies in developing countries by simultaneously considering and balancing environmental, safety, and health risks and economic risks with the required technological and sociopolitical infrastructure[46] needed to ensure regulation enforcement and policy implementation.

Probabilistic risk assessment. As discussed earlier, risk is the product of the probability of an event occurring over a given period of time and the consequence(s) of the event, should it occur. The purpose of a risk assessment is—for a particular system of interest—to identify events that can have a deleterious effect on the performance of the system, assess the likelihood of their occurrence, evaluate their potential consequence(s), and estimate the risks that they pose. The likelihood of occurrence of the event is provided by a probability. It was also discussed in Sec. 1.3.1, under "Technical uncertainties," that the evaluation of the potential consequence(s) of hazardous events is plagued by uncertainties associated with the models used to simulate the events, processes, and phenomena that it may initiate, as well as the numerical values of the parameters contained in the models. These uncertainties are typically propagated to the numerical value of the consequence(s) via statistical sampling with Monte Carlo simulation. This risk assessment framework is commonly known as *probabilistic risk assessment,* or *PRA* for short.

The most widely known use of PRA was pioneered by the nuclear power industry for the conduct of safety analyses of nuclear reactors[49]; however, PRA is now widely used in waste disposal,[16] environmental, safety, and health management,[11] the chemical industry,[42] the aircraft industry,[40,45] and reliability analysis,[47] to name but a few applications. A PRA, independent of the particular system being analyzed, consists of five generic steps:

1. Understanding of the system and the gathering of all available relevant data and information

2. Identification of initiating events and the construction of scenarios from the events, including assessment of the likelihood of occurrence of the scenarios in terms of a probability

3. Identification and quantification of the uncertainties that will affect estimation of the consequences of the scenarios (i.e., uncertainty in models and uncertainty in parameters)

4. Consequence modeling, including Monte Carlo simulation

5. Estimation of risk

PRA methodology. Morgan and Henrion[5] suggest that a successful PRA methodology, particularly one that will be used to support decision making, should adhere to the following guidelines:

1. Do your homework (i.e., understand the problem and the associated issues).

2. Let the problem drive the analysis.

3. Make the analysis as simple as possible, but do not eliminate important complexities.

4. Identify all significant assumptions.

5. Specify the decision criteria.

6. Explicitly identify the important sources of uncertainty.

7. Perform systematic uncertainty analyses and sensitivity analyses.

8. Refine the problem statement and the accompanying analysis by performing successive iterations.

9. Document the analysis clearly.

The generic PRA methodology shown in Fig. 1.3, even though it was not developed following the guidelines of Morgan and Henrion,[5] exhibits all the attributes listed above. This methodology has been demonstrated for a wide range of problems, such as PRA for nuclear power plants,[19] radioactive waste disposal,[48] prioritization of contaminated-site cleanup,[49] and reliability analysis in component manufacturing.[50] As just pointed out, the strength of the methodology is its adaptability to a wide variety of applications, which reinforces the notion that PRAs should follow the generic steps presented in Sec. 1.4.2 under "Probabilistic risk assessment" regardless of the application. This is particularly important in risk communication when one attempts to compare risks from uncommon or unfamiliar situations with risks that the public has learned to tolerate. However, as will be discussed shortly, there still remain key open issues related to the application of this methodology.

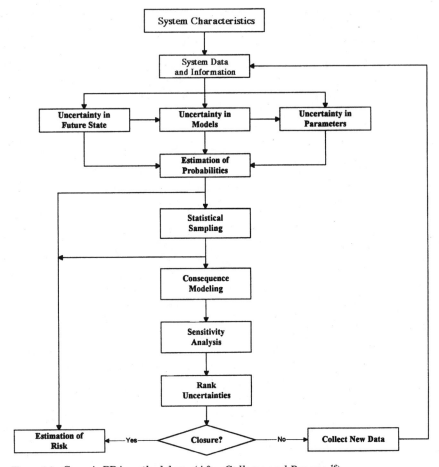

Figure 1.3 Generic PRA methodology. (*After Gallegos and Bonano.*[16])

One important aspect or component of this PRA methodology is sensitivity analysis. It is quite common for uncertainty analysis and sensitivity analysis to be equated with each other because often the results of an uncertainty analysis are used to carry out sensitivity analyses. In reality, these are two different types of analyses conducted for different purposes. In an *uncertainty analysis,* one seeks to identify, quantify, and propagate the uncertainties to the estimate of risks, and as such, it is a necessary component of a PRA. In a *sensitivity analysis,* one seeks to determine those uncertainties with the highest influence on the uncertainty in the value of the consequence(s). A sensitivity analysis is not essential in PRA, but it is highly recommended. Sensitivity analysis can have a considerable positive contribution to the reduction of uncertainty, for it is the main approach used to identify the significant sources of uncertainty. Results from a sensitivity analysis can provide the necessary guidance to ensure that data-collection strategies are focused on those uncertainties with the greatest impact on the decision.

The PRA methodology shown in Fig. 1.3 is iterative in nature. It is highly unlikely that the data or information needed to support the application of the PRA methodology will be sufficiently complete in the first iteration; this is particularly true for complex systems. Therefore, following the first iteration, the uncertainties are likely to be too large to support a defensible decision. Through sensitivity analysis, new or additional needs for data or information are identified. In principle, the data or information is collected, the database for the PRA is updated, and another iteration of the methodology is carried out. This iterative process continues until it has been determined that the results are sufficiently reliable and defensible to proceed with the decision. This iterative process sounds fairly reasonable in theory; however, reality is quite different. The resolution of two key aspects of the approach remains elusive: (1) traditionally, sensitivity analyses are conducted through regression analysis from the results of a Monte Carlo simulation, and the latter may not capture all the potentially significant uncertainties, and (2) an adequate "stopping rule" is needed to determine when key uncertainties have been resolved and defensible results have been obtained.

This methodology considers the main sources of uncertainty and the methods and techniques available to treat the uncertainties, as discussed in Sec. 1.3.1. The methodology permits the examination of intermediate results and is modular in nature to accommodate the exchange of models and approaches to treat the uncertainties with relative ease as more advanced techniques become available. Finally, it results in a direct mapping of the uncertainty in the results of the risk assessment to the different sources of uncertainty. This is extremely important because it allows the decision maker to (1) identify the most significant sources of uncertainty with respect to the decision to be made, (2) prioritize research and development (R&D) efforts, (3) manage finite resources in an effective manner, and (4) set appropriate and practical risk-reduction targets.

The methodology tracks the propagation of uncertainty to the estimate of total risk. Total risk can have several components: (1) the risk of health effect hazards, (2) economic risk, and (3) programmatic risk. Dividing the risk into the appropriate components allows the decision maker to incorporate and consider all available information likely to have an impact on the decision at hand. An example of the latter is the development of a BRC policy for either radioactive or hazardous wastes. As mentioned earlier, commonly, BRC is equated with a *de minimis* level; however, while the two terms are directly related, they are not synonymous. A *de minimis* level is solely based on health risk, whereas BRC considers both health risk and other factors, such as economic impacts. Therefore, it is reasonable to expect that a BRC risk level is often somewhat higher than a *de minimis* level.

Benefits and limits of risk assessment. Risk assessments provide managers and decision makers with a tool that allows them to

1. Determine whether or not the risks posed by a problem or situation are unacceptably high and thus warrant remedial action

2. Select appropriate actions or alternatives that will reduce the risk to acceptable and practical levels

3. Assign priorities to needed technological developments and thus increase the likelihood that R&D investments will have high payoffs

By using risk assessments as the technical basis supporting the decision-making process, managers and decision makers should be able to implement solutions that withstand the scrutiny of the technical community, the regulatory authorities, and the general public.

The results of a risk assessment are only as good as their use in risk management. A risk assessment will be no more than an academic exercise if the decision makers choose not to use the results. Emphasis should not be on the specific numerical values that the risk assessment yields but rather on the identification of potentially hazardous events, the ranking of the consequences and risks that they pose, and the selection of appropriate mitigating actions. Decision makers may shy away from using the results of a risk assessment because of the inherent uncertainties; however, the advantages and strengths of a risk assessment lie in the fact that it deals with the uncertainties explicitly. In this sense, if used in the proper context, risk assessment can guide decision makers through the process of making informed decisions and minimize the likelihood of repeating past mistakes.[51]

1.4.3 Risk management

Risk management deals with the policy and societal issues about risk and the cost, practical feasibility, and timing of risk-mitigating actions. As such, a key attribute of a "good" risk-management program is consistency in the manner decision makers respond to risk.[10,52] Consistency starts with ensuring that all hazardous events and the associated risks have been considered in the same context so that there is a common basis for risk comparisons and the tradeoffs that accompany such comparisons. Thus determining adequate "margins of safety" or "how clean is clean" are two examples of decisions that fall under the purview of risk managers.

The tolerance of risk ranges from risks that are totally unacceptable—tolerating them cannot be justified under any set of circumstances—to negligible risks in which expenditures to reduce or mitigate them would be a waste of valuable resources (*de minimis* risks). Between these two extremes lies a "gray area" in which the tolerance of risks depends on (1) the benefits that can be reaped from such actions and (2) the cost of risk reduction. Decisions regarding the tolerance of given risks—because the benefits make the risk worth taking—are a key element of risk management.

Use of risk assessment in policymaking.   In the 1980s, for example, the U.S. Environmental Protection Agency (EPA) implemented policies that separated risk assessment from risk management, and such a divorce had detrimental effects on the development of environmental policies. This separation, Silbergeld[32] argues, can lead to abuses in scientific research and misleading interpretations and uses of scientific results. The resolution of uncertainty lies at the center of Silbergeld's argument. A practical element of risk management is that the resources available for the reduction of an uncertainty are not without limit. Those who advocate the separation between risk assessment and risk management do not seem to appreciate, recognize, or accept the fact that resolution of uncertainties relies on value judgments or tradeoffs. Scientists typically advocate fundamental research without due regard to the reality that the resource constraints present. On the other hand, policymakers tend to be ambivalent toward the fact that policy decisions need to rely on scientific evidence.

Let's consider the decision to construct, license, and operate a deep geologic repository as the example to illustrate this point. Regulations governing such a system in most countries prescribe either explicitly or implicitly that the safety of the system be demonstrated by conducting a risk assessment—more commonly known as a *performance assessment* in waste-management jargon.[16] The methodology employed to conduct the performance assessment is identical to the PRA methodology discussed in Sec. 1.4.2 under "PRA Methodology." The concept of iterative PRA is being widely used in the conduct of performance assessment for radioactive waste-disposal facilities. The basic tenet for the iterative approach, as discussed earlier, is that a sensitivity analysis will identify and rank the important sources of uncertainty and that this ranking will provide the necessary guidance for data collection. This ranking, however, is solely based on the technical impact of the uncertainties on the results of the performance assessment. It could very well be that the reduction of the highest-ranked uncertainty presents a technical feasibility challenge that will require prohibitive expenditures of resources. In this case, programmatic risks posed on the construction, licensing, and operation of the repository need to be ascertained; i.e., it must be determined if not reducing the uncertainty will negate the successful development of the necessary safety case for the facility. One approach to deal with this problem is to assess the impact of resolving—or otherwise—the highest-ranked uncertainty and compare it with the impact of resolving a set of several lower-ranked uncertainties.[53] This comparison constitutes a risk assessment to evaluate the programmatic risk associated with alternative approaches for the resolution of technical uncertainties. Several different outcomes are possible from such an assessment: (1) the programmatic risk of not resolving the highest-ranked uncertainty is intolerable, and therefore, more resources should be devoted to its resolution, (2) the programmatic risk, while high, can be effectively balanced by resolving a set of lower-ranked uncertainties without requiring additional resources, and (3) the programmatic risk is not as high as originally anticipated, and resources may be better spent on the resolution of other issues. The risk assessment in this case allows a policy decision on the alternative route for resolution of uncertainties that will have the biggest payoff within programmatic constraints.

Policymaking—although often viewed as pertaining only to decisions in the public sector—is also an important aspect of "business" in the private sector. Whether a government regulatory authority is concerned with establishing adequate margins of safety on which to base an emerging regulation or a company is trying to select a new medical insurance plan for its employees, the decision is a policy decision that requires an analysis. Such analysis is aimed at evaluating and structuring the available information in order to make an informed decision that considers the state of knowledge and its limitations (i.e., uncertainties).[5] Throughout this chapter I have argued that due to the unavoidable presence of uncertainties, their explicit consideration enhances—rather than diminishes—the defensibility of the decision making.

Policy analysis seeks to examine different alternatives, their effects, and the costs and benefits of each. Policymaking uses this information as the basis for making a decision and selecting a given alternative. When policymaking has to do with making decisions regarding actions to mitigate certain risks (i.e., risk management), risk assessment is the underpinning for the associated policy analysis. FFI,[10] in an argument for the development of a national environmental risk-management policy, advocates the use of risk assessment as providing the supporting analysis in which risks are evaluated and characterized. Similarly, the U.S. Department of Energy[54] has proposed a risk-management strategy for environmental restoration and waste management that aims at reducing risks. The first step in this strategy is estimation of defensible risks to health and safety and to the environment for each of the department's facilities.

Earlier, Sec. 1.4.1 discussed the lack of a BRC policy in the United States for both radioactive and chemical wastes. The underpinning for the development of a much-needed BRC policy is the concept of *de minimis* risk levels. This arises because there may be some risks related to the health and safety of the public and to the environment that are too low to merit or justify being regulated. In order to determine whether or not risks are small enough to be classified as *de minimis,* two factors must be considered: (1) a risk value below which the risks are considered negligible and (2) the character of the risks. The first is a value judgment, whereas the second requires an analysis (i.e., a risk assessment). The EPA and the U.S. Food and Drug Administration—from a policy point of view—regard risks of less than 1 in 1 million ($<10^{-6}$) to be negligible.[36]

Scientific evidence and public perceptions.   Upon making a decision, risk managers face the extremely challenging task of communicating the decision to the public. Whether the risk manager is a government official charged with the development of a new environmental regulation or a chemical plant manager responsible for reducing air emissions, the public needs to be convinced that the decision made does not jeopardize their health and safety in particular and their quality of life and well-being in general. Risk managers hopefully used risk assessments to characterize the different risks presented by the different alternatives and explicitly and systematically considered the uncertainties that affect the risk estimates.

The issue is how risk managers present (1) the available factual evidence for the risk assessment and the risk-management decision, (2) the manner in which the evidence influenced the decision, and (3) the other nontechnical factors (e.g., economics, social and political) that were considered. Together, these three components provide the basis for justifying and explaining the rationale supporting the decision. Risk managers must be able to clearly articulate this information if they are to be successful in convincing the public that the decision was made with their long-term benefits in mind. In communicating such information, risk managers must strike a critical balance between public awareness of the uncertainties associated with the decision and the defensibility and robustness of the decision. The public must be convinced that the best available information—though not perfect—was used in making the decision. The public also needs to recognize that delaying the decision in order to collect more data or information to reduce uncertainties would not have been an acceptable option. Risk managers must feel and seem confident about the decision, for perceptions of lack of confidence may raise doubts in the public's mind about the competence of the individuals to make the decision. However, expressions of overconfidence also would be foolhardy, for these tend to generate mistrust.[31]

Section 1.4.1 presented five factors proposed by Kemp[34] for risk tolerance. One of these factors is "comparisons" of different risks. Rodricks[31] and Covello et al.[41] also recommend comparative risk assessments as effective means of communicating the results of risk-management decisions.

1.5 Concluding Remarks

This chapter has hopefully provided the reader with a general picture of the decision-making process and the impact that the inherent uncertainties can have on the results of the process. It has advocated in the strongest of terms that meaningful decisions must recognize the impact of the uncertainties and therefore must deal with these in an explicit and systematic manner. It also has discussed risk assessment and risk management as the frameworks for the consideration and analysis of uncertainties in decision making. Finally, it attempts to contrast the more technical and quantitative aspects of decision making with those pertaining to policy or societal issues.

It would be foolish to claim that this is a comprehensive treatise on the aforementioned topics. On the contrary, only the surface has been scratched. Therefore relevant works in the open literature have been referenced to allow the interested reader to delve deeper into one or more of the topics herein presented.

1.6 References

1. P. Goodwin and G. Wright, *Decision Analysis for Management Judgment,* Wiley, New York, 1991.
2. S. H. Kim, *Statistics and Decisions: An Introduction to Foundations,* Van Nostrand Reinhold, New York, 1992.
3. D. V. Lindley, *Making Decisions,* 2d ed., Wiley, New York, 1985.
4. A. M. Finkel, *Confronting Uncertainty in Risk Management: A Guide for Decision-Makers,* Center for Risk Management, Resources for the Future, Washington, 1990.
5. M. G. Morgan and M. Henrion, *Uncertainty: A Guide to Dealing with Uncertainty in Quantitative Risk and Policy Analysis,* Cambridge University Press, Cambridge, England, 1990.

6. Barakat & Chamberlin, Inc., *Uncertainty in Forecasting,* CU-6855, Electric Power Research Institute, Palo Alto, Calif., 1990.
7. K. Shrader-Frechette, "Reductionist Approaches to Risk," in D. G. Mayo and R. D. Hollander (eds.), *Acceptable Evidence: Science and Values in Risk Management,* Oxford University Press, New York, 1991, pp. 218–248.
8. D. von Winterfeldt and W. Edwards, *Decision Analysis and Behavioral Research,* Cambridge University Press, New York, 1986.
9. E. J. Bonano, "The Formal Use of Expert Judgments in Environmental Management," in A. Avogadro and R. C. Ragaini (eds.), *Technologies for Environmental Cleanup: Soil and Groundwater,* Kluwer Academic Press, Amsterdam, The Netherlands, 1993, pp. 409–433.
10. FFI (Federal Focus, Inc.), *Toward Common Measures: Recommendations for a Presidential Executive Order on Environmental Risk Assessment and Risk Management Policy,* Federal Focus, Inc. and The Institute for Regulatory Policy, Washington, 1991.
11. E. J. Bonano, "Decision Making, Risk Assessment, and Uncertainty Analysis in Environmental Management," in A. Avogadro and R. C. Ragaini (eds.), *Technologies for Environmental Cleanup: Soil and Groundwater,* Kluwer Academic Press, Amsterdam, The Netherlands, 1993, pp. 13–46.
12. E. W. Colglazier, "Evidential, Ethical, and Policy Disputes: Admissible Evidence in Radioactive Waste Management," in D. G. Mayo and R. D. Hollander (eds.), *Acceptable Evidence: Science and Values in Risk Management,* Oxford University Press, New York, 1991, pp. 137–159.
13. R. L. Keeney and D. von Winterfeldt, "On the Uses of Expert Judgment in Complex Technical Problems," *IEEE Transactions in Engineering Management,* 36: 83–86, 1989.
14. S. C. Hora, *The Acquisition of Expert Judgment: Examples from Risk Assessment,* School of Business Administration, University of Hawaii, Hilo, 1992.
15. R. M. Cooke, *Experts in Uncertainty: Opinion and Subjective Probability in Science,* Oxford University Press, New York, 1991.
16. D. P. Gallegos and E. J. Bonano, "Consideration of Uncertainty in the Performance Assessment of Radioactive Waste Disposal from an International Regulatory Perspective," *Reliability Engineering and System Safety,* 42: 111–123, 1993.
17. E. J. Bonano and R. M. Cranwell, "Treatment of Uncertainties in the Performance Assessment of Geologic High-Level Radioactive Waste Repositories," *Mathematical Geology,* 20: 543–565, 1988.
18. *Uncertainty Analysis for Performance Assessments of Radioactive Waste Disposal Systems,* Nuclear Energy Agency, Organization for Economic Cooperation and Development, Paris, 1987.
19. *Reactor Risk Reference Document,* NUREG-1150, U.S. Nuclear Regulatory Commission, Washington, 1987.
20. *Systematic Approaches to Scenario Development,* Nuclear Energy Agency, Organization for Economic Cooperation and Development, Paris, 1992.
21. W. W. Doerr, "WHAT-IF Analysis," in H. R. Greenberg and J. J. Cramer (eds.), *Risk Assessment and Risk Management for the Chemical Process Industry,* Van Nostrand Reinhold, New York, 1991.
22. A. L. Gutjahr, E. J. Bonano, and R. M. Cranwell, "Treatment of Parameter Uncertainties in Modeling Contaminant Transport in Geologic Media: Stochastic vs. Deterministic Models with Statistical Sampling," *Proceedings of the International Symposium on Stochastic Approaches to Subsurface Flow,* pp. 332–350, Montvillargene, France, 1985.
23. G. F. Wilkinson and G. E. Runkle, *Quality Assurance (QA) Plan for Computer Software Supporting the U.S. Nuclear Regulatory Commission's High-Level Waste Management Programs,* NUREG/CR-5393, SAND89-1432, Sandia National Laboratories, Albuquerque, N.M., 1986.
24. N. de Finetti, *Theory of Probability,* Wiley, New York, 1974.
25. G. Apostolakis, "The Concept of Probability in Safety Assessment of Technological Systems," *Science,* 250: 1359–1364, 1990.
26. R. von Mises, *Probability, Statistics and Truth,* Allen & Unwin, London, 1957.

27. D. L. Ray, *Trashing the Planet: How Science Can Help Us Deal with Acid Rain, Depletion of the Ozone, and Nuclear Waste (Among Other Things)*, Harper Perennial, New York, 1992.
28. S. Ahmed, D. R. Metcalf, and J. W. Pengram, "Uncertainty Propagation in Probabilistic Risk Assessment: A Comparative Study," *Transactions of the American Nuclear Society: 1981 Annual Meeting,* 38: 483–484, 1981.
29. Y. S. Sherif, "On Risk and Risk Analysis," *Reliability Engineering and System Safety,* 31: 155–178, 1991.
30. S. Kaplan and B. J. Garrick, "On the Quantitative Definition of Risk," *Risk Analysis,* 1: 11–27, 1981.
31. J. V. Rodricks, *Calculated Risks: The Toxicity and Human Health Risks of Chemicals in Our Environment,* Cambridge University Press, Cambridge, England, 1992.
32. E. K. Silbergeld, "Risk Assessment and Risk Management: An Uneasy Divorce," in D. G. Mayo and R. D. Hollander (eds.), *Acceptable Evidence: Science and Values in Risk Management,* Oxford University Press, New York, 1991, pp. 99–114.
33. W. W. Lowrance, *Of Acceptable Risk: Science and the Determination of Safety,* William Kaufmann, Los Altos, Calif., 1976.
34. R. V. Kemp, "Risk Tolerance and Safety Management," *Reliability Engineering and System Safety,* 31: 345–353, 1991.
35. P. Slovic, "Beyond Numbers: A Broader Perspective on Risk Perception and Risk Communication," in D. G. Mayo and R. D. Hollander (eds.), *Acceptable Evidence: Science and Values in Risk Management,* Oxford University Press, New York, 1991, pp. 48–65.
36. S. Jasanoff, "Acceptable Evidence in a Pluralistic Society," in D. G. Mayo and R. D. Hollander (eds.), *Acceptable Evidence: Science and Values in Risk Management,* Oxford University Press, New York, 1991, pp. 29–47.
37. R. Neider, "Exemptions Limits for Contaminated Materials to be Recycled and for Low Level Radioactive Waste from Nuclear Power Stations and Uranium Mining and Milling Areas in South-Eastern Germany," *Proceedings of Waste Management 1992,* University of Arizona, Tucson, Ariz., 1992.
38. 10 CFR Part 20, "Radiological Criteria for Decommissioning, Draft for Comment, U.S. Nuclear Regulatory Commission, Washington, January 26, 1994.
39. D. G. Mayo and R. D. Hollander (eds.), *Acceptable Evidence: Science and Values in Risk Management,* Oxford University Press, New York, 1991.
40. M. G. Morgan, "Risk Analysis and Management," *Scientific American,* 269: 32–41, 1993.
41. V. T. Covello, P. M. Sandman, and P. Slovic, "Guidelines for Communicating Information about Chemical Risks Effectively and Responsibly," in D. G. Mayo and R. D. Hollander (eds.), *Acceptable Evidence: Science and Values in Risk Management,* Oxford University Press, New York, 1991, pp. 66–90.
42. *Risk Assessment: A Survey of Characteristics, Applications, and Methods Used by Federal Agencies for Engineered Systems,* U.S. Nuclear Regulatory Commission, Washington, 1992.
43. H. R. Greenberg and J. J. Cramer (eds.), *Risk Assessment and Risk Management for the Chemical Process Industry,* Van Nostrand Reinhold, New York, 1991.
44. G. Zorpette, "Keeping the Phones Lines Open," *IEEE Spectrum,* 26: 32–36, 1989.
45. E. E. Murphy, "Aging Aircraft: Too Old to Fly?" *IEEE Spectrum,* 26: 28–31, 1989.
46. E. J. Bonano, "Examination and Recommendations for the Improvement of Environmental Standards in Mexico," A Concept Paper, Beta Corporation International, Albuquerque, N.M., 1993.
47. M. Modarres, *What Every Engineer Should Know about Reliability and Risk Analysis,* Marcel Dekker, New York, 1993.
48. E. J. Bonano, R. M. Cranwell, and P. A. Davis, "Performance Assessment Methodologies for the Analysis of High-Level Radioactive Waste Repositories," *Radioactive Waste Management and the Nuclear Fuel Cycle,* 13: 229, 1989.
49. R. P. Rechard, M. S. Y. Chu, and S. L. Brown, *SRS: Site Ranking System for Hazardous Chemical and Radioactive Waste,* SAND86-2994, Sandia National Laboratories, Albuquerque, N.M., 1988.
50. J. E. Campbell, B. M. Thompson, D. E. Longsine, and P. A. O'Connell, *RAMP (Reliability Analysis and Modeling Program), Version 2 User's Reference Manual,* Sandia National Laboratories, Albuquerque, N.M., 1993.

51. T. E. Bell, "Managing Risk in Large Complex Systems," *IEEE Spectrum,* 26: 22–23, 1989.
52. R. W. Myers, J. J. Cramer, and R. T. Hessian, Jr., "Risk Management Programs," in H. R. Greenberg and J. J. Cramer (eds.), *Risk Assessment and Risk Management for the Chemical Process Industry,* Van Nostrand Reinhold, New York, 1991.
53. E. J. Bonano and J. A. Thies, "Bridging the Gap Between Performance Assessment and Data Collection for Waste Disposal Systems: A Proposed Approach Using Genetic Algorithms," presented at Waste Management 1994, Tucson, Ariz., February 1994.
54. *Risk Management Strategic Plan,* Draft, U.S. Department of Energy, Washington, January 1993.

Regulatory Guidance

Robert D. Zimmerman
Fluor Daniel, Inc.

2.1 Introduction

Most regulatory documents and industry-recognized texts on risk assessment make only brief mention that the risk assessment should be conducted in a cost-effective manner, even though the distribution of costs and risks is fundamental to the political forces that create the regulations in the first place. Typically, little, if any, guidance is given in regulatory or industry-recognized texts on how to deal with the most contentious issues, such as (1) the intrinsic value of life, health, or aesthetics, (2) institutional biases and ethical conflicts, and (3) the fairness of the distribution of costs, risks, and benefits. The regulations that assign legal and financial responsibility to individuals for the hazards they impose on society also establish authority and responsibility for the governmental agencies who interpret and administer the laws. The Occupational Safety and Health Administration (OSHA), the Environmental Protection Agency (EPA), and the Nuclear Regulatory Commission (NRC) all recommend that the depth of the risk analysis should be in some measure proportional to the level of risk at the facility under consideration. Sources of guidance on the degree of effort appropriate for risk analyses are identified in Table 2.1.

Risk assessments that are used by proponents and regulators to communicate with the public go through a series of review and approval steps. This process has gotten increasingly complex as more and more special interests have succeeded in obtaining legal recognition.

TABLE 2.1   Guidance on Appropriate Degree of Effort for Risk Analysis

Source	Application	Guidance
DOE 6430.1A[1]	U.S. Department of Energy facilities	Depth of analysis should be proportional to the level of risk
OSHA 29 CFR Part 1910.119, Sec. (e)[2]	U.S. facilities with potential for catastrophic releases of toxic, reactive, flammable, or explosive chemicals	Analysis shall be appropriate to the complexity of the process
DOE 5480.23, Attachment 1, Sec. 4.f (1)b[3]	U.S. Department of Energy nuclear facilities	The level of effort should be proportional to the magnitude of hazards, complexity of the facility and systems, and the stage of facility completion
API RP750[4]	Facilities in the U.S. petroleum industry with potential for catastrophic release of toxic, flammable, or explosive material	Recommends refs. 5 and 6 for acceptable methodologies
Evaluating Process Safety in the Chemical Industry[7]	Chemical process facilities	Provides a decision tree for determining if quantitative analysis is the efficient approach
MIL-STD-1629A[8]	Originated for defense projects; applied many places	The foreword is devoted to effectiveness. The body contains guidance on approach and discusses the importance of choosing the level of detail

Although the analyst and the sponsor have the initial say, they are not the final decision makers. Initially, the analyst recommends how much work is required; the sponsor decides how much is appropriate given the economic constraints (profitability on private projects, political support on public works, special interest support on civic projects); and the regulators balance the project sponsor's interests with those of other stakeholders (private property and public environmental, health, and safety interests). Ultimately, each party decides how much study it feels is enough, balancing its own vested interest with its own perception of its personal risk.

2.2   Analyst Judgment

Regulatory guidance on the effectiveness of risk analysis is purposely general, allowing room for the expert judgment of the analyst.

Industry, EPA, and OSHA agreed that performance-based standards would be more effective than prescribing specific equipment requirements or analyses. *Performance-based standards* are defined as those which require a hazard-assessment program that anticipates potential accidents, a risk-management program that ensures that the plant has safeguards to prevent or mitigate credible accidents, and an emergency-response program for responding to potential worst-case accidents. This approach was adopted in recognition of the fact that the various industry and trade groups had initiated the effort to manage risks.

Many risk professionals have observed that there is considerable overlap among the various recommended risk-management programs.[9] From their perspective, the most significant change imposed by recent legislative actions was to require public review and approval of safety management programs. Others point out that the old system, which relied on voluntary implementation of consensus standards, tended to penalize the short-term profits of companies who implemented them and did not provide any penalties for companies who did not implement them. From a legal standpoint, no one was held responsible. From a political standpoint, everyone in the industry was held responsible. Perhaps the most significant change was to provide a mechanism that requires industry and government facilities to address catastrophic accidents specifically and community planning issues generally. This requires input from a broad-based team of people, including operators, engineers, and management. To do so, the risk analysis not only must include hazards analysis, engineered features, and operating procedures, but it also must demonstrate technical thoroughness and credibility and take into consideration negative impacts that an accident or normal operations could have on the community. Consideration also must be given to the industry's safety record.

Regulations generally can be divided into two categories. One type is very prescriptive and requires a minimum of analysis or judgment. The regulators establish both the criteria and the methods; the analyst applies them. Examples include many of the fire and safety codes and many of the OSHA regulations. The second type is goal-oriented and simply states the broad performance standards that must be met. The latter type is preferred by industries that are undergoing a lot of technical innovation and works best when the risk assessment is performed concurrently with the plant design. This approach allows (1) considering unique combinations of technologies, many of which may be new or unfamiliar to regulators or others in the same industry, (2) eliminating ineffective features and undue risk, and (3) having the most efficient and reliable plant. Examples include the recent OSHA regulations for process safety management of hazardous chemicals. The primary disadvantage is that the project proponents have the burden of establishing the adequacy of the analytical methods and safety criteria they have chosen; both the regulators and project opponents can challenge them.

In principle, the license applicant should select an effective method for meeting the statutory requirements, and the regulatory agencies concentrate on reviewing whether the method was appropriate and applied correctly in that specific analysis. In cases where opponents perceive significant risks, scientifically implausible but impossible to disprove claims can cause expensive delays unless those issues are identified early and addressed properly in the analysis; see Chap. 11 for more detail on suggestions on conflict and issue resolution. Most agencies use a hybrid approach, allowing license applicants flexibility on some items while prescribing others.[2,10,11] This is so partly because of differences in approaches, methods, and scientific know-how and partly because of differences in perspectives between those who benefit from a project and those who do not. For example, regulatory agencies often force analysts to use assumptions that bias analytical results toward one particular agency's policies. On the other hand, many risk analysts have observed that they have never seen a risk assessment that seriously conflicts with its sponsor's position, whether they be an advocate or detractor of a particular project. Indeed, the level of effort spent on risk analysis is often a better reflection of the sponsor's financial position than of environmental, health, or safety risks. A more detailed discussion and example can be found in Mazur.[12]

Many regulatory agencies are willing to comment on preliminary design input during a preapplication review. Although the agencies cannot make a final determination based on this information, this type of review is helpful to both parties. For example, the agency will usually identify areas of concern, including recommended practices, emergency planning guidelines, risk reduction/mitigation, hazard screening criteria, measures of completeness (e.g., checklists, review guides), and identification of technologies and systems which it feels require in-depth analysis.

The NRC has instituted specific safety assessment methods in regulatory guides. These methods have been established in a legally defensible public review process and cannot be challenged during the license application process. This generally deterministic approach is preferred by some because it presumably reduces the opportunity for litigation. On the other hand, the deterministic approach requires each applicant to use the same approach as the "worst-case" plant without allowing credit for unique features it may have included in the design. This escalates costs and often results in inflated risk estimates. It can also have the undesirable effect of diverting resources away from areas where greater risk reduction could be achieved at the same cost. Chapter 3 discusses approaches for avoiding this problem.

OSHA uses both prescriptive and performance standards. The older standards for common occupational accidents tend to be prescriptive. The newer accident standards tend to be performance-based. The newer standards include threshold quantities that are used to determine if in-depth analysis is required. The requirements for more detailed analysis resulted from public and worker concern over the increasing frequency of major accidents. Industry, workers, and government agencies all agreed that the accident statistics demonstrated that the command-and-control approach failed to prevent accident propagation in the larger and more complex plants. OSHA 29 CFR Part 1910.119, "Process Safety Management of Highly Hazardous Chemicals,"[2] was written as a performance-based standard to address this problem by requiring the plant designer to identify the most significant hazards based on threshold quantities of chemicals that are particularly reactive or hazardous, even when one adheres to the more traditional design and OSHA codes and standards.

The new OSHA chemical process safety standard (29 CFR 1910.119), Section 112(r), "Prevention of Accidental Releases," of the Clean Air Amendments of 1990, and the Emergency Planning and Community Right-to-Know Act (Title III of the Superfund Amendments and Reauthorization Act of 1986) created the general duty to identify hazards, to design and maintain a safe facility, and to minimize the consequences of accidents.[13] These regulations allow the analyst to determine an appropriate method and to document and defend the adequacy of his or her analysis before regulators. Reasonable estimates of the hazards located in adjoining areas also must be considered if they could either initiate or contribute to a credible accident within the plant boundary. In case there is not sufficient information to rely on, the analyst should clearly identify safety-related support systems, hazard zones, and emergency planning zones.

2.3 Analysis Approach

The most difficult aspect of deciding on the extent of the analysis is the fact that the analyst will never have perfect understanding of all the real and perceived risks in the plant. An analyst should try to obtain as much input as possible from all sources, including designers, operating staff, researchers, and people who are knowledgeable about adjoining areas and their hazards. Section 4.4 contains guidance for evaluating whether nearby areas and supporting systems should be analyzed in detail. Several of the professional societies have developed recommended practices that include qualitative rankings of risk to determine whether the significance of the hazard and complexity of the plant warrant the expense of a qualitative risk assessment.[5–7]

General guidance on the appropriate method is contained in recent texts on risk-assessment methods. The OSHA standard *Process Safety Management of Highly Hazardous Chemicals* lists acceptable methods for a process hazards evaluation. The American Petroleum Institute (API) publication RP750, *Management of Process Hazards,*[4] refers to the Center for Chemical Process Safety (CCPS) *Guidelines for Hazard Evaluation Procedures*[5] and the Chemical Manufacturers Association (CMA) *Process Safety Management*[6] for recommended methods. The CCPS guidelines cover all the methods mentioned in the OSHA document. Other useful references on methodology are readily available.[7,9,14,15] These texts refer to many other sources. A summary of important references and guidance is given in Chap. 5.

In OSHA 29 CFR 1910.119, the greatest risks to the public are addressed first. Risks such as hydrogen fluoride and ammonia are to be analyzed extensively. Lesser risks can be analyzed in less detail. This regulation uses a performance-based standard; the plant owner-operator has to demonstrate that the design has properly considered hazards and has incorporated adequate provisions to prevent serious health problems or injury or require off-site emergency response if an accident were to occur. This regulation was developed as a consensus standard after considerable review and comment by both the public and the EPA.[2,16,17] The intent of developing a consensus regulatory standard is to have a single administrative review process. Despite this intent, the EPA issued its own draft risk-management program (40 CFR 68), which proposes using different criteria than the ones contained in 29 CFR 1910.119 to determine which systems require in-depth analysis.[18] The justification given for the second standard is to overcome differences in statutory jurisdictional authority, not risk reduction. A comparison of the proposed EPA risk-management program with the existing OSHA program concluded that the proposed rule will double the regulatory burden on approximately two-thirds of the facilities regulated by either agency.[18] Obviously, this proposal will increase the cost of any plant's regulatory compliance. At the time this was written, the Office of Management and Budget had not completed its review process on the need for and effectiveness of the proposed regulation.

Performance-based standards give the analyst the responsibility for determining the appropriate level of detail. In some portions of the facility, it may only be necessary to demonstrate that credible accidents cannot cause significant consequences. This can be accomplished at a low level of detail using a risk survey, as discussed in Chap. 4.

References on methodology provide flexibility for different approaches, such as top-down failure modes and effects analysis (FMEA) and high-level FMEA.[8] In the top-down approach, the level of detail is adjusted according to the failure effects. A high-level FMEA can be used during conceptual design to determine whether there is sufficient depth of defense in the design at the system and subsystem levels. Although hazard and operability (HAZOP) study guides often state that each item on the piping and instrumentation diagram should be analyzed, sometimes it may be appropriate to go into greater detail or to envelop similar items. In general, with any methodology, analysis should be performed in sufficient detail to ensure that there are no unexpected effects on interfacing systems. See Chap. 5 for more discussion.

Most hazards and safety review processes emphasize the early data-gathering process. One also should consider review and approval as part of this process, since the analyst is not the person who makes the decision. In most practical situations, there is no single decision maker; instead, there are different "interests" who will have their own opinions on the subject and will want to review and comment on the analyst's assessment. Many of these people are the very people who *should* be giving the analyst their input early on in the evaluation process: plant operators, researchers, designers, managers of neighboring facilities and utility services, and emergency responders. These groups "know" and "own" the information. The analyst's job is to gather accurate and complete input, which is almost inevitably a two-step process. The first step is based on the staff's initial input, which typically is information based on their personal experience with similar systems. The second step occurs during the formal review process. By its nature, the second step is more in-depth and thorough. The reviewers not only have the benefit of more complete design information regarding adjoining systems and the balance of plant, they also have had time to think about potential hazards and interactions they may not have raised during the initial hazard review.

It is philosophically desirable to concentrate most of the risk-assessment effort on identifying, analyzing, and mitigating the areas that contribute the most significant risks to the plant owners, operators, and neighbors. The goal is general agreement between analyst, decision makers, and stakeholders that the remaining risks are acceptable. In practice, except for low-frequency events, actual operating experience is the best objective yardstick of residual risk; one must deal with individual decision makers' perceptions.

It is important to realize that there are numerous decision makers involved in developing risk standards and for implementing those standards. The analyst cannot completely anticipate who will review his or her analysis during the process of deciding when enough is enough. The regulatory process used by federal, state, and local agencies includes input from a broad spectrum of scientific, legal, and political organizations and from special-interest groups and other stakeholders. That process should consider the following[17]: (1) the appropriateness of government policies, (2) scientific principles, (3) the need for additional research, (4) whether the principles for risk assessments are rational and scientifically based and whether they adequately address nonfatal effects such as neurotoxicologic and reproductive effects, and (5) ethical values (e.g., fairness) and benefits such as quality of life.

Most risk analysts recognize that risk assessment is both a subjective and an objective process, since most people evaluate risk in terms of their individual experiences.[20,21] This provides an opportunity for considering cost-effectiveness when planning and performing the analytical portion of the risk assessment. The analyst and decision makers can focus on the most significant risks, increasing the level of detail in specific areas when their level of importance to individual decision makers becomes an issue. The whole issue of "how much is enough" is about minimizing the individual decision makers' perceptions of the differences between predicted and real-life experience. The cost-effective approach uses the risk models to resolve these issues and allows for variations in local practices, ethical values, legal positions, and political and cultural issues that will arise as different reviewers make their own individual decisions. See Chap. 1 for a description of the elements of a risk model and how to develop one and Chap. 3 for a description of how to apply the model to evaluating risk and resolve issues. Using a risk model allows an evaluation of the sensitivity of the estimated residual risk to those variations without passing judgment on claims that are scientifically implausible but impossible to disprove. The model can then be used to facilitate communications and develop approaches for managing those risks. In most cases, it is possible to achieve mutually acceptable solutions. In others, such as where the results are highly sensitive to implausible scenarios, the project sponsor may have to abandon consideration of that technology or site.

There are four institutional approaches to managing risk, all of which have to be considered in developing any risk model[21]: (1) laws related to negligence, liability, nuisance, and trespass, (2) private and government liability insurance, (3) voluntary standards (American National Standards Institute), and (4) mandatory government standards and regulations. The National Research Council recommends maintaining the current strict separation between the scientific process of risk assessment and the value-laden process of management and regulation.[13] This approach (1) has the benefit of allowing unbiased comparisons between public opinion and scientific assessments of environmental, health, and safety risks, (2) identifies areas where the public is concerned about the limits of scientific knowledge, and (3) facilitates establishing priorities for future research.

2.4 References

1. DOE Order 6430.1A, *General Design Criteria,* U.S. Department of Energy, April 1989, Sec. 1300-1.3.
2. OSHA 29 CFR Part 1910.119, "Process Safety Management of Highly Hazardous Chemicals," *Federal Register,* July 1993, pp. 364–385.
3. DOE Order 5480.23, *Nuclear Safety Analysis Reports,* U.S. Department of Energy, 1992, Attachment 1, p. 16.
4. API Recommended Practice RP750, *Management of Process Hazards,* American Petroleum Institute, Washington, 1990, Sec. 3.2.1.
5. *Guidelines for Hazard Evaluation Procedures,* 2d ed., Center for Chemical Process Safety of the American Institute of Chemical Engineers, New York, 1992.
6. R. E. Knowlton et al., *Process Safety Management,* Chemical Manufacturers Association, Washington, 1985.
7. J. S. Arendt, D. K. Lorenzo, and A. F. Lusby, *Evaluating Process Safety in the Chemical Industry,* Chemical Manufacturers Association, Washington, 1989.
8. MIL-STD-1629A, *Procedures for Performing a Failure Mode, Effects and Criticality Analysis,* U.S. Department of Defense, 1984 (available from Naval Publications and Forms Center, Philadelphia).
9. D. A. Walker et al., "Managing Safety," *Chemical Engineering,* March 1993, pp. 90–100.
10. EPA 40 CFR 68, Clean Air Act Amendments (CAAA), November 1990, Secs. 301 and 304, January 19, 1993.
11. EPA 40 CFR 355, "Superfund Amendments and Reauthorization Act (SARA)," *Federal Register,* April 22, 1987, p. 13395; as amended in the *Federal Register,* July 26, 1990, p. 30645.
12. A. Mazur, "The Hazards of Risk Assessment," *Chemical Engineering News,* October 12, 1992, pp. 76, 77, 106.
13. *Chemical Process Safety Report,* "Laws and Regulations," App. 1-G, "The Clean Air Act Amendments of 1990: How They Affect Chemical Process Safety," Thompson Publishing Group, Washington, April 1993, pp. 307–405.
14. *Guidelines for Chemical Process Quantitative Risk Analysis,* Center for Chemical Process Safety of the American Institute of Chemical Engineers, New York, 1989.
15. *Guidelines for Technical Management of Chemical Process Safety,* Center for Chemical Process Safety of the American Institute of Chemical Engineers, New York, 1989.
16. T. Seymour, Occupational Safety and Health Administration, "OSHA's Process Safety Management Standard," American Institute of Chemical Engineers, 1992 Spring National Meeting, March 1992.
17. *Proceedings of the 27th Annual Loss Prevention Symposium, Session III: Regulatory Issues with Respect to Loss Prevention,* American Institute of Chemical Engineers, March 1993.
18. *Discussion and Summary of U.S. EPA's Draft Proposed Risk Management Program Regulations (40 CFR 67),* Primatech Inc., Columbus, Ohio, June 1993.
19. U.S. Environmental Protection Agency and the Department of Health and Human Services, "Risk Assessment Practices in the Federal Government," *Federal Register,* 56(204): 54580–54582, Notices, Tuesday, October 22, 1991.
20. S. Jasanoff, "Bridging the Two Cultures of Risk Analysis," *Risk Analysis,* 13(2): 123–129, 1993.
21. T. S. Glickman and M. Gough, *Readings in Risk,* Resources for the Future, Washington, 1990.

Measuring Engineering Effectiveness: How Much Study Is Enough?

R. Peter Stickles
Arthur D. Little, Inc.

3.1 Introduction

As evidenced by many papers and books on the subject, there is no lack of tools and techniques for identifying hazards and quantitatively assessing the associated risks. The problem for the design engineer is knowing when a given approach is appropriate and whether the specific safety concern justifies the additional time and cost of quantifying the magnitude of the risk. This chapter discusses important constraints to the application of risk analysis and provides practical guidance on what to use when and how much. This will be done in the context of the phases of an engineered project. The following delineation of project phases applies throughout the text:

- Project conceptualization
- Basic engineering
- Detailed engineering
- Procurement/construction
- Pre-start-up/commissioning

- Operation
- Decommissioning

3.2 Constraints

The constraints imposed on the use of risk-analysis techniques can be broadly grouped into the following three categories:

- Project information
- Economic issues
- Quantification uncertainties

To a large degree, these constraints influence decisions on the level of detail and extent of risk analysis. The constraint limits change as the project develops. For example, comprehensive quantitative risk assessment should not be attempted until process equipment and piping have been sized, since release quantities and rates cannot be characterized accurately without such information.

3.2.1 Project information constraints

Risk management for a new design should be an ongoing activity from the initial process concept through active operation. The earlier in the project cycle the risk assessment is applied, the lower is the impact on cost and schedule from incorporating preventive or mitigative design changes.[1] The main constraint to applying quantitative risk-assessment methods early in the project is the availability of sufficiently detailed information. Figure 3.1 lists project information that is generally available during different project stages. While it is possible and appropriate to begin risk-management activities during project conceptualization, available information will limit which analysis techniques can be used. A very effective technique that can be used at the conceptual stage is the process materials interaction or compatibility matrix. A discussion of this technique is presented later.

3.2.2 Economic constraints

As discussed in the previous chapters, economic considerations are a necessary factor in risk management. A major concern is always the cost of implementing required risk-mitigation measures. Such mitigation measures have the potential to add significant cost to the project. However, properly executed, a risk-management program can identify the design deficiencies that are the major contributors to unacceptable

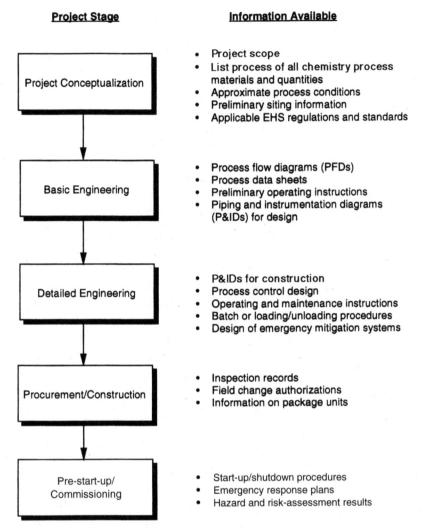

Project Stage

Information Available

Project Conceptualization

- Project scope
- List process of all chemistry process materials and quantities
- Approximate process conditions
- Preliminary siting information
- Applicable EHS regulations and standards

Basic Engineering

- Process flow diagrams (PFDs)
- Process data sheets
- Preliminary operating instructions
- Piping and instrumentation diagrams (P&IDs) for design

Detailed Engineering

- P&IDs for construction
- Process control design
- Operating and maintenance instructions
- Batch or loading/unloading procedures
- Design of emergency mitigation systems

Procurement/Construction

- Inspection records
- Field change authorizations
- Information on package units

Pre-start-up/ Commissioning

- Start-up/shutdown procedures
- Emergency response plans
- Hazard and risk-assessment results

Figure 3.1   Basic project design stages.

risk and can provide comparative risk-reduction information for mitigation alternatives. Coupled with cost estimates for the mitigation alternatives, project management can make an informed decision regarding selection of the most cost-effective mitigation.

Another pertinent aspect of risk-mitigation costs is that what was considered acceptable risk in the past is less tolerable now. Yet there is a tendency to use past frames of reference for project costs when trying to justify or discard risk-mitigation alternatives. Mitigation should not be eliminated on the basis that it is "too expensive" until the consequences and likelihood of the unmitigated accidents have been evaluated. The objective of the risk management should be to implement the most cost-effective risk-reduction solution.

Planning and scheduling of the risk assessment need to be properly addressed to avoid unnecessary economic ramifications. For example, initial screening might reveal the need for detailed analysis in a system that is ordinarily unimportant. Conversely, an extensive assessment might be initiated before detailed information is available, resulting in major reductions of remaining budget but little reduction of uncertainty. Project planning should anticipate the type of risk assessment required so that there are no unpleasant budget surprises midway through the project. Scheduling of the risk assessment needs to be coordinated with the project engineering efforts so that engineering and detailed design activities are not delayed. Such delays can increase project management cost and ultimately project cash flow.

As a guideline for use of comprehensive risk quantification, full quantitative risk assessment (QRA), when its cost, compared with the cost of mitigation, is less by a factor of 5 to 10, should be considered.

3.2.3 Uncertainty constraints

All risk assessments involve a degree of uncertainty. Risk assessment is performed so that the uncertainty can be reduced sufficiently to allow a decision (as opposed to a guess). After a risk assessment, there will be some uncertainty that cannot be eliminated or is not worth reducing. Some of the residual uncertainty is associated with the stochastic methods used (i.e., modeling of hazard phenomena and failure analysis). For some analyses, such as air-dispersion modeling, the magnitude of uncertainty can be bounded. Such bounded uncertainties can be dealt with in the decision-making process.

More troublesome is the uncertainty due to lack of understanding or ability to quantify. The issue of completeness arises in the hazard-identification step.[2] Hazards not uncovered during a process hazards analysis (PHA) will very seldom be discovered during the more-focused analyses that may follow. This reinforces the need to have the proper mix of expertise and experience represented on the PHA team. While no single PHA will identify 100 percent of the hazards, having a multidisciplinary, skilled team increases the probability of identifying the major hazards. Even when a potential hazard has been identified, there is no certainty that the subsequent analysis will address all the possible causes and effects. However, one can reasonably expect trained and experienced practitioners using systematic techniques and relevant experience to identify the most important accidents, causes, and effects.[2]

Another important uncertainty can be unknown chemical instabilities that exist outside the envelope of process knowledge. Starting the risk assessment during process development can help identify areas where thermochemical data must be developed.

In Chap. 1, the uncertainties in criteria were discussed. More important are uncertainties in public acceptance. The public may even question the variables that are used to express risk. The best way to reduce this uncertainty is to involve the community early in the analysis, as discussed further in this chapter.

As an example showing the uncertainties that must be dealt with, future population growth around a site can be modeled in relation to potential release contours. The maximum population may be limited by land-use regulations. The susceptibility of the population will depend on factors such as age, lifestyle, and mobility, for which statistics are available. Even if population changes could be ignored, there are other uncertainties: The release of chemicals is subject to physical limitations. There is variability among available models in regard to how well they simulate the physical phenomena. These model biases should be considered during risk assessment.[3] In addition, the skill of the users is a variable. Consequently, there are wide variations in calculated dispersion from a release.

Likewise, operator actions under stress, which may worsen the situation, can be unpredictable. There are unbounded uncertainties involved in using acute human health effects predictions that are based on extrapolations from laboratory animal experiments and are subject to uncertainties in data and methods.

Some uncertainties that are not easily bounded can be characterized by sensitivity analyses. A sensitivity analysis can be used to decide which design and external factors are important enough to require further analysis or design revision. The effectiveness of process safety management systems (e.g., mechanical integrity program) after startup is a significant uncertainty. However, the comprehensive risk assessment can prioritize for operating management those areas where procedures and inspection programs are being relied on to mitigate risk.

Consequences from complicated accident scenarios are naturally more difficult to model. Spatial orientation of piping and equipment layout can contribute to knock-on or domino effects during a fire or explosion, resulting in a much more serious incident, an example being a pump seal leak or flange leak igniting, which causes failure of structural components or a stagnant line, thereby escalating the event. The potential for knock-on events depends on the coincidence of several location- and orientation-specific circumstances. Applying fault-tree analysis without recognizing this potential generally will suggest that the scenarios that result from these knock-on events are very unlikely. Yet anyone who has been involved in postincident reconstruction knows that "Murphy's law" certainly applies during facility catastrophes. The best approach during initial design and layout is to follow industry standards and codes regarding exclusion distances and equipment location, provide ample access to equipment, and avoid congested piping arrangements. Furthermore, the addition of fixed fire protection systems to susceptible pumps, pipe racks, etc. is worthy of consideration. If details of plant layout are not available, it may be necessary initially to adopt a conservative approach, because consideration of all potential individual interactions becomes prohibitively expensive and the uncertainties become almost impossible to quantify. To ensure that a reasonably simple analysis can provide acceptable limits on knock-on events, barriers sometimes must be added to the design.

Chapter 9 discusses a qualitative approach to an assessment of the defenses against common-cause failures and, in particular, the use of barriers as a defense. This approach also can be used as a basis for a review of defenses against potential knock-on failures. In fact, the example of the analysis of barriers was developed from the method for analysis of spatial interactions such as fires and floods.

3.3 Case Study

The incident described in this section occurred in the mid-1980s at a major olefin plant. The loss in assets alone was $55 million. Miraculously, no one was killed in the incident. After a description of the chain of events, the implications for dealing with uncertainty will be addressed.

Just prior to the incident, there was an upset condition at the acetylene hydrogenation system in the deethanizer overhead stream. The automatic trip system blocked in the reactors, but the bypass failed to open. The deethanizer column pressure increased until the relief valves located on the reboiler vapor return line opened. The operators continued to attempt to alleviate the problem in the overhead system, while the relief valve was intermittently venting. This continued for some time, but no action was taken to reduce feed to the cracking section. Eventually, the vibration of the venting relief valve loosened the flange bolts underneath the valve, and a vapor jet appeared.

An operator was sent to manually block in the reboiler (the deethanizer had two reboilers provided with isolation valves). As the operator attempted to close an isolation valve, the vapor jet ignited. The orientation of the jet flame was such that it impinged on a spring hanger rod holding up the blowdown line from the column relief valves. The rod failed, causing the blowdown line to collapse and breaking the relief valve inlet lines (there were two relief valves per vapor return line) where they connected to the reboiler return line. This resulted in two large flame jets, one of which impinged on an elbow in the ethylene column reboiler vapor line. This 36-in (0.91-m) elbow weakened and failed, rapidly depressuring the ethylene column.

Across the road from the ethylene column was a battery of vertical pressurized storage bullets for ethylene and propylene product. The force or flame engulfment from the ethylene column failure knocked over or caused a boiling liquid, expanding vapor explosion (BLEVE) in one of the storage bullets. The resulting inferno caused most of the other bullets to undergo a BLEVE. The fire destroyed three main fractionation columns and six 90,000-gal (340-m^3) storage tanks.

This incident provides several lessons for the risk analyst. Because of the number of knock-on events, the predicted likelihood of the top event was incredibly low. A postincident fault-tree analysis established the frequency to be less than 10^{-8} per year. This is well below even nuclear industry risk-acceptability levels for catastrophic events.[4] Therefore, classic risk analysis would not have indicated a concern, assuming a process-hazard analysis could have identified the actual chain of events. Furthermore, the likelihood is so low that a PHA review during project design would not have characterized the entire incident. However, there were deficiencies in the design that a skillful hazard and operability (HAZOP) team could have found and, had they been corrected, could have prevented or greatly reduced the magnitude of the damage.

A review of the system for bypassing the acetylene hydrogenation system without blocking the deethanizer overhead should have raised questions about preventive maintenance and proof testing of emergency shutdown and interlock systems. Investigation of the deethanizer pressure-relieving capability would have revealed that the relief valve was sized for loss of overhead condenser cooling, which was a much larger flow than the event that occurred. This resulted in relief valve "chatter" at the lower flow conditions and contributed to the loosening of the bolts. Alternate sizing or set-point criteria and valve configurations could have reduced the potential for chattering. A tight, congested equipment layout with little stationary fire protection was another contributing factor. Clearly, the performance of the operators during the incident, especially the delay in stopping the feed once a fire had been reported, exacerbated the situation. This supports the need for a PHA review of shutdown and emergency operating procedures and operator training requirements.

This case study also reinforces the fact that risk analysis begins with thorough hazard identification. The importance of this aspect of risk

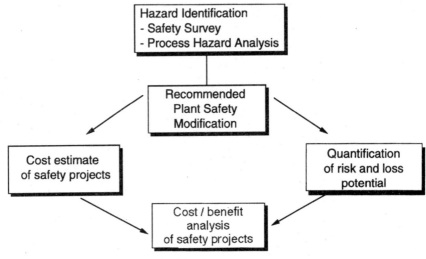

Figure 3.2 Block diagram of methodology.

assessment cannot be overstated. Hazards that are not found during the identification step seldom get incorporated into subsequent risk-analysis and design considerations.

3.4   Cost-Effective Methodology

A stepwise procedure is appropriate to study the costs versus benefits of the complete plant and individual safety recommendations. Figure 3.2 illustrates the activities leading to a cost-effective project. The steps are

1. Identify and prioritize accident scenarios using the techniques outlined in Sec. 3.4.1. These survey methods provide a rough, quick ranking of hazards.

2. For the significant accident scenarios identified in the first step, recommend plant modifications that will prevent or reduce the magnitude of accident damage.

3. Estimate mitigation project costs using an order-of-magnitude estimating approach (Sec. 3.4.2).

4. Estimate the impact (consequence) and statistical frequency of accident scenarios using hazard-evaluation methods outlined in Sec. 3.4.3.

5. Generate the loss profile described in Sec. 3.4.4 to determine the statistically expected financial loss. Then compare the costs from step 3 with the avoided risk from step 4. At this point, the public perception of plant risks and benefits should be considered.

In this approach, an attempt to evaluate human life in financial terms has been avoided for several reasons:

- It would imply an acceptance of human fatality.
- It would lead to placing a value on human life, with many ethical issues arising if different values are assigned to different locations.
- It would suggest that fatalities are regarded as part of the cost of doing business.

Nevertheless, it is clear that projects that reduce the chance of injury or death also will lessen the potential for financial loss. This cost-benefit methodology identifies such projects based on the proposition that safe operation is good business.

The basic methodologies that exist for risk assessment will be reviewed. A methodology for incorporating mitigation cost into a risk analysis is also described. Since much has been written in texts and the technical literature on this subject, the reader should consult the references at the end of this chapter for additional information. The chapter ends with guidelines for scheduling risk-analysis activities.

3.4.1 Hazard identification and prioritization

Interaction matrix. The interaction matrix is a deductive technique for identifying potential hazards due to chemical interactions. A representative interaction matrix is illustrated in Table 3.1. Applying the method first involves determining generic chemical interaction hazards, followed by identifying specific process areas or steps where such potential exists. It is especially applicable to reactive chemical systems. It can be applied before detailed design information is available, and the results may trigger consideration of inherently safe process alternatives. Alternatively, the results may indicate that the chemistry of some potential interactions is not well understood and that additional thermochemical analysis (differential scanning calorimeter, accelerated rate calorimeter, etc.) is warranted. Completing the interaction matrix prior to a PHA also can be beneficial for orienting the team and focusing the review activities.

A potential drawback of this method is that it takes into consideration only binary interactions. However, as shown in Table 3.1, the matrix can be expanded to cover mixtures and other cause-effect relationships. Naturally, the more complex the matrix, the more effort is required to complete it.

TABLE 3.1 Dimethyl Badstuff Project: Interaction Review Matrix*

	Chemical A	Chemical B	Chemical Z	Mixture 1	Notes	References
Chemical A		x	x	x		
Chemical B			x	x		
Chemical Z				x		
Mixture						
Water						
Steam						
Acid						
Base						
Air/O_2						
N_2						
Detergent						
Rust						
Lube oil						
Contaminant 1						
Hi temp						
Lo temp						
Hi pressure						
Construction material						
Acute limit						
Chronic limit						
OSHA PSM						
EPS RMP						

*An x denotes duplicate interaction of chemicals; consideration not required.

Screening techniques. Hazard and risk screening techniques include some metric to obtain a relative index or ranking or hazard and risk potential. Three widely applied indices are the Dow Fire and Explosion Index,[5] the Chemical Exposure Index,[6] and the ICI Mond Index. There are also several risk screening models available[7,8] that combine semirigorous consequence algorithms with exposed population factors to generate a process risk-ranking score. These models incorporate a chemical physical properties database, and certain ones can handle mixtures.[8]

As a result of legislation regarding the handling and storage of highly hazardous substances, some states (e.g., Delaware and New Jersey) have adopted the Substance Hazard Index (SHI) to define and rank hazardous materials. The SHI is defined as EVC/ATC, where EVC is the equilibrium vapor concentration (ppm) and ATC is the acute toxicity concentration (ppm). The equilibrium vapor concentration (ppm) at 20°C (68°F) can be calculated by

$$EVC = \frac{\text{vapor pressure of substance at } 20°C \times 10^6}{760 \text{ mmHg}}$$

For gases and liquids with vapor pressures greater than 760 mmHg at 20°C, the EVC reduces to 1 million parts per million.

Of interest to the analysis is that different jurisdictions have selected different minimum values for the SHI, i.e., the cutoff for highly hazardous materials. The SHI value above which a substance is defined as extremely hazardous is indicated below for certain jurisdictions:

Jurisdiction	SHI value	Reference
Delaware	8000	9
API RP750	5000	10
New Jersey	1388	11

The value for New Jersey is derived from 36% hydrochloric acid, which was listed in the original legislative bill.

It also should be noted that ATC values used to calculate the SHI vary according to jurisdiction. Therefore, the analysts should consult the specific regulation or standard to determine the appropriate ATC value.

The Occupational Safety and Health Administration (OSHA) and Environmental Protection Agency (EPA) have created other lists of "highly hazardous chemicals" or "regulated substances" ranked according to threshold quantities above which risk-management programs apply.[12,13]

The beauty of screening techniques is that they require minimum data (chemical inventory and hazard properties) and do not require a large investment in time to apply. However, they provide only a relative indication of hazard and risk potential, which can identify high-hazard process areas and process sites. Even though some of the techniques incorporate risk concepts, they are not a substitute for comprehensive risk quantification. The results can be used to flag processes or plant sections that should be subjected to more rigorous risk assessment. Alternatively, ranking scores should be used to determine and prioritize high-risk facilities that are candidates for a more detailed risk survey. Chapter 4 contains further discussion on the use of these techniques.

Process hazard analysis. Hazard-identification techniques sanctioned for process hazards analysis include checklist, what-if, hazard and operability (HAZOP) study, and failure mode and effects analysis (FMEA). A description of these techniques can be found in other references.[2,10] Some features of these methods are discussed below.

Since HAZOP study and FMEA are systematic hazard-identification procedures, they have certain features in common:

- Documentation of possible disturbances in the form of cause/consequence/countermeasure spreadsheets.
- Use of search aids (guide words, failure mode list).

Therefore, the generic procedure consists of systematic investigation, according to the given scheme, of all deviations from the design intent.

The value of these methods, over less formalized design hazard reviews, is that they impose a certain degree of organization and structure on the investigation of safety aspects. If properly applied, they offer the following advantages:

1. Due to the structured methodology, it is more likely that teams made up of people with different types of qualifications will achieve similar good results.

2. Process improvement can result from the repeated systematic questioning of process functions and conditions and the need to consider the effects of deviations.

3. The use of search aids and a structured documentation format allows the result to be easily understood by those who did not participate in the review.

There are also pitfalls associated with such methods that users should recognize, namely,

- New or previously unknown hazards are not likely to be discovered. Knowledge of chemical bond reactivity, coupled with thermochemical testing and analysis, is the only way to identify unknown chemical hazards. This factor reinforces the benefit of using the interaction matrix during project conceptualization. However, the methods can determine how hazards may evolve (e.g., loss of cooling, contamination).

- There is a tendency to consider specific disturbances without regard to concerns beyond the immediate cause-effect relationship. This is especially the case for FMEA. However, a properly facilitated HAZOP study should require considering consequences (resulting from deviations) regardless of where they occur in the process.

- The hazard-identification findings are not final. Problem areas are indicated, and potential solutions presented. Others are empowered to determine the ultimate fix, which may not receive subsequent review. This issue can be dealt with by flagging PHA findings that need to receive follow-up review by the team.

- In its classic form, the FMEA method is quite rigid. Process conditions (pressure, temperature) and functions (reaction, mixing) are not addressed directly. Therefore, some practitioners have modified the procedure to include two levels of effects. For example, the "primary effect" of a temperature transmitter false low signal is a steam valve wide open. The "secondary effect" is temperature increase in the reactor with runaway potential. This forces the team to look beyond the immediate effect of the failure.

- Systematic approaches can involve a significant allocation of staff and financial resources, depending on the complexity of the process. Given the regulatory requirements in certain jurisdictions and more comprehensive corporate standards, this is generally the rule rather than the exception. This means that the review process needs to be well planned and managed to obtained the best value for the money spent.

Prioritization of PHA findings.   When companies perform process hazard analysis to meet regulations, a large number (literally thousands in some instances) of findings and recommendations can be produced. Since available resources generally do not permit implementation of all the recommendations at once, it is desirable to prioritize the projects so that items with high risk-reduction potential relative to cost are done first. The approach discussed here incorporates means of balancing project cost and risk-reduction benefit to aid in the prioritization of a large number of mitigation projects.

An important part of the approach is a common basis for the evaluation of both safety-related and production-related spending.[14] Any program to implement risk reduction entails the following.

- Selection of the order in which work is to be done.
- Effective project management of implementation.

It is desirable to have plans in place to deal with all safety-related inadequacies, although the available resources may dictate that some work be scheduled on a more urgent basis than others.

To determine the order of project work, it is necessary to quantify the potential losses from incidents that could arise if the project were not done. To make a start on the project management, it is necessary to make some definition of the scope of work and to derive a cost and feasible schedule for implementation. The combination of quantified loss potential and cost estimate permits a cost-benefit analysis on the safety project that serves as the basis for prioritization of the work.

Risk quantification can be achieved in some measure using risk-ranking tables to prioritize findings, as illustrated in Table 3.2, used for ranking findings. The table comprises a matrix of consequences described by the terms *negligible, marginal, substantial, critical,* and *catastrophic.* Each term is defined by a loss range that is estimated to include loss of both property and profits. The ranges also can be defined in terms of numbers of accidents or fatalities for safety ranking. The two scales are treated separately (it is not implied that an event causing one fatality also will cause losses of between \$1 and \$10 million). In this table, frequency is covered by three ranges: *occasional, infrequent,* and *rare.* These terms are similarly specified by ranges of annual frequency. The ranking table needs to be adapted to suit the needs of the client and the site being surveyed. In many cases, a 4 × 4 matrix is pre-

TABLE 3.2   Matrix for Ranking Events*

	Negligible	Marginal	Substantial	Critical	Catastrophic
Fatalities	Accident	Accident	1	2–10	>10
Damage cost ($ millions)	<0.1	0.1–1.0	1–10	10–100	>100
Rare (less than once in 1000 years)	Low	Low	Low	Medium	High
Infrequent (between once in 10 and once in 1000 years)	Low	Low	Medium	High	Immediate
Occasional (more than once in 10 years)	Low	Medium	High	Immediate	Immediate

*The three rankings used—high, medium, and low—were allocated using this matrix.

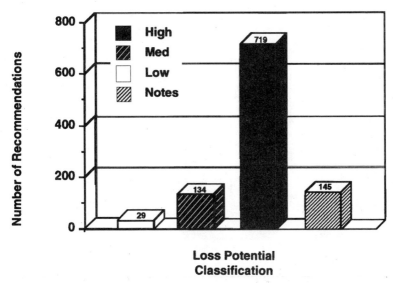

Figure 3.3 Loss potential classification according to the HAZOP study recommendations.

ferred that gives equal emphasis to frequency and consequence rankings. Figure 3.3 illustrates the results of an overall ranking of a large HAZOP study covering a number of plant sections.

If greater precision is required, a quantified risk analysis can be performed in which the frequency of potential releases and their consequences are systematically enumerated. Frequencies are typically analyzed using a fault-tree approach quantified with failure data from industry sources modified to the individual circumstances of the plant in question. Consequences are calculated using dispersion models and probit functions for toxic releases or flammability limits and overpressure radii for materials that are explosive. Again, these methods are well established and widely described in the literature.[10]

3.4.2 Cost estimation

Much can be done without going to the extent of a detailed planning and cost-estimating exercise on each project. It is useful to classify the potential project work into items that can be managed with plant resources (small projects) and those requiring external support (large projects). Costs can then be range-estimated using order-of-magnitude steps:

- Minor: below $10,000
- Small: $10,000 to $100,000

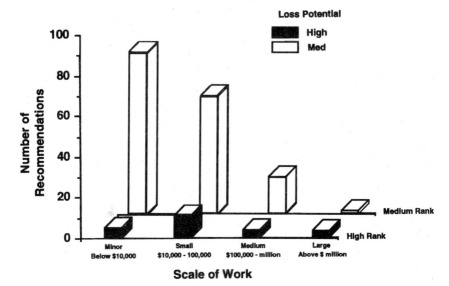

Figure 3.4   Project cost classification, showing scale of project work and recommendation ranking.

- Medium: $100,000 to $1 million
- Large: above $1 million

Although this may seem crude when considering an individual project, the range-estimating approach can give useful results if a large number of recommendations are involved, e.g., grouped by schedule requirements.

Figure 3.4 illustrates the cost-ranking approach applied to the data from Fig. 3.3. High- and medium-rank recommendations have been assigned to four cost ranges.

3.4.3   Hazard evaluation

The preceding section discussed methods and their limitations for identifying hazards. To properly answer the question "How much study is enough?" requires the use of hazard-evaluation methods. Evaluation methods differ considerably from identification methods not only in their ultimate objective but also in some other important respects[15]:

1. Potential hazardous events are not considered in isolation but combined to assess deviation interactions and total risk.

2. They permit quantitative evaluation of risk parameters.

3. They require a certain level of knowledge and application skill to obtain meaningful results.

The principal hazard-evaluation methods include

- Failure or frequency analysis
- Consequence analysis
- Quantitative risk analysis

Failure analysis uses logic or sequence diagrams to establish the frequency of undesirable outcomes. Two techniques are employed: *event-tree analysis* based on incident sequence and *fault-tree analysis* based on failure states. *Consequence analysis* involves the application of simulation models, which mathematically describe complex hazard phenomenon, to estimate the hazard impact (consequences) that can be released. *Quantitative risk analysis* (QRA) combines the results of fault-tree analysis and consequence analysis with influencing factors, such as weather data, population distribution, and ignition potential, to determine the frequency of a range of impacts (fatality, financial loss). A more extensive treatment of these topics is presented in later chapters. The objective of management of the risks from the identified hazards that cannot be eliminated is that they be reduced to sufficiently low levels.[16] A quantified hazard evaluation may address the likelihood of the hazard and/or the extent of the consequences. When applying such techniques, the analysis is taken only so far as is necessary to aid with a decision.[16]

Some governments have imposed numerical standards of risk for certain endeavors (i.e.. core damage from nuclear power generation).[17] Where this is not the case, there can be some balancing of risk against benefit in considering what is reasonable mitigation. In order to judge the significance of estimated levels of risk, some form of risk-acceptability criteria is required. Before discussing acceptability criteria, the overall approach to hazard evaluation will be presented.

Approach.   A sequential approach to hazard evaluation, with increasing degree of quantification, affords the flexibility to stop once the results indicate that the risk of identified hazards meets the accepted criteria. The first step is setting some form of damage and risk-acceptability criteria. The hazard-evaluation techniques are then applied in ascending order of complexity and effort, namely, consequence analysis, failure analysis, and finally, full risk quantification. The evaluation is continued to the point where a decision can be made, with a reasonable level of certainty, that the remaining risk is acceptable.

TABLE 3.3 Sample Damage Criteria for a Variety of Hazards

Hazard type	Sample damage criteria	Impact level
Toxic chemical release, LC_{50}	Lethal dose ERPG, IDLH, ATC	Fatality Health effects
Pool/jet fire	12.5 kW/m^2 (4000 Btu/h · ft^2)	Fatality
Flash vapor fire	LFL or 1/2 LFL	Fatality
Explosion overpressure	3 psi	Fatality from building damage

Damage criteria. Damage or impact criteria are threshold values for impact of particular hazards (fire, explosion, etc.) that are set at the estimated hazard effect limit for a given level of impact (irreversible health effects, fatality). An example is a criterion for fatality from fire radiation of 12.5 kW/m^2. Damage criteria are used in conjunction with consequence models in order to delineate the extent of the hazard impact (zones). Table 3.3 lists sample damage criteria for a variety of hazards.

Damage criteria are used in the context of the production-site physical layout and demographics. That is, the specific criterion must be met some acceptable distance downwind of the release. This distance is usually the plant or site fence line or the nearest affected member of the public. The site boundary is generally preferred because it provides a margin for error. One jurisdiction[9] uses a nominal 100 m, which can be adjusted upward for large sites.

Risk-acceptability criteria. Risk-acceptability criteria goals are established to protect organizations, their employees, and society from potential acute effects of accidents or abnormal events resulting from industrial operations. The use of quantitative criteria to evaluate risk acceptability can help ensure consistency and fairness in corporate decision making.[18]

Acceptability criteria for the three principal types of risk are defined below:

Critical event/release: Threshold frequency for events or releases with potential for environmental/facility damage or human fatality potential.

Societal risk: Frequency of affecting general populations at one or more and multiple fatality levels.

Individual risk: Frequency of affecting an individual member of the population.

Sample numerical criteria for fixed facilities are presented in Table

TABLE 3.4   Sample Numerical Criteria for Fixed Facilities

The following criteria are appropriate for chemical industry process-related risks from toxic vapor clouds, explosions, and fires. These sample criteria are based on a synopsis of current process industry practice and societal attitudes in western Europe and the United States.

Individual Risk

The average individual risk level for the public should be less than 1 in 1 million per year with a goal of 1 in 10 million per year or less. Maintaining this level will ensure that the facility does not significantly increase background risk levels.

The maximum individual risk level for the public should be less than 1 in 100,000 per year with a goal of less than 1 in 1 million per year. This criterion recognizes that risks increase with proximity to a facility but still keeps the risks at controllable levels. No more than 10 to 20 people should be exposed to this risk level.

The maximum individual risk level for employees should be less than 1 in 20,000 per year, based on historical experience for low levels of employee risks.

Societal Risk

The probability of one or more public fatalities should be less than 1 in 1000 per year with a goal of less than 1 in 10,000 per year.

The probability of 100 or more public fatalities should be less than 1 in 1 million per year with a goal of less than 1 in 10 million per year.

Similarly, the likelihood of numerous employee fatalities in one accident also should be several orders of magnitude less than the likelihood of one or more employee fatalities.

Release Frequencies

All releases with frequencies greater than 1 in 10,000 per year should be contained on site.

SOURCE: Bendixen.[18]

3.4. Numerical criteria such as these must be applied with an understanding of their limitations. Such criteria are goals or targets rather than universally accepted limits, standards, or requirements. Therefore, any judgment regarding the acceptability of risk also must (1) take into account the uncertainty of the risk assessment and (2) address the various qualitative issues affecting public perception.[18]

Although the sample values are a useful starting point, there are no universally accepted risk criteria. Attempts of various jurisdictions to set criteria have been based on political resolution of social and industrial issues, not on optimization of any model. As a result, criteria differ widely (including even zero risk). Provided that there are benefits to the public from a proposed project, agreements are possible on a local level based on perceived fairness. Any explicit or implied criteria from previous agreements will only be the starting point within the social values and political climate of another jurisdiction or time. Ultimately, the fair standard of risk is determined by public consideration of the alternative benefits that could be achieved for comparable risk. As discussed in Chap. 11, public concerns must be determined and considered in the early phases of design; this avoids loss of public confidence and the need for design revisions in the late phases of the project.

A generally unwritten risk criterion used in design is that catastrophic failure of process piping and equipment is unacceptable. Therefore, emergency relief vent sizing is based on the maximum credible event. In addition, external fire is usually a design case, even when it is only remotely probable.

Use of hazard evaluation. As stated earlier, the guiding principle is to employ quantitative risk analysis only to a level sufficient to aid in a decision. Figure 3.5 presents a flowchart for use of hazard-evaluation techniques that helps meet this objective. The logic incorporates consequence analysis, fault-tree analysis, and full QRA methods. While the tree is structured to start with identified hazards, other entry points are possible. For example, if it is already known that the hazard extends beyond the plant boundary, the entry point might be fault-tree analysis or developing mitigation.

This approach is generally applicable to many situations involving new or existing facilities; however, variations of the approach are acceptable. For example, depending on the number of events and level of risk, some practitioners will replace consequence analysis and fault-tree analysis with full QRA at the upper part of the flowchart. This might be warranted when dealing with extremely toxic chemicals with many potential hazardous events, and it is recognized that management needs to know the overall risk after mitigation. However, not all hazards need to be evaluated to this level of detail. The results of a process hazard analysis usually include mitigation concepts that do not cost a lot to implement or involve modifications to management systems. In such instances, the proper decision is generally obvious, and applying quantitative analysis is a waste of resources.

An example to illustrate the use of Fig. 3.5 is provided. The project involves the design of an emergency vent and containment system for several batch process reactors. The process materials undergo exothermic decomposition and produce hydrogen chloride (HCl) as one of the products. The design problem is whether to discharge the HCl from an elevated vent or provide a passive scrubber to mitigate the release. The problem is approached by first applying consequence analysis to determine the stack height needed to achieve the established damage criteria, in this case, ERPG-2 concentration for HCl. Given the distance to fence line and the peak discharge rate, the height required is nearly

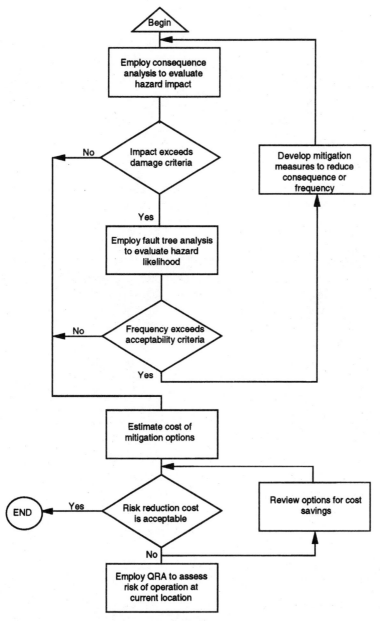

Figure 3.5 Hazard evaluation for risk mitigations.

90 m (300 ft). While feasible, this option was not considered practical at the plant location.

At this point, fault-tree analysis can be employed to determine the likelihood of initiating a runaway reaction and blowing the rupture disk. If the frequency does not exceed the established criteria, then management may consider installing a shorter vent stack and exceeding the ERPG-2 concentration (ground level) at the fence line. Other factors of conservatism that can be investigated at this point are

How close is the nearest neighbor?

What is the population density?

Given the event duration, what is the likely dose? (ERPG is a limiting concentration for a 60-minute exposure time.)

If the frequency is higher than acceptable, then other mitigation options including a scrubber design need to be considered. Consequence analysis is again employed to evaluate the tradeoff between stack height and scrubber capacity in order to meet the damage criteria ground-level concentration. Mitigation to reduce the event frequency also should be evaluated with the aid of fault-tree analysis. At this point, a budget cost estimate should be prepared for the design concepts. If the costs are acceptable, then decide among the alternatives and conclude the analysis. If there are no cost-effective alternatives, then designs need to be reviewed for potential cost savings. If the cost cannot be reduced, management should consider undertaking a full QRA to assess the risk of future operation at the site.

3.4.4 Loss potential

The risks that have been identified by survey or HAZOP study and ranked as illustrated in Fig. 3.3 provide the basic means of estimating the potential losses from the facility. Two rankings are used. One ranking is for financial losses, including

- Business interruption
- Asset losses
- Litigation expense

A separate ranking is used for injuries or fatalities.

Generation of the loss profile (mentioned in step 5 of Sec. 3.4) shows the relationship between probability and the size of the loss. It is readily estimated using a Monte Carlo simulation based on the ranges of frequency and consequence assigned from the ranking matrix. Figure 3.6 illustrates the results obtained from the HAZOP study recommen-

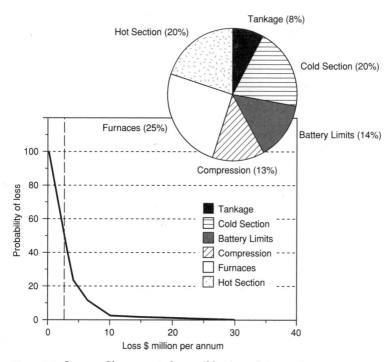

Figure 3.6 Loss profile: property loss and business interruption.

dations ranked in Fig. 3.3. The loss profile is calculated for the rankings of financial impacts. A similar profile can generated for fatalities. The HAZOP study recommendations for each plant section have been taken separately to show their contribution to the overall loss.

The chart shows which sections of the plant (e.g., feed reaction) can be important sources of financial loss.

Next, the mean of the loss profile is computed, which gives the average loss. If the assigned frequency ranges are annual frequencies, this is the average loss per year. The probability corresponding to the mean value indicates the chance of this loss occurring. The loss history available for the particular plant can be used to check the calculation, if there are sufficient data points in relation to the probability of the mean.

The cost-benefit analysis compares the average annual loss with the expected cost of project work. This may be done for the hazard recommendations for the plant as a whole or for recommendations grouped by priority. Evaluating the costs versus benefits of individual engineering recommendations is generally not worthwhile because of the relatively large error bounds on a quick, individual calculation. However, for groups of calculations, random variations in data will average out. The group must be large enough to provide an acceptable level of uncertainty for the "go/no go" decision on the group. Therefore, small groups with similar priority should be lumped together.

A comparison between potential loss and mitigation cost is possible only if unbiased data on cost, consequence, and frequency are available. If order-of-magnitude data are not available, conservative bounding values may be applied. In some cases, expenditure on the entire group of recommendations is justified by the loss reduction from those which can be calculated.

Each calculation must take into account any residual risk remaining after the mitigation work is completed. In this way, the net loss averted by the expenditure is compared against the cost of the recommended modifications.

Figure 3.7 shows the result of such a comparison based on the loss profile from Fig. 3.6. The example results show that including all the projects leads to costs that are likely to outweigh the loss averted. However, the small projects and the medium-sized, high-priority projects do show a positive balance between loss aversion and cost. This is significant, since over 130 recommendations are shown to have a positive benefit-to-cost ratio.

The purpose of the cost-benefit analysis is to sort recommendations in order to permit decisions between alternatives. The uncertainties discussed early in this chapter result in losses and costs that cannot be

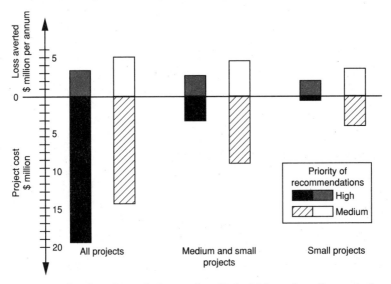

Figure 3.7 Cost-benefit analysis: cost benefit for high- and medium-priority recommendations. Loss averted has been estimated from the recommendation ranking. Ranges of cost have been assigned depending on scope of work involved. Small projects are cost-effective, as are medium-sized projects with high ranking.

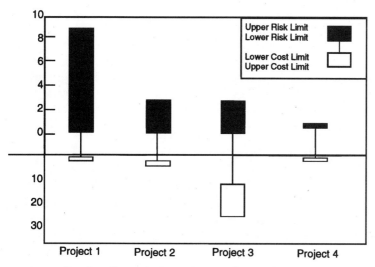

Figure 3.8 Cost-benefit analysis: estimate of uncertainty. Projects are ranked by the size of the risk averted.

evaluated exactly. Rather, the values can only be placed within bands, as indicated in Fig. 3.8. To this extent, it is necessary to define the potential losses and costs just sufficiently to distinguish between them. More detailed work is only justified to narrow the range of uncertainty when the loss band and cost band overlap.

The cost-benefit ratio for individual projects can be tabulated as shown in Table 3.5. It is important to note that the examples with poor cost-benefit ratios are reanalyzed rather than discarded. This is so because the

TABLE 3.5   Cost-Benefit Analysis: Prioritization

HAZOP rec. no.	Description of project	Cost of implementing ($MM)	Loss potential ($MM)	Fatality potential	C/B ratio	Action
2	Install emerg vent hdrs & scrubber system	5.10	100.0	11	0.1	Implement
21	Install ROVs on all rxr & tank outlets w/SSD	2.00	10.0	5	0.2	Implement
5	Reduce and reroute piping	0.45	1.0	1	0.5	Implement
13	Install independent HP alarms on rxrs & stills	1.20	1.0	1	1.2	Reanalyze
7	Install deluge systems in all class I tk farms	5.00	4.0	1	1.3	Reanalyze
10	Install independent HHL on all tanks	3.00	1.0	1	3.0	Reanalyze

recommendations, while being unattractive in financial terms, may nevertheless be important investments for their improvement in safety.

In such cases, the potential accident rate can be compared against cost. This serves to rank the projects in terms of the effectiveness of investment for reducing accidents. The analysis may be completed by determining at what point in the ranking to divide the work into items that will be implemented and those which will be delayed. Several methods can be applied:

- Identify the relationship between accident aversion and cost for a part of the design required by regulations or code. Implement all work with a cost-benefit ratio greater than that corresponding to the regulatory requirement.

- Set a particular fatal accident rate (FAR) that will apply to the facility (corresponds to the mean of the fatality loss profile), and identify the minimum-cost combination of work needed to reach the desired FAR.

3.4.5   Applicability of risk analysis

Every technique for hazard identification or evaluation can be carried out at preliminary or detailed levels. The timing and level of detail for a risk assessment involves a tradeoff: It should be late enough so that the design is well defined and can be accurately analyzed but early enough that required design changes will not unnecessarily delay the project. Some techniques may be applied more than once to different sections or different degrees of analysis. Some companies apply screening techniques at initial stages, perform a complete analysis during detailed engineering, and revisit the results once more before project commissioning.

The application of certain risk-analysis techniques is more appropriate as more detailed project information is available. The general applicability of these techniques to stages of a project is indicated in Table 3.6.

Project conceptualization.   During the initial period of the project, only preliminary information concerning the process may be available. The focus of the risk assessment at this point should be identifying the major hazards and performing initial risk screening. Hazard-identification techniques using basic process knowledge can be applied at this stage. Chemical interaction matrices are commonly used to define areas with potential for uncontrolled reactions with release of chemical energy or undesirable by-products. Results from these techniques include the potential hazard of all chemicals used in the process, either individually or in mixtures, and the potential for fire or explosions.

At this point, project planners also should look at the risk in the broadest context, evaluating the major tradeoffs relative to process and

TABLE 3.6 Array of Typical Methods of Risk Analysis for the Phases of a Project*

Project phase	Inter-action matrix	Hazard-screening index	Hazard/safety review	Process hazard analysis				Consequence analysis	Fault-tree analysis	Event-tree analysis	Quantitative RA
				Checklist	What-if	HAZOP	FMEA				
Conceptualization	x	x		x							
Basic engineering				x	x	x		x			
Detailed engineering				x	x	x	x	x	x	x	x
Procurement/construction			x	x	x	x					
Pre-start-up/commissioning			x	x	x						
Operation			x	x	x	x	x	x	x	x	x
Decommissioning			x	x	x						

*An x indicates a frequently used method.

site selection. Risk-screening techniques allow a top-down review of the potential worst-case risks. The results allow the designer to prioritize areas within a process that pose the highest risk or to compare broad design alternatives.

Early risk-screening techniques are often based on hazard indices, which rank the potential risk based on the type, quantity, and physical state of each chemical used in the process. Hazard rankings are assigned from the potential hazards for each material and the consequences of a catastrophic release. Several approaches are discussed in Chap. 4.

The techniques used in developing hazard rankings also have been refined in the development of risk-screening software. Software packages include additional factors, such as the storage conditions and surrounding population density and distances, to incorporate more fundamental estimates of potential consequences into the hazard ranking. Although these packages may not include any consideration of the frequency of undesirable events, they do allow rough screening of alternate approaches based on a comparison of scores.

Checklists also can be utilized effectively, especially to establish environmental, health, and safety regulatory requirements and industry and internal design codes or standards.

Basic engineering.   During basic engineering, the design becomes more generally defined, including the development of process flow diagrams, operating conditions, and preliminary operating instructions. This information allows a more detailed hazard review. Several process hazard analysis (PHA) techniques, including hazard and operability (HAZOP) studies and what-if analysis, are commonly used to systematically review a process flow sheet. Other techniques, such as checklists or what-if checklist studies also can be applied in greater depth.

The goal of a hazard-identification study at this stage should be a summary of significant hazards, with an indication of potential consequences and recommended actions to reduce the risk. Often the solution is obvious, and the hazard can be readily eliminated through redesign. Recommended actions generated through the study must be documented and assigned to members of the project team for design consideration.

Where the solution is not obvious, hazard assessment may be necessary to ensure the effectiveness of protective measures in meeting risk criteria. For example, consequence modeling could be used to determine the viability of reducing the flammability risk in material storage areas by adding secondary containment and water curtains. Application of consequence modeling may help provide specifications or guidelines for the detailed design, such as special requirements for site layout based on explosion hazards.

Occasionally, preliminary analysis may show that the risk in some aspect of the process cannot be easily reduced to acceptable levels. A complete quantitative risk assessment may be necessary to evaluate cost versus risk reduction for several alternatives. If the cost of risk reduction is high, decision makers may use risk analysis to make a "go/no go" decision for project approval.

Detailed engineering. The focus of risk assessment after project approval shifts from risk evaluation to minimizing overall risk within project cost and schedule constraints. At this stage, complete descriptions of the process and site allow detailed studies to be conducted and results incorporated into the final design.

If systematic hazard-identification studies of the process were not conducted during the basic engineering phase, this is the final opportunity. Studies should be conducted once the plant location and the process diagrams have both been fixed but before the detailed piping and instrument diagrams are approved for construction. In this way, any changes recommended by the study team are readily incorporated into the final design. Certain hazard-identification techniques, such as sequential HAZOP studies or what-if studies, also can be used to identify potential hazards in operating instructions and batch procedures, including loading/unloading and maintenance. Because a disproportionate number of chemical plant accidents occur during the start-up and shutdown, hazard analysis of these procedures can be especially critical.

FMEA is particularly effective for identifying and prioritizing the risks associated with failure of critical process control systems. Detailed information about such systems will be available at this stage of the project.

Alternate measures to reduce the frequency of failure also can be explored at this point using fault-tree or event-tree analysis. Results can be used to quantify what level of reliability is required for a particular process section, protective system, or utility to meet the specific risk criteria.

All or part of a process may be analyzed using either focused hazard assessment or full risk quantification to determine cost versus risk reduction for the detailed design. For example, risk assessment could be used to find the most cost-effective means of reducing the risk of a toxic gas release: increasing equipment reliability or designing redundant levels of control and mitigation.

The design of critical control or mitigation systems may call for either consequence modeling or frequency analysis. For example, fault-tree analysis might be used to break down the ways in which a reactor control system could fail. Consequence modeling could be used to design the fire-suppression systems for a flammable material storage area.

Procurement/construction. Generally, design information on package units (e.g., refrigeration system, dryers) becomes available during this stage. These systems should undergo a review using one of the PHA techniques. Field change requests can be reviewed using the what-if checklist method.

Pre-start-up/commissioning. Prior to start-up, safety review inspection[19] ensures that all results from previous assessments have been incorporated into the design. Results may include recommendations applied to operating instructions and procedures and emergency response plans. A checklist can be applied as a final review for compliance with applicable regulations, codes, and standards. Finally, the safety review should ensure that all areas associated with the process have been reviewed—including loading, transfer, and chemical storage areas.

Operation. During the operating phase of the project, all the detailed risk-analysis techniques are applicable, and the selection and scope depend on the objectives of the risk assessment.

Plants being designed today may be operating 50 years from now. Great changes in risk are possible due to facility aging, adoption of new technology, site changes, social and regulatory reform, cultural changes among operators and management, prevalence of sabotage, and so forth. For these reasons, risk assessments must be reviewed every few years.

Decommissioning. Methods such as safety review or what-if analysis are appropriate to ensure that demolition personnel or the public is not exposed to any process material hazards. A checklist may suffice for review of equipment decontamination procedures.

3.5   References

1. B. Ex and R. P. Stickles, "Risk Assessment in Design: Techniques and Tools," presented at the American Institute of Chemical Engineers Summer National Meeting, 1992.
2. *Guidelines for Hazard Evaluation Procedures,* 2d ed., Center for Chemical Process Safety of the American Institute of Chemical Engineers, New York, 1992.
3. S. Jasanoff, "Bridging the Two Cultures of Risk Analysis," *Risk Analysis,* 13(2): 123–129, 1993.
4. K. Solomon et al., "An Evaluation of Alternative Safety Criteria for Nuclear Power Plants," *Risk Analysis,* 5(3): 209–216, 1985.
5. *Fire and Explosion Index Hazard Classification Guide,* 6th ed., CEP Technical Manual, American Institute of Chemical Engineers, New York, 1987.
6. *Guidelines for Safe Storage and Handling of High Toxic Hazard Materials,* Center for Chemical Process Safety of the American Institute of Chemical Engineers, New York, 1988, App. B.
7. "Risk Rank," *CEP Software Directory,* Special Supplement to *Chemical Engineering Process,* October 1992, p. 72.
8. Facility Initial Risk Screening Tool, commercial software, Arthur D. Little, Inc., Cambridge, Mass.

9. Delaware Department of Natural Resources and Environmental Control, Division of Air and Waste Management, *Regulation for the Management of Extremely Hazardous Substances,* June 1989.

10. *Guidelines for Chemical Process Quantitative Risk Analysis,* Center for Chemical Process Safety of the American Institute of Chemical Engineers, New York, 1989.

11. J. H. Berkowitz, *Basis and Background Document for Proposed New Rule N.J.A.C. 7:31,* Toxic Catastrophe Prevention Act Program, New Jersey, Bureau of Release Prevention, September 1987.

12. OSHA 29 CFR, Part 1910.119, "Process Safety Management of Highly Hazardous Chemicals, Explosives and Blasting Agents: Final Rule," *Federal Register,* July 1993, pp. 364–385.

13. EPA 40 CFR, Part 68, "Risk Management Programs for Accidental Release Prevention: Proposed Rule," *Federal Register,* October 20, 1993.

14. G. Stevens and R. P. Stickles, "Prioritisation of Safety Related Plant Modifications Using Cost-Risk Benefit Analysis," *International Conference on Hazard Identification and Risk Analysis, Human Factors and Human Reliability in Process Safety,* American Institute of Chemical Engineers, New York, January 1992.

15. V. Pilz, "Safety Analyses for the Systematic Checking of Chemical Plant and Processes—Methods, Benefits and Limitations," *German Chemical Engineering,* 9: 65–74, 1986.

16. J. L. Hawksley, "Process Safety Management: A UK Approach," Presented at the American Institute of Chemical Engineers Spring National Meeting, 1988.

17. NUREG/CR-2300, *A Guide to the Performance of Probabilistic Risk Assessment for Nuclear Power Plants,* U.S. Nuclear Regulatory Commission, Washington, 1982.

18. L. M. Bendixen, "Risk Acceptability in the Chemical Process Industry—Working Toward Sound Risk Management," *Spectrum,* Arthur D. Little Decision Resources, March 1988.

19. *Guidelines for Hazard Evaluation Procedures,* 2d ed., Center for Chemical Process Safety of the American Institute of Chemical Engineers, New York, 1992.

4

Getting Started:
The Risk Survey

Robert Deshotels
Fluor Daniel, Inc.

Thomas C. McKelvey
Four Elements

4.1 Purpose

A risk survey prioritizes the order of assessment, which can be useful for planning the detailed risk analyses described in later chapters. The survey is brief and conducted at a system level, neglecting the component interdependencies that are modeled in the detailed analysis. The intent is that when the detailed analysis is complete, no one will say, "We spent most of our time analyzing things that turned out to be unimportant, and with a little initial thinking, we could have been much more effective."

The effort to achieve cost-effectiveness begins with a risk survey, which provides a quick characterization of potential risk. The survey applies to health and safety risk, environmental risk, or financial risk. The main result of the survey is a ranking or, in some cases, order-of-magnitude estimates for the risk. Also, the survey clarifies the functional hierarchy· among the systems that make up the facility. These results are used to formulate a work plan, from which schedule and cost estimates for the detailed analysis are developed. The work plan includes the choice of appropriate methods, level of detail, and order of analysis for the systems to be designed. In addition, the survey creates a critical items list for quality-assurance planning.

Managers may object to a survey. If the method of detailed analysis, the budget, and the schedule already have been determined, the survey seems (at first glance) like a waste of time and effort. This situation is common. Project schedules are often inflexible, being dictated by the customer schedule. Presumably, the value of the facility has been roughly estimated. Management may have tacitly decided on the detailed analysis method and cost based on similar projects. If the detailed analysis will involve only a few areas of concern and there is little doubt that all areas need to be analyzed as planned, a risk survey is necessary only for planning the order of analysis and ensuring that all design interfaces are addressed.

The benefits of a risk survey may be shown by further consideration of the situation. The methods, budget, or schedule assumed earlier may be unworkable. By identifying where the depth of analysis can be reduced, cost savings may be realized. On the other hand, the survey may indicate the potential for serious accident scenarios involving systems that had been perceived as unimportant. If so, it is better to find out early. Depending on potential accident consequences, financial liability may greatly exceed the worth of the facility. When there is a large potential liability, managers need to have an early estimate of the residual risk that would remain after detailed analysis and possible improvement. Management should know as soon as possible if the design could result in unacceptable financial risk. A preliminary risk survey thus complements the preliminary cost estimate.

The survey may reveal that one siting choice or design concept is superior to another or that other options should be considered. Perhaps more data must be developed in certain areas before detailed analysis will be worthwhile. In some cases, detailed analysis cannot reduce the uncertainties in accident consequences until the influences of various process parameters are better understood. In other cases, estimates of accident frequency may be subject to conjecture. Early discovery of such information is well worth the small time and effort required.

4.2   Survey Scope

The following information is needed to begin: a process material balance, process system diagrams, support system diagrams, and a location (layout) plan. All systems in the design are surveyed, as well as the interfaces with systems that are designed by others or will be designed in the future. The functional dependencies among systems are considered in the survey.

The risk survey provides information so that the detailed analysis effort is allocated in a cost-effective manner to produce a design with acceptable risk. Recalling the definition in Sec. 1.4, risk is a combination of consequence and likelihood. The next chapter shows how decisions on the acceptability of the facility design can be made with a risk matrix. The matrix contains accident-consequence categories ranging from minor to catastrophic and accident-likelihood categories ranging from noncredible to likely. For a severe-consequence scenario, the likelihood must be especially low, to ensure that risk is acceptable. To reduce the likelihood, severe-consequence scenarios usually need

- Greater depth of safety defenses in the design.

- More detailed safety analysis to find low-probability failure scenarios (which may require design modification). Greater depth of analysis will give greater confidence that safety systems are justified and that they perform their intended functions.

- More review of the detailed analysis to catch overlooked scenarios (which may require additional safety analysis).

Although peer review or independent evaluation improves the outcome of the detailed analysis, no risk analysis is perfect. A comparison study showed that each of two experienced teams using similar techniques missed about 25 percent of the hazards in a chemical facility.[1] In this case, each team conducted an extensive analysis.

A suggested logic for the survey is shown in Fig. 4.1. Design and interfacing systems are sorted into three consequence categories: those containing no significant hazard or liability, those with potentially catastrophic hazard or liability, and those in between. The consequence categories are determined quickly and conservatively. Because *hazard* is a relative term, criteria must be established.

Among the systems that are nonhazardous by themselves, the potential for affecting the hazardous systems must be considered. A hierarchy of effects is established between primary systems that contain hazards and the inherently nonhazardous secondary systems that affect primary systems.

Likelihood of an accident cannot be conservatively determined from a system-level survey. Therefore, all hazardous systems and the systems that can affect them should be included on the list for detailed analysis. A rough likelihood ranking can be used for planning the order of detailed analysis. If necessary, the plan can be corrected during detailed analysis in order to concentrate on the important areas.

It is a good policy to let those responsible for the detailed analysis determine which systems should be eliminated from further consider-

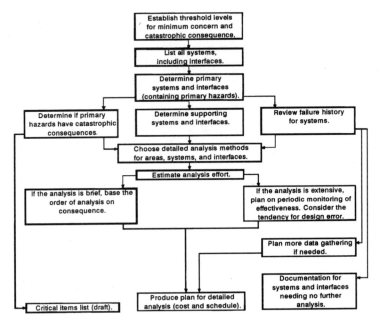

Figure 4.1 A suggested survey method.

ation. This gives the decision to those with the most expertise. Also, this policy keeps a clear distinction between the analysis plan (generated from the survey) and analysis results that affect the design. If those managing the survey regardlessly decide to eliminate some systems, it should be carefully documented that the risk from ignoring these systems is within criteria for acceptable risk.

The survey can provide a rough, relative prediction of potential risk. For a detailed analysis requiring extensive effort, the work plan should be reviewed at predetermined intervals and modified if needed, as described in Chap. 3, based on risk results from the completed portions of the detailed analysis.

4.3 Survey Method

The survey can involve four rating scales: potential consequence, system hierarchy, system failure history, and design difficulty. Each has a different function. The potential consequence and system hierarchy provide information for choosing the method and order of analysis. The system failure history can indicate whether detailed analysis is necessary for support systems or whether more data are needed for primary systems. The design difficulty provides optional information for improving the order of analysis.

4.3.1 Potential consequence

Criteria are chosen to compare the contents of systems and areas in the survey with threshold quantities of hazardous material, energy potential, and financial loss or liability. Chapter 2 identified regulatory minimum standards for hazardous substances.

One convenient measure of catastrophic consequences for highly hazardous chemicals is by comparison of potential (unmitigated) release quantities with the threshold quantities of highly hazardous chemicals, toxics, and reactives in App. A of OSHA 1910.119.[2] A more extensive list of chemicals, with different catastrophic threshold quantities, is found in the Environmental Protection Agency's (EPA's) extremely hazardous substances list.[3] Proposed EPA regulations on risk-management programs (40 CFR Part 68) contain additional chemicals and different threshold quantities.[4] Although the Occupational Safety and Health Administration (OSHA) and the EPA lists contain the chemicals that are commonly used in large quantities, some reactive and toxic chemicals are absent. In addition, several other lists of threshold limits have been proposed, based on concentration rather than quantity. If concentration values are used, consequence modeling (Chap. 7) must be applied in order to determine the quantities of concern. One can refer to guidance[5,6] on the suitability of the different threshold concentrations proposed by various national committees. Financial or intangible considerations (such as impact of the company reputation on sales or public acceptance) may dictate more stringent criteria.

The potential for unmitigated energy release should be ranked according to the net heat of combustion, expansion work, or other measure of energy potential. OSHA and the EPA use 4500 kg (10,000 lb) as the threshold quantity for flammable materials.[2,4] However, a lower threshold might be justified by economics. Vapor cloud explosions have accounted for the largest dollar losses in the hydrocarbon and chemical industries.[7] As another benchmark for catastrophic explosions, the Flixborough disaster is estimated to have developed from a total reactor loop inventory of 120,000 kg (260,000 lb) of cyclohexane, producing a heat of combustion of 18 million kcal (70 MBtu).[8]

A critical items list is typically created for use in the facility design. The list includes components and structural elements that are designed for more extreme (less probable) stress conditions and which require more extensive quality assurance. The critical items list begins with a listing of systems from which failure could result in catastrophic consequences from an unmitigated accident. Critical items should have an increased multiplier in the facility cost estimate. Thus an evaluation of unmitigated release can improve quality-assurance planning and cost estimation.

Several alternative ranking correlations consider mitigating factors such as the existence of safety systems and the distance to the affected population. Correlations that consider mitigation are more representative of actual risk but require more time than correlations based only on consequence. The cost of the detailed analysis (and perhaps the entire facility) is related to the ratio of *un*mitigated risk to acceptable risk. The ranking of mitigating features involves nonconservative, generic correlations and subjective rating. Thus the survey may overlook design shortcomings that would be noticed in the detailed analysis. Therefore, more benefit may be gained by considering mitigating factors in the detailed analysis rather than in the planning survey.

Ranking methods that consider mitigating factors are summarized in texts.[9,10] Historical data and expert opinion have been combined in several methods, including the Dow Fire and Explosion Index,[11] the Mond Index,[12] and the Chemical Exposure Index.[13]

4.3.2 System hierarchy

The systems can be sorted into three categories based on system function: (1) primary systems containing significant hazards, (2) secondary systems that do not contain a hazard but can affect protective functions of primary systems, and (3) systems that cannot significantly affect hazards and should not be analyzed further.

The primary hazardous systems contain enough material, energy, or loss potential to exceed minimum threshold limits. Systems that contain less than the minimum threshold quantities merit detailed analysis only if they support a protective function of a primary system or are located close enough to adversely affect the primary systems during an accident.

For systems and areas without primary hazards or liabilities, the potential for adversely affecting primary systems must be reviewed, based on the functional dependency among the connected systems. When the potential for severe consequences exists, multiple-failure scenarios are often important. If the secondary system failure modes are not well known, then effects on other systems must be presumed (and explored during detailed analysis).

For an existing facility, it is very likely that system failure modes are well known. As discussed in Sec. 4.3.3, it may be possible to show that connected systems cannot significantly affect hazardous systems.

Even support systems that cannot cause an above-threshold accident in any of the connected primary systems should be considered for possible common-cause factors. During the layout of the facility, components from unrelated systems are located next to each other. Failure of nearby, unconnected components can affect primary hazards or prevent operator intervention by causing physical impact, flooding, electromagnetic interference, or other unwanted effects. Such common-cause failures (Chap. 9) should be considered during detailed analysis if there is the potential for catastrophic consequences. It is important that any decision to eliminate a system (or system interface) from detailed analysis be fully considered, reviewed, and documented.

The risk ranking of systems in the facility can be based on the general expectation that an accident of unacceptable consequences is more likely to result from a failure in a primary system than a failure in a secondary system. Although a few secondary systems (e.g., emergency power) can be important contributors to serious accident scenarios (e.g., by failing to protect hazardous systems), it is easier to analyze secondary systems after the failure effects of the primary systems are known. Consequently, the primary hazardous systems are ranked above the secondary systems.

During detailed analysis, secondary systems may not have to be considered in as great detail as primary systems. By considering only the interfaces with primary systems, it may be possible to avoid detailed consideration of the secondary system internal components.

4.3.3 System failure history

A study of failures and accidents from similar systems can be beneficial during the survey, detailed analysis, or analysis review. A study of system failures requires the same effort, whether done as part of the survey or as part of the detailed analysis. The advantage of beginning this study during the survey is earlier improvement of the work plan, especially if further data may be needed.

Accident records have been compiled by insurers, industry associations, consultants, and regulatory agencies. System failure history and near-miss records are often available within an operating company. Design companies often fail to use this information. As a result, facility areas or operating modes that are less interesting from a design viewpoint seem to receive less safety attention. For example, a survey of large accidents in the hydrocarbon and chemical industries showed that, year after year, the greatest percentages of losses occur from piping systems and tank failures.[7] Most of the dollar losses occur during other-than-normal operation (such as start-up or on-line maintenance), although such operation occurs a small percentage of the time.[7] Several useful databases and reports of accident information can be found.[14–19]

System failure history and system design parameters can be used to rank the probability that a system without hazardous material can cause an accident in a connected or nearby primary hazardous system. As discussed in the next-to-last paragraph of Sec. 4.2, "Survey Scope," the decision not to analyze further usually should be made during the detailed analysis. To determine the potential effects of system failure, the failure modes of the system must be known. The possible effects on other systems can be developed by checking differences in the design limits between the primary hazardous systems and supporting systems, by reviewing potential contaminants in the connected systems for reactivity in the primary system, and by reviewing in-house or published accident records of similar systems. Hazard-identification methods (discussed in Sec. 4.5 and Chap. 5) are used for this review.

During hazard identification for a system or system interface, connected process and utility systems should be analyzed in sufficient detail to reveal the potential for contamination or other abnormal conditions. Contamination through unexpected flow paths may eventually lead to creation of a flammable mixture, unexpected corrosion, pluggage, or other undesired reactions in a primary system. Unexpected flow paths can result from heat-exchanger leakage, sample system errors, diaphragm-pump leakage, transfer through hose connections, valve leakage, operator error, pressure upsets, failed separation devices, vessel overflow, etc. The results of the system effects review should be documented in a matrix form, similar to a failure mode and effects analysis (FMEA) or hazard and operability (HAZOP) study.[20] A risk matrix based on categories of consequence and likelihood can be used to decide whether further analysis is needed.

4.3.4 Design difficulty

Some systems may have a greater tendency for design faults, depending on the design engineering work environment. Rating this tendency can improve the order of detailed analysis. The design difficulty rating can be used to predict whether design engineers have overlooked important failure mechanisms. Design difficulty includes the factors that deter communication between the various involved design groups. Poor design communication and poor coordination increase the tendency for design engineering mistakes; lack of design integration causes poor communication between different operators. Meshkati,[21] reporting on accidents in complex human-machine systems, has collected many examples showing that the effectiveness of technical decision makers in a work domain is a function of communication and coordination.

A relative weighing factor can be assigned to account for the varying degree of isolation, or lack of integration, among the design teams responsible for a system. If all the systems have about the same degree of team integration, no rating is needed. If there are obvious differences in the design integration of different systems, then factors should be assigned, using the following relative ranking as a guide:

1. Integrated

    a. One small team with previous similar experience
    b. One large team from same discipline in one location

2. Less integrated

    a. Different discipline teams used to working together
    b. Different discipline teams at the same company

3. Isolated

    a. Teams from the same company with a lapse of time
    b. Different companies in the same industry and country
    c. Companies with different practices, cultures, laws, design standards, or languages

The design-difficulty rating involves quick judgment; this rating is merely a pointer for planning the detailed analysis, not an analysis result.

4.4 Survey Results

The survey produces system rankings that can be used to determine the appropriate sequence and methods of detailed analysis. The choice of method should consider the system consequence category and functional hierarchy. These ratings, along with availability of failure data and tendency for design faults, can be combined into a priority list for analysis.

The plan for detailed analysis begins with the prioritized list of systems and areas of the facility that are candidates for further analysis. Obviously, systems with primary safety hazards and financial liabilities should be included. This includes systems containing minimum-threshold levels of hazardous material, stored energy, or potential recovery cost. In addition, secondary systems that can affect the primary systems are included, but lower on the ranked list. The secondary systems include directly connected supporting systems such as utilities, controls, venting, draining, and sampling. Other, nearby unconnected systems that may initiate common-cause failures should be included if there is the potential for catastrophic consequence.

There is always a slight risk associated with any design, even with completely analyzed systems that have ample multiplicity and diversity of protection. Management must decide in the beginning what level of risk is acceptable for low-consequence hazards. If systems are eliminated from future analysis because adverse effects are sufficiently unlikely (based on analysis using failure mode experience from similar systems), then the results must be documented.

Interfaces with outside systems and areas must be considered. There are a number of valid reasons why outside systems may have been excluded from the design:

- The system (e.g., an outside supplier of raw material via pipeline) was designed by others and cannot be changed.

- The system (e.g., a connected unit in the facility) has been recently analyzed.

- The system (e.g., a standard, vendor-supplied package) will be designed in the future.

- The system (e.g., a utility system) has no primary hazards and its effects on the areas to be analyzed are well known.

The interfaces with areas outside the design provide hiding places for hazards.

If some utility and support systems will be designed later, the interfaces with these secondary systems should be considered during the analysis of the primary system. Detailed analysis of the interfaces with the primary systems can be used to develop design requirements on the secondary systems.

The detailed analysis will proceed down the prioritized list of systems, areas, and interfaces. For a detailed analysis of brief duration, the ordering of systems can be based on consequence alone (to save survey time), presuming that the entire list will be analyzed. For an extensive analysis, the cost-effectiveness of the analysis effort should be monitored at predetermined points in progress. If further analysis is clearly not cost-effective (and not required by regulations), the effort should stop. As a result, systems or areas of low priority on the list may not be analyzed.

The order for the analysis is determined by rearranging the consequence ranking, using judgment to account for likelihood factors. Systems with a greater design difficulty are expected to have more design faults. The administration of the detailed analysis also must be considered: the availability of personnel, when necessary information will be available, and whether some systems become easier to analyze after others have been done. Secondary systems are usually easier to analyze after the failure effects of the primary systems are known. Often, worst-case accidents can be used as bounding conditions for other accidents to reduce the number of calculations.

The choice of detailed analysis methods to be employed for a system or area should be guided by the following:

- Whether there is a potential for catastrophic consequence (for the catastrophic case, multiple failures and common-cause failures should be explored).

- Whether similar systems have been in operation long enough for the types of failure and abnormal conditions to be well known.

- Whether the system itself contains a hazard or whether the system only has an interface with a hazardous system.

- Whether the detailed analysis effort also could serve for team building or start-up training among operating, engineering, maintenance, and facility safety groups.

The choice among detailed analysis methods (except checklists) is discussed in later chapters. When the cost-effectiveness of the detailed analysis is monitored, the choice of methods should be left to the experts who will perform the analysis.

4.5　Use of Checklists for Hazard Identification

When the practical limitations of checklist methods are observed, the use of checklists can ensure safe and cost-effective designs. Checklists, like the survey methods discussed in this chapter, do not consider the component interdependencies that are addressed in modeling methods. Checklists are useful for considering what has happened in the past in analogous situations but cannot by themselves propose accident scenarios that have not yet occurred nor predict the probability of infrequent scenarios.

HAZOP studies have justifiably earned the reputation of being one of the best ways to identify process hazards. However, in the context of the early stages of cost-effective facilities design, HAZOP is excessively detailed and time-consuming. It is also difficult to use as input for establishing plant design priorities, because the level of design detail necessary to conduct a valid HAZOP study probably will not be available at such an early stage in a project. At the other extreme, checklists are limited to the experience of the author(s) of the lists and therefore cannot adequately account for new hazards that might be associated with developing technologies and other novel designs. What-if checklists offer a better choice but still lack the structure necessary to ensure the degree of systematic thoroughness and completeness that is needed. One viable and proven option is to use a structured what-if checklist to conduct the preliminary hazards analysis needed during the early stages of design. It can be effectively and efficiently used to identify and prioritize hazards and to provide the necessary insights to enable the designers to finalize critical aspects of the safety design.[22,23]

Preliminary hazards analyses (PHAs) are less time-consuming than HAZOP studies and with proper preparation are still able to identify atypical hazards in processes. By definition, such studies are restricted to identifying only the major anticipated hazards and safety-critical protective systems. However, preliminary analysis making efficient use of a study team comprising two or three process specialists from the facility, a trained HAZOP study leader, and a risk analyst can effectively identify the major hazards while spending from 2 to 8 hours per operation surveying each process unit.

For each process or subsection selected, the leader will focus the team discussion by encouraging the team to pose what-if questions that identify potential deviations from the intended normal design conditions. The discussion is structured by asking questions that fall into a series of experience-based, cause-related discussion elements (e.g., human factors, errors and ergonomics, mechanical failures and maintenance, utility and service failures). Where documentation is insufficient or not yet available, the team of experts, based on their experience, can simultaneously define the process and analyze the potential hazards by

- Developing lists of safety features they would expect to find on the major subsystems or alarm and interlock system schedules.

- Systematically considering what failures and errors might challenge these anticipated safeguards.

- Identifying hazards that might result if the safeguards failed to perform.

- Specifying upgraded design and process safety features.

- Recommending the completed specification information database to be used by the design team to develop piping and instrument diagrams (P&IDs) for the project.

- Review the completed P&IDs to ensure that they are consistent with the specifications developed during the study.

This procedure is carried out for each unit operation, addressing one discussion element at a time. Use of specially designed, industry-specific checklists will help prompt additional what-if questions specific to the discussion element under analysis and ensure that all appropriate experience is made available.

Selection of a balanced study team is very important. An experienced engineer, trained and accomplished as a HAZOP study leader, can help guard against slighting sections of the process with subtle but potentially serious hazards, while a skilled risk analyst will ensure that the necessary information for prioritizing the results according to risk potential is developed. The scope of such a structured what-if checklist analysis enables a design team to identify the unexpected reactions, fires, explosions, and toxic releases and to some degree their potential size and from what parts of the process these events might originate.

The use of a structured what-if checklist–based approach enables an efficient and effective preliminary hazards analysis through ensuring a systematic and thorough exploration of the process safety knowledge of the facilities' experts while avoiding the unnecessary examination of details that are likely to change. Furthermore, it helps to establish the relative risk-related priorities of hazards that require further analysis or study prior to design completion, construction, and actual start-up of the finished facility.

4.6 Conclusions

The ranking method outlined in this chapter can produce order-of-magnitude estimates of risk at best. Estimating the potential benefits of the detailed analysis involves predicting where hidden hazards will be uncovered. This situation can be improved if companies that perform detailed risk analysis track their estimates of risk (with uncertainty range) before and after analysis. To aid in planning future projects, reliability growth in the aerospace industry is tracked as a project develops.

Provided the scope of work can be adjusted for developments in the analysis, cost-effectiveness can be ensured by monitoring, despite the difficulty of prediction. Examples of monitoring cost-effectiveness can be found in literature.[24,25]

The risk survey is intended primarily to assist in developing the work plan for the detailed risk analysis. The brief time spent on the survey is intended to improve the overall cost-effectiveness of the analysis effort. Planning for cost-effectiveness involves compromising one kind of uncertainty for another. In the traditional plan, the consultant or in-house specialist team uses guidelines (based on previous experience) to develop a scope of work with a specified level of detail, fixed budget, and schedule. Progress and analysis effort are monitored to ensure that the scope is completed within close tolerance of the original budget and schedule. Alternatively, in a cost-effective analysis plan, the scope has specified options (based on results of the actual analysis), while the budget and schedule depend somewhat on the options. The detailed analysis effort and estimate of risk are monitored to ensure that cost-effectiveness is within an acceptable tolerance. The range of acceptable tolerance needs to be wide enough to account for the uncertainties of evaluating risk. An effective survey reduces these uncertainties.

4.7 References

1. J. Soukas, "Evaluation of the Coverage and Validity of Hazard and Operability Study," *5th International Symposium on Loss Prevention and Safety Promotion in the Process Industries,* Société de Chimie Industrielle, Paris, 1986.
2. OSHA 29 CFR Part 1910.119, "Process Safety Management of Highly Hazardous Chemicals," *Federal Register,* July 1993, pp. 364–385.

3. EPA 40 CFR Part 355, App. A, "The List of Extremely Hazardous Substances and Their Threshold Planning Quantities," *Federal Register,* April 22, 1987, p. 13395; amended by *Federal Register,* July 26, 1990, p. 30645.
4. EPA 40 CFR Part 68, "Risk Management Programs for Chemical Accidental Release Prevention" (proposed), *Federal Register,* October 20, 1993, pp. 54190–54219.
5. *Handbook of Chemical Hazard Analysis Procedures,* Federal Emergency Management Agency, Washington, 1988, Chap. 6.
6. G. Melhem and P. Croce, *Advanced Consequence Modeling: Emission, Dispersion, Fires and Explosions,* Van Nostrand Reinhold, New York, 1993.
7. D. G. Mahoney, *Large Property Damage Losses in the Hydrocarbon-Chemical Industries,* 14th ed., Marsh and McLennan, Chicago, 1992.
8. F. P. Lees, *Loss Prevention in the Process Industries,* Vol. 2, Butterworths, London, 1980, pp. 238, 877.
9. *Guidelines for Hazard Evaluation Procedures,* 2d ed., Center for Chemical Process Safety of the American Institute of Chemical Engineers, New York, 1992.
10. M. Sawyer, M. Livingston, and W. Early, "Screening Analysis Techniques," in *Risk Assessment and Risk Management for the Chemical Process Industry,* Van Nostrand Reinhold, New York, 1991, Chap. 2.
11. Dow Chemical Company, *Fire and Explosion Index Hazard Classification Guide,* 7th ed., American Institute of Chemical Engineers, New York, 1989.
12. *The Mond Index,* 2d ed., Imperial Chemical Industries, Winnington, Northwich, Cheshire, U.K., 1985.
13. R. Smith and G. Miller, "Chemical Exposure Index," in *Guidelines for Safe Storage and Handling of High Toxic Hazard Materials,* Center for Chemical Process Safety of the American Institute of Chemical Engineers, New York, 1988, App. B.
14. L. R. Hathaway, *A 25-Year Study of Large Losses in the Gas and Electric Utility Industry,* Marsh and McLennan, Chicago, 1990.
15. *FACTS,* a database available from TNO, P.O. Box 342, NL-7300 AH Apeldoorn, Netherlands.
16. *MHIDAS (Major Hazards Incident Data Service),* a database available from Safety and Reliability Directorate, Wigshaw Lane, Culcheth, Warrington WA3 4NE, U.K.
17. *WOAD (World Offshore Accident Data),* a database available from Veritec Offshore Technology and Services A/S, Oslo, Norway.
18. A. Bertrand and L. Escoffier, "Offshore Data Base Shows Decline in Rig Accidents," *Oil and Gas Journal,* 89:72–78, September 16, 1991.
19. *Guidelines for Chemical Process Quantitative Risk Analysis,* Center for Chemical Process Safety of the American Institute of Chemical Engineers, New York, 1989, Table 5.1.
20. R. Deshotels and R. Goyal, "HAZOP Methods Applied to Project Design Interfaces," *Proceedings of the International Symposium on Risk Identification and Risk Analysis,* Center for Chemical Process Safety of the American Institute of Chemical Engineers, New York, 1992.
21. N. Meshkati, "A Framework for Enhancement of Human and Organizational Reliability of Complex Technological Systems," *Proceedings of the International Conference on Probabilistic Safety Assessment and Management,* Elsevier, New York, 1991.
22. T. McKelvey and J. Shah, "Using Major Hazards Review to Identify Atypical Hazards in Quantitative Risk Assessment," *Proceedings of the AIChE Spring National Meeting,* American Institute of Chemical Engineers, New York, 1993.
23. T. McKelvey and B. Harvey, "Recommendations: Not Just a Result, but an Integral Part of a Successful Hazard Identification Study," *Proceedings of the AIChE Summer National Meeting,* American Institute of Chemical Engineers, New York, 1992.
24. G. Stevens and R. Stickles, "Prioritization of Safety-Related Plant Modifications Using Cost-Risk Benefit Analysis," *Proceedings of the International Symposium on Risk Identification and Risk Analysis,* Center for Chemical Process Safety of the American Institute of Chemical Engineers, New York, 1992.
25. J. Arendt, "Management of Quantitative Risk Assessment in the Chemical Process Industry," *Plant/Operations Progress,* October 1990, 9:266–268.

5

Hazard Identification

Mardy Kazarians
Kazarians & Associates

5.1 Introduction

Hazard identification is the first step of any hazard analysis (or risk analysis, using the accurate definition of the terms). It provides the basis for many other analyses that often need to be done to support the decision process for making a system or operation safer.

The focus of this chapter is on planning and conducting the hazard-identification task of risk analysis. An important part of planning is defining the scope of the analysis.

5.2 Purpose of Risk Analysis

Before we can discuss the scope of a risk analysis, it is necessary to establish the reasons behind conducting the analysis in the first place. The purpose of risk analysis is to gain an understanding of the risks in a facility so that decisions can be made to enhance safety. Three questions arise from this statement—What is meant by risk (so that there can be an analysis of it)? What is meant by understanding? and How can one use risk analysis to enhance safety?

Portions of this chapter were presented previously in "Hazard Analysis for Compliance with Process Safety Regulations," in G. E. Apostolakis and J. S. Wu (eds.), *Proceedings of PSAM II,* University of California, Los Angeles, March 1994.

Risk is defined as the possibility and magnitude of receiving harm, and *hazard* is defined as the source of harm. Thus risk encompasses information about potential release scenarios, likelihood of occurrence of the scenarios, and their levels of damage. Although this definition is widely accepted by risk and safety practitioners, many regulatory statutes use the word *hazard* loosely in a way that also can be interpreted as *risk*. This chapter will use the exact definitions of these two words as provided in this paragraph. Often, in the petroleum and chemical industry literature, the phrase *hazard analysis* is used for studies that are done to establish the elements of risk. In this chapter, the phrase *risk analysis* stands for hazard analysis.

To gain an understanding of the risks, two issues need to be dealt with—Is the existing plant safe enough? and How can one use the risk-analysis results to make a plant safe enough in a cost-effective manner? Risk analysis provides a method for ranking risk and for providing a rational basis for choosing among different alternatives.

Whether a plant is safe enough, acceptability of risk, is of course a difficult subject. It is difficult because individuals and communities must balance risks against benefits. It is practically impossible to create an all-encompassing and generic set of procedures for the use of decision makers to determine whether a certain operation is safe enough. This difficulty is circumvented by owners, operators, and regulators by adopting accepted practices. The accepted practice, as seen by the progress of engineering codes and standards, changes continually with the growth of industry experiences and knowledge gained from research and experimentation. Also, the accepted practice changes with changes in our culture, values, and community expectations.

5.3   Scope of Hazard Identification

It is necessary to have a clear understanding of the objectives of the study to be able to define the scope of the hazard-identification task. In practice, there has been a wide variation in the scope and depth of the analyses conducted for various facilities in different industries. The reason for the differences in the scope of these analyses is rooted in the very objectives of the people who commission the study. The objectives could be any combination of the following:

- Regulatory compliance
- Economic loss estimation
- Due diligence for a business transaction
- Environmental impact
- Worker safety

- Public safety

- Decision support for system modification

In the recent times, often the objective is to satisfy the requirements of 29 CFR 1910.119,[1] 47 CFR Part 68, API RP-750,[2] or a local regulation. In the case of regulatory compliance—for example, to comply with the risk management and prevention program regulation[3]—a facility needs to identify those parts of the system where acutely hazardous materials are present and conduct a hazard analysis for only those parts. However, if prevention of economic losses is the main objective, the analysis should address all possible events that could lead to equipment damage, system downtime, worker and public safety, and environmental impact.

The scope of the analysis should include such issues as the systems to be analyzed, the operational status of the systems (e.g., normal operation, start-up, and emergency shutdown), the consequence attributes, and the acceptable level of uncertainty. Consequences can be expressed via such attributes as percentage of system damage, number of days that the system could be rendered inoperable, and the number of people from the public exposed to a certain concentration of a hazardous chemical. Uncertainty in the final answer is related to the level of effort expended in determining the risk level. This is further discussed in Sec. 5.10.

5.4   A General Procedure for Hazard Identification

A risk analysis involves a string of studies that includes the identification of the hazards, identification of the chain of events that leads to a release, analysis of the behavior of the hazardous materials after a release, and analysis of the adverse effects of the hazardous materials. Hazard identification is the first step in the string of studies. To complete a risk analysis, and especially a hazard-identification task of a risk analysis, the following steps should be undertaken:

1. Definition of objectives, scope, and ground rules

2. Selection of analysis team

3. Planning and preparation

4. Undertaking the study

5. Report production and review

5.4.1   Objectives, scope, and ground rules

Before a study can begin, it is necessary for the team leader (see the discussion below on the team leader) to obtain consensus among the members of the team and from the "client" on the ground rules. The client is the decision maker. The client is the group of people who will eventually review the final results of the risk analysis and decide how much safety is necessary to manage the risks of the system under study. The ground rules should be consistent with meeting the objectives of the client. Ground rules include such issues as level of detail for defining components, inclusion of utilities and other related systems, and specification of what constitutes a safeguard. For example, a compressor may be considered as a component in one study, and in another it may be considered as a system that includes a motor, a compressor, valves, and pipes that provide the cooling medium.

5.4.2   Team selection

Hazard identification is often done by a team of experts. The team is selected from professionals who have detailed knowledge of the way the facility is intended to work. This may require several specialists and members of operations personnel. It is essential that the team include people with sufficient knowledge and experience to provide the answers to a majority of the questions regarding system design and operations. For a new system or facility that is not in operation yet, typically the team may comprise a design engineer, a chemist, a safety engineer, and an instrumentation engineer. The team also may include a production supervisor and an operator who are either familiar with the system or are expected to be working with the system under design. For a study of an existing facility, the team could be made up of the unit supervisor, a few operators, members of the engineering staff, and an instrumentation specialist. Occasionally, very specialized questions are brought up (e.g., metallurgical characteristics of a certain part) that require the participation of a specialist in the risk-analysis discussions on a part-time basis.

In addition to specialists and experts, the team includes a team leader and often a "scribe." The team leader is responsible for carrying out the analysis and producing the final report for the client's review. The main reason for including the position of a scribe on the team is that hazard identification is often done in a brainstorming session. The scribe is responsible for taking notes, allowing the team leader to stay focused on leading the discussions.

It is helpful if the majority of the hazard-analysis team members have had some formal training in hazard-analysis techniques. It is essential for the team leader to have such training.

The authority to make changes is also important when selecting the hazard-analysis team. This facilitates the process of making recommendations, especially when the analysis is conducted to comply with the requirements of a specific regulation. The proper method for conducting the hazard-identification discussions is to ensure that all original members of the team are present when a specific record, recommendation for change, or item for discussion is altered. This ensures that all the multidisciplinary issues that were raised during the original set of discussions will be recalled and properly considered before the alteration is finalized. This practice provides the proper authority to the authors of the study.

5.4.3 Planning and preparation

Planning includes such activities as scheduling meetings with key personnel to define the scope of the analysis, to collect and review the necessary data, and to conduct a brainstorming session where the hazard-identification method is followed. A thorough and well-executed plan guarantees efficient use of personnel time and hence is an important element for ensuring cost-effective hazard identification.

To prepare for the hazard-identification task, the relevant information should be collected and reviewed. In some facilities, formal procedures have been developed for conducting hazard analysis. The procedures specify a set of information items to be collected and reviewed for accuracy. The following list of items ideally would be included in a risk analysis:

- Piping and instrument diagrams (P&IDs)
- Layout and elevation drawings
- Operating procedures
- Systems design philosophy and process description
- Information on instruments and control valves
- Information on alarms and trip settings
- Materials specifications and standards
- Information on relief valves and rupture disks
- Chemical, physical, and hazardous properties of all process materials, and intermediates
- Process-flow diagrams and material balances
- Electrical single-line diagrams

The latest version of each document should be obtained. Ambiguities and discrepancies in the database should be resolved before the study begins. For a study of an existing facility, it is necessary that documents be up to date. It is vital that all plant modifications be reflected on P&IDs; this could require a detailed facility review to determine drawing accuracy.

5.4.4   Undertaking the study

Hazard identification generally constitutes a brainstorming session with participation of the hazard-analysis team members. Some hazard-identification methods can be conducted by an analyst in isolation; however, the preferred method in the petroleum and chemical industries is group brainstorming led by the team leader. The product of the brainstorming sessions is generally a set of record sheets that gives a detailed account, often in an organized fashion, of what had been discussed during the sessions.

5.4.5   Report production and review

A report is the final product of the hazard-identification task. It should include all the information necessary for the client to make the proper decisions. It should address the scope of the study, the methodology e...; loyed, the data (and quality of the data) used for the analysis, the results (conclusions) of the analysis, and the basis of the results. Some facilities have adopted a standardized format for the report. If the analysis is done for compliance with regulations, the regulatory agency (e.g., some fire departments in California) have specific formats for the report that may include such items as dates and duration of the brainstorming sessions and a list of hazard-analysis team members.

5.5   Selecting a Methodology

A number of methods are available for hazard identification. Several books have been written on the subject; the most well known[4] provides a catalog of methods with worked examples. The main requirement is to be complete. To achieve this, a method should be rigorous, systematic, and structured. The following is a list of methods that have had more acceptance than others:

Hazard and operability (HAZOP) study

Failure mode, effects, and criticality analysis (FMECA)

Fault-tree analysis (FTA)

Event-tree analysis (ETA)

Quantitative risk assessment (QRA)

HAZOP study is the most commonly used and is perhaps best suited for a facility that processes hazardous chemicals because it addresses all those areas of the process where the hazardous materials may exist and it focuses on the ways by which an adverse condition may develop.

FMECA is an excellent tool for identifying the ways a complex component or equipment item may fail. It identifies the failure modes of every component in a system (complex component or equipment item) and the impact of those failures on the entire system.

Fault-tree and event-tree analyses are often used together. A fault-tree analysis is best suited for analyzing safety systems, for systems with many built-in redundancies, for systems where the source of harm, the hazard, is concentrated in one area, or for analyzing a subsystem or equipment item that has been identified in a HAZOP study as extremely important to safety. An event tree is used to identify a chain of events, especially when several layers of safeguards must fail for a release to manifest itself.

QRA is the complete risk analysis. The final results of the QRA are presented in terms of the probabilities of different levels of harm. A QRA includes hazard identification (e.g., using a HAZOP study), chain-of-event identification (e.g., using the event- and fault-tree approach), and release and dispersion modeling (this is accomplished by using sophisticated computer programs). A QRA also may include demographics of the area around the plant, the weather patterns, and the toxic or other adverse effects of the hazardous material. If the material is flammable, the adverse effects may include modeling of fire and explosion conditions and heat and shockwave impact on people and structures. QRA is seldom undertaken. In Sec. 5.10, the conditions under which QRA may be the method of choice are discussed.

Many HAZOP study practitioners use a specialized version of QRA, *risk matrix methodology,* for deciding whether a recommendation is warranted and to measure whether the recommended changes provide sufficient risk reduction. FMECA uses the same method.

5.6   HAZOP Method for Hazard Identification

HAZOP study is perhaps the most commonly used method for complying with process safety regulations. The focus of the HAZOP method is on identifying trends in the system that could lead to adverse conditions. The way a HAZOP study is generally done is that the possible causes of the trends (deviations) are clearly identified in terms of system component status or operator actions. The next item in a HAZOP study is the identification of consequences. The consequences are identified in terms of changes in system operation or the possibility of adverse effects. The safeguards that may reduce the likelihood of occurrence of the adverse trend or the magnitude of the consequences are also identified as a separate item. Figure 5.1 provides a sample HAZOP record sheet gleaned from an analysis done for an ammonia refrigeration system.

Sheet Number: 1
Revision: 0

Company:
Facility:
Unit:
Team Leader/Scribe:
Team Members:
Hazop Date:

System: Ammonia Refrigeration System
Subsystem:
Drawing Number: R-4 (June 15, 1993)
Reference:
Drawing Number:
Print Date:

Nodes (from/to): From suction side of the compressors to evaporative condense EC-1, fan speed pressure switches, including part of the condenser.

Design Intent: To provide high-pressure ammonia at sufficient flow rate for receiver makeup

Parameter: Flow

Item No.	Deviation	Cause	Consequence	Indication/ Protection	Recommendations/ Questions	Comments
1.1	High flow	- None identified	- No adverse consequences			
1.2	Low or no flow	- Evaporative condenser inlet valve closed	- Compressor overheat and potential for release from a failed compressor	- High-pressure switch - Compressor relief valve may not be sufficient - Not readily accessible	R1.2.1 - Consider a secondary high-pressure cutoff for compressors	
1.3	Back flow	- Check valve leaking after a shutdown	- NH3 leak into crankcase / operability problem / No adverse consequences			
1.4	Loss of containment	- Mechanical seal failure - Gasket connection failure - Fitting failures	- Small ammonia leak	- Building is occupied normally except on weekends when small compressor (C-2) cycles to keep pressure low	R.1.4.1 - Conduct a study on the need and specification of area ammonia detectors	

Figure 5.1 HAZOP record sheet: An example.

HAZOP analysis requires breaking the system down into nodes or segments. The level of detail incorporated into this breakdown has almost a direct relationship with the amount of time that needs to be expended to complete the brainstorming sessions. A *node* is defined as a continuous segment of a system that has similar characteristics. Thus *node boundaries* should be defined at those places where such parameters as temperature, pressure, and flow undergo a change. Some businesses insist on the accurate application of the definition. However, it is a common practice, to make efficient use of time, to combine several nodes into one and select the boundaries based on major changes in system characteristics.

The methodology used for identifying the adverse trends includes the use of a standard set of guide words that depict deviations from the norm applied to the parameters that define the design intent of a portion of the system. At this stage of the analysis, including the enumeration of the causes for the trends (deviations), it can be claimed that completeness is achieved in the HAZOP study. The identification of the equipment or component failures that may lead to adverse conditions is the main result of a HAZOP study. In terms of quantitative risk-assessment (QRA) methodology, these causes identify the initiating events of the chain of events needed for risk analysis (this is further discussed in Sec. 5.10).

To minimize duplications and thus facilitate the efficient use of time, it is a common practice to limit the causes of a deviation to the node under study. In contrast, the consequences of a deviation are identified to the fullest extent possible, regardless of node or event system boundaries. This is important for the team to fully realize the potential hazards of a system and operation.

The level of rigor, as compared with the identification of causes for deviations in the system parameters, is significantly less for consequences. HAZOP analysts generally do not use any tools to evaluate the level of the consequences except for their experience and judgment. Consequences are dependent on the type of failures that may occur. The available safeguards often influence the outcome of the consequences. For this reason and for the purpose of minimizing the potential for optimistic notions of a system's risk level, some businesses have adopted the requirement that, in HAZOP studies conducted for their facilities, consequences should be identified hypothesizing that all safeguards are rendered ineffective.

The assumption that safeguards are ineffective is one method for taking into account the possibility of multiple failures. The lack of treatment of multiple failures is an often-quoted limitation of HAZOP methodology.

After identifying the consequences and safeguards of a deviation, the analysts often consider risk-reducing modifications to the hardware and administrative elements of the system. The decision to make a recommendation often depends on the mind-set of the analysts. Thus the type and scope of recommendations vary significantly among HAZOP studies. At one extreme, a HAZOP study may contain virtually no recommendations, and at the other extreme, for every HAZOP line item that indicates a possibility of adverse consequences, a recommendation may be noted. In the first case, the HAZOP analysts are considering the risk level of the existing system as acceptable. Of course, since the analysts have not evaluated the risk in such a fashion that they could compare it against other risks, the notion of acceptability of the risk level cannot be substantiated. In the second case, the business manager is burdened with a long list of recommendations that may prove to be expensive and have diminishing returns in terms of risk reduction.

This problem has long been recognized by the practitioners of safety studies, and a solution is found in the application of the risk-assessment method. The two parameters of risk, likelihood and consequence, are used to rank the different events identified in the HAZOP study. This approach has been used extensively by the military as part of FMEA methodology[5] and preliminary hazard analysis.[4] Use of the risk-ranking approach is discussed in Sec. 5.9.

5.7   FMEA Method for Hazard Identification

The focal element of failure mode and effects analysis (FMEA) methodology is identification of the failure modes of a component and the effects of that failure mode on the system. The FMEA methodology is rather simple. A group of experts gathers system drawings and other documents describing system functions and conducts a component-by-component review of the system. For each component, all possible failure modes and operating conditions (phases) are first identified and enumerated. The effects of each failure mode are examined next, and the corresponding safeguards are identified. At this point, the group may propose recommendations to improve the system: to either minimize the chances for the failure mode to occur or to enhance the safeguards. To facilitate recording of the FMEA discussions and review of the results at a later stage, a standardized record sheet is used. Figure 5.2 provides an example.

As with to a HAZOP study, the preferred approach for conducting an FMEA is to limit the causes for failure to the component under study, to assume that all safeguards are ineffective when specifying the consequences, and to carry out the consequence identification to the fullest extent possible, regardless of component and system boundaries.

IDENT.	DESCRIPTION	FUNCTION	PHASES	FAILURE MODES	CAUSES	EFFECTS	SAFEGUARDS	RECOMMENDATIONS
V-1	Gas supply valve	Isolate gas supply to water heater burner	Normal operation	Close inadvertently	Human error, Valve failure	Long-term shutdown, no hazards		
				Leak	Valve failure	Gas release in the area, potential for explosion and fire.	Ventilated area	Post sign next to heater not allowing to store anything near it.
			Long-term shutdown (pilot off)	Open inadvertently	Human error	Assuming that GC-1 leaks, gas leak and potential for explosion and fire if ignition source is present.	Ventilated area GC-1 is shut	
				Leak	Valve failure	Gas cloud in the area, potential for explosion and fire.	Ventilated area	See above
			Short-term shutdown (pilot on)	Close inadvertently	Human error, Valve failure	Long-term shutdown, no hazards.		
				Leak	Valve failure	Gas cloud in the area, potential for explosion and fire.	Ventilated area	See above
			Lighting the pilot	Left closed	Human error	Failure to light the pilot		
				Leak	Valve failure	Assuming user ignores the gas odor - gas leak and potential for explosion and fire upon lighting a match to light pilot.	Odor from leaking gas	
GC-1	Gas control valve	Control gas flow into the burner	Normal operation	Close inadvertently	Valve failure	Heater fails to provide hot water		

Figure 5.2 FMEA record sheet: An example.

Often the failure modes or the recommendations are prioritized according to a risk (criticality) index. The index is based on an estimate of the likelihood of occurrence of the failure mode and the severity of its effects. The prioritization scheme is used for preparing the implementation plan of the recommendations. When a risk index is used, the methodology is often referred to as FMECA. This method is the same as the risk-ranking method mentioned in the preceding section and is discussed in Sec. 5.9.

FMEA (or FMECA) can be conducted by a single analyst or by a group. For process systems, the preferred approach is to use a brainstorming type of setting similar to a HAZOP study, where a team leader leads the discussions and the team consists of experts in system design and operation.

5.8 Treatment of Multiple Failures

It is common understanding that most well-accepted hazard-identification methods (e.g., HAZOP or FMEA) address single failures and are incapable of identifying "double jeopardy" types of scenarios. Actually, this is not the case. For an adverse consequence to manifest itself, an initiating event must occur. This is an event that perturbs the balance of the plant and may lead to an adverse consequence if automatic systems or operators fail to intervene. Thus, if there are any safety features incorporated into a system, the initiating event (a single event) would not lead to a release. To properly identify the consequences of a deviation in a HAZOP study or the effects of a failure mode in an FMEA, analysts should consider the influence of safety features on the chain of events. For estimating the level of consequences, as mentioned in the preceding sections, many businesses have adopted the procedure of assuming that all safeguards are rendered ineffective. In such cases, analysts list the safeguards that could influence the consequences or the likelihood of occurrence. This list represents the additional failures (in addition to the initiating event) of the chain of events.

The assumption of loss of safeguards is the same as considering multiple failures. The simultaneous occurrence of two initiating events is very small. Therefore, if the list of initiating events is complete, it can be claimed that the HAZOP study or FMEA has properly addressed a complete list of "worst case" scenarios. They are worst case because, in some cases, the safeguard limits the damage level.

Thus, by recognizing the effects of safeguards, HAZOP and FMEA methods can identify multiple failures. However, for each initiating event, only the chain of events that leads to the worst possible consequence is identified. This is so because, typically, it is assumed that all safeguards are ineffective. Using such an assumption, the analyst may overlook chains of events that are more likely to occur but with less damaging effects than those identified in the analysis.

It is important for the hazard-analysis team to distinguish between *mainline systems* and *safety systems.* A mainline system needs to operate according to its design intent for the final product of the facility to be possible. If part of the mainline system fails, the production of the entire facility or a major part of it may either stop or reduce significantly. For example, in a gas separation plant that includes two separator vessels, if the level-control valve on one of the separators fails closed, plant production may drop to about half the intended capacity. Therefore, the separators and associated control devices should be considered as mainline components or subsystems.

Each separator vessel may be equipped with a level alarm and high-level shutdown switches. If the alarm or shutdown switch fails (unable to produce an output signal to activate the alarm or pump shutdown relay), the operation of the plant would not be affected as long as the plant is running and the alarm is not needed. This is an example of a *latent failure.* Another example can be gleaned from redundant systems, where for the sake of reliability, an additional, identical train is included that can be put on line if the first train fails to operate properly. Such components or systems that do not affect the main operation of the system are referred to either as *standby* or, in the context of hazard analysis, as *safety systems.*

The hazard-analysis team should take into account two important points about standby and safety systems. First, when discussing standby or safety systems, it is not necessary to search for the conditions that would require activation of the standby or safety system. In this situation, it is not necessary to assess the release or damaging event. This point is further discussed below. Second, safety systems are usually addressed as part of safeguards.

For a hazard analysis of a system that includes mainline, standby, and safety systems, the team should explore the effects (consequences) arising from failure of nonmainline systems in terms of capabilities that would be lost. It is not necessary to identify the adverse consequences (releases) that could result. For example, failure of a standby pump of a two-pump train configuration leads to loss of redundancy in the pumping system. It is not necessary for the team to try to envision the further implications of loss of redundancy.

A standby or safety component may fail either passively or actively. In the case of *passive failure,* the system where the component is located is not affected, and in the worst case, the operators do not become aware of the subsystem condition until an upset occurs in the system (an initiating event). An *active failure* is like an initiating event; it leads to a chain of events. For example, a relief valve (a safety system), if opened inadvertently, can lead to a release and rapid system depressurization. A high-level alarm, if activated inadvertently, may lead to operator actions that result in adverse conditions. If the focus of a hazard analysis is solely on a standby or safety system, the team should ascertain that the effects of active and passive failures of the subsystem are properly identified.

5.9 Risk Matrices for Recommending and Implementing Changes

To facilitate the decision on whether the risk of a scenario is acceptable or a scenario is more risky than another, an *index of criticality levels* (a risk-ranking scheme) is often used. This approach is based on the two elements of risk: the likelihood and consequences of an event. It should be stressed here that often the focus of all hazard-analysis methods (be it HAZOP, FMEA, FTA, or ETA) is the identification of scenarios that start from an initiating event and end with either no impact on facility operation or some adverse effect (damaging consequences).

A prespecified set of likelihood and consequence (severity) levels is used to establish the criticality index. Figure 5.3 provides an example. The categories presented in Fig. 5.3 were developed for HAZOP studies of refrigeration systems that use anhydrous ammonia. The categories can be defined in many different ways and in different levels of detail. The specific conditions and needs of the facility or system should dictate how the categories are defined.

Based on the likelihood and consequence (severity) categories, a matrix of criticality (risk) levels is established. The criticality levels can then be used to establish a decision rule for proposing recommendations. Figure 5.4 gives a risk matrix, criticality levels (the numbers provided for each combination of likelihood and consequence categories), and a decision rule. For example, Fig. 5.4 indicates that a criticality level of 3 should be assigned to an event that is judged to be of medium likelihood (category B) and small consequence (category II). For such an event, a set of recommendations must be proposed so that after the implementation of the recommended changes, the criticality level will be 2 or lower.

An important pitfall of the risk-matrix approach is that it can be manipulated by its users to justify risk acceptance of a scenario without violating any of the rules of the methodology. Each scenario (chain of events) that leads to adverse consequences can be redefined in terms of several more narrowly defined scenarios that are individually less likely to occur but collectively are the same as the original scenario. For example, the combination of "valve *XX* fails to close" and "level switch

Likelihood

A	Frequent	May occur a few times in a year.
B	Occasional	May occur a few times in the life of the facility.
C	Rare	Has occurred a few times when the life of about 50 ammonia refrigeration systems is considered.
D	Very rare	Has occurred a few times in the history of ammonia refrigeration industry.
E	Improbable	Has never occurred in the history of ammonia refrigeration industry.

Consequence

I	Limited	The effects of release are limited to the boundaries of the site. Small amount of ammonia vapor release.
II	Small	Ammonia gas travels a short distance (on the order of a few ten feet) outside facility boundaries. Ammonia vapor release from low-pressure side.
III	Medium	Ammonia gas travels a few city blocks from facility boundary. Small amount of liquid ammonia release. Ammonia vapor release from low-pressure side for a long duration.
IV	Large	Ammonia gas travels an extended distance from facility boundaries. Large amount of liquid ammonia release.

Figure 5.3   Categories of likelihood and consequences: An example.

YY fails to operate" can be redefined as "valve stem stuck" and "level switch float failed in position" and several other permutations of the causes for the two failure modes. Clearly, "valve stem stuck" is one of the many causes for valve failure, and therefore, it is less likely. Thus one can see that an analyst who has the intention can redefine the scenarios in such a way that the likelihoods could fall below the unacceptable level. To circumvent this pitfall, the decisions should be based on the total frequency of the class of scenarios that lead to the same level of consequences. This often is not simple to do, because the analysis team uses qualitative terms to define the likelihoods.

5.10   When to Use QRA?

The risk-matrix approach is an approximation of a QRA approach using rough definitions for likelihood and severity of consequences. In QRA, all possible scenarios are addressed, their likelihoods are estimated using

Risk Matrix

Likelihood	Consequence			
	I	II	III	IV
A	2	3	4	5
B	2	3	4	4
C	1	2	3	4
D	1	1	2	3
E	1	1	1	2

Decision Rules

Criticality Level	Description
5	Shut down the facility immediately and implement measures that will reduce the risk to level that the decision rule will require "Consider Options" or better.
4	Implement measures within 3 months of RMPP due date that will reduce the risk to a level that the decision rule will require "Consider Options" or better.
3	Implement measures within 12 months of RMPP due date that will reduce the risk to a level that the decision rule will require "Consider Options" or better.
2	Those risk-reducing measures that do not impact the economics of the business severely will be considered for implementation.
1	The risk level is acceptable.

Figure 5.4 Risk matrix, criticality levels, and corresponding decision rules.

proper statistical methods (including quantitative assessment of uncertainties), and the consequences are assessed using sophisticated modeling methods. The results of a QRA can display the overall risk of an operation in such formats as risk curve or average loss. QRA can show how each element of the system contributes to the risk. QRA is hazard analysis in its complete form. It encompasses all the necessary elements to produce risk estimates that are defensible and rational. To obtain a quantitative estimate of the risk, the analyst should identify sources of hazard, establish the initiating events and chain of events that can result in a release in an exhaustive fashion, evaluate the likelihood of the various chains of events, define the various release conditions, evaluate dispersion of the hazardous materials, estimate the level of damage (e.g., to the workers and the public), and present the risks in different formats.

It can be claimed that all hazard-analysis methods are relevant to QRA. They are QRA with some of the elements missing. A HAZOP study without the risk-ranking part deals with the initial steps of a QRA. When risk ranking is included in a HAZOP study, the study tries to mimic the QRA methodology but in a crude fashion. If a hazard-analysis method yields information that is sufficient for the decision maker, the conduct of any analysis more detailed than that undertaken will be fruitless and ineffective for the plant. However, there are situations where the detail required for a full-scope QRA should be considered.

Detailed QRA is the hazard-analysis method of choice when an emotionally charged opposition is fighting the facility plans. The only way to exchange opinions regarding risk, in a rational manner, between two opposite parties is to use quantified results that explicitly address uncertainties. Only through a detailed study is it possible to address the concerns of the opposition. A detailed study will contain the scenarios that could be the focus of the opposition. QRA will provide the medium for a rational dialogue. Any study less detailed than a QRA has to include simplifying assumptions. A simplifying assumption that may not be conservative can be used by the opposition to assert that the risk level of the facility is unacceptable. In the case of a HAZOP study, for example, the high-likelihood and yet low-consequence-level scenarios that may potentially be ignored by the analyst could be used by the opposition as proof that the entire risk picture has not been properly considered by the facility owners in their decisions to reduce risk.

Theoretically speaking, QRA should be the method of choice when facing either very expensive alternatives or very risky operation. However, other, less detailed methods often can prove to be sufficient for reaching a rational decision, given that the users are clear about the pitfalls mentioned above.

5.11 Conclusions

Hazard analysis is a central element of all process safety regulations and industry-suggested practices. The purpose of hazard analysis is to understand the level of hazards in a facility so that decisions can be made to enhance safety, prevent accidents, and control losses. Hazard analysis is actually the analysis of risks (the possibility and magnitude of receiving harm), since the effects of the safeguards are crucial in containing the hazards (the sources of harm). The scope of the risk analysis (or hazard analysis as it is used in the regulations) is a different issue. Depending on the specific characteristics of the hazardous materials and operations, a wide spectrum of options is available to management and its analysts for defining the scope of the analysis, level of detail, and methodology. Risk analysis, in its complete form, should be interpreted as a detailed quantitative risk assessment (QRA). However, except when facing emotionally charged opposition, methods other than detailed QRA can be effective as well.

Risk ranking can afford sufficient detail and the most economical approach when the alternatives are somewhat expensive or the risk level is rather high. It is important for the users (i.e., the management and hazard-analysis team) to understand the pitfalls of risk ranking. Since the likelihood and consequence levels are often estimated by non-experts, the so-called hidden agenda of the analysis team may influence the results. This can be circumvented by ensuring that a third-party expert has verified the results and that management has reviewed the recommendations. If an expensive recommendation is considered, a detailed analysis (a mini-QRA) may be necessary to strengthen the basis of the decision. Also, a detailed analysis of specific issues may be necessary to verify the estimates provided by the analysis team and disputed by the technical reviewer. "Worst case" analysis should be adopted only when it is suspected that the worst possible release scenario leads to an acceptable consequence level. For this approach to be acceptable, the analysts should ensure that there are no scenarios, no matter how unlikely, worse than the so-called worst scenario. Otherwise, the analysts should adopt the risk-ranking method. HAZOP studies or other such methods (e.g., FMEA) can be sufficient when the risk is low and alternatives are inexpensive.

Risk analysis provides a basis for almost all safety-related activities. Unit operations can use HAZOP study and fault-tree results to show the operators what to look for to mitigate adverse conditions. The release scenarios and results of consequence analysis can be used in design of the emergency response plan to ensure that the likely and severe release conditions are properly considered in the plan. Changes in operation, hardware, and administrative policies and programs need to take into account the lessons learned during the risk analysis. The maintenance program can be altered to ensure that the most "critical" equipment is addressed properly.

5.12 References

1. OSHA 29 CFR Part 1910.119, "Process Safety Management of Highly Hazardous Chemicals; Explosives and Blasting Agents; Final Rule," *Federal Register*, July 1, 1993, pp. 364–385.
2. EPA 40 CFR Part 68, "Risk Management Programs for Chemical Accidental Release Prevention; Proposed Rule," *Federal Register*, October 20, 1993, pp. 54190–54219.
3. "Hazardous Materials Management," Article 2 of Chapter 6.95 of the California Health and Safety Code, *West's Annotated California Codes*, Health and Safety Code Sections 18200 to 25699, Vol. 40B, West Publishing Co., Saint Paul, Minn., 1992.
4. *Guidelines for Hazard Evaluation Procedures*, 2d ed., Center for Chemical Process Safety, American Institute of Chemical Engineers, New York, 1992.
5. MIL-STD-1629A, "Procedures for Performing a Failure Mode, Effects and Criticality Analysis," U.S. Department of Defense, Washington, November 1984 (available from Naval Publications and Forms Center, Philadelphia).

Chapter

6

Human Factors
in Process Plants
and Facility Design

Najmedin Meshkati
Institute of Safety and Systems Management,
University of Southern California

6.1 Introduction

A common characteristic of large-scale technological facilities such as chemical processing plants, refineries, energy conversion and generation systems (e.g., nuclear, fossil fuel, thermoelectric power plants, gas processing facilities), offshore rigs, and high-capacity compressor and pumping stations is that large amounts of potentially hazardous, flammable, combustible, or pressurized materials are concentrated and processed in single sites under the centralized control of a few operators. The immediate effects of human error in these facilities are often neither observable nor reversible; therefore, error recovery is either too late or impossible. Catastrophic breakdowns of these systems, resulting from human and natural causes, pose serious, long-lasting health and environmental threats. For the foreseeable future, despite increasing levels of computerization and automation, human operators will remain in charge of the day-to-day controlling and monitoring of these systems. Thus the safe and efficient operation of these technological systems is a function of the interactions among their *human* (i.e., personnel and organizational) and *engineered* subsystems. This chapter

attempts to (1) review critical human factors (micro- and macroergonomic) considerations that play a significant role in the safe and efficient performance of industrial facilities and (2) present an actual
example demonstrating the instrumental effect of the lack of such considerations in a major accident at a chemical plant.

6.2   Significance

Human ingenuity can now create technological systems whose accidents
rival in their effects the greatest of natural disasters, sometimes with
even higher death tolls and greater environmental damage. Potential
catastrophic breakdowns of the above-mentioned technological systems,
caused by an error or an accident, could pose serious threats with long-
lasting health and environmental consequences for the workers, for the
local public, and possibly for the neighboring region and country.[1]

The accidental release of methyl isocyanate (MIC) at the Union
Carbide pesticide plant in Bhopal, India, on December 4, 1984, was
caused primarily by a series of "design-induced" human and organizational systems' errors.[2,3] It resulted in the death of "more than 4000
people"[4]; some estimates said "as many as 15,000 have died since the
time of the accident."[5] More than 300,000 others had been affected by the
exposure; "about 2000 animals had died, and 7000 more were severely
injured."[3] On average, two of the people who were injured at the onset of
this disaster died every day in 1990.[6] Those who survived the gas initially "are continuing to suffer not only deterioration of their lungs, eyes,
and skin but also additional disorders that include ulcers, colitis, hyste-
ria, neurosis, and memory loss."[7] Moreover, the MIC exposure has even
affected the second generation, "mortality and abnormalities among children conceived and born long after the disaster to exposed mothers and
fathers continue to be higher than among a selected control group of
unexposed parents."[7] Also, according to a report issued by the National
Toxic Campaign Fund, on the basis of laboratory tests, several toxic substances were found in the Bhopal environment, raising further questions
about the additional long-term environmental effects of the disaster.[8]

6.2.1   The requirements for incorporation
of human factors in chemical processes
and plant design

Human factors and organizational problems have, historically, plagued
the safety and operation of petrochemical plants and refineries. According to many accident investigations, including several by the U.S.
Occupational Safety and Health Administration (OSHA), between 19
and 80 percent of all incidents and accidents at these facilities are caused

by "human error." Moreover, the Chemical Manufacturers Association, which is the major U.S. trade association of petrochemical companies, has acknowledged that "Managers in the [petro-] chemical process industry have found human errors to be significant factors in almost every quality problem, production outage, or accident at their facilities" (p. 1).[9]

OSHA has estimated that between 1983 and 1987, an average of 265 fatalities and 901 injuries or illnesses were associated with major accidents involving hazardous materials.[10] One way to reduce these numbers is by regulation and rule making.

On February 24, 1992, OSHA released the Final Rule of the Process Safety Management (PSM) Standard, 29 CFR 1910.119. According to paragraph (e)(3)(vi), "the process hazards analysis shall address human factors."[11] As OSHA has admitted, it "finally added" this paragraph, which requires that employers address human factors in the process hazard analysis (p. 6377).[11]

OSHA further elaborates: "The Process Hazard Analysis (PHA) focuses on equipment, instrumentation, utilities, human actions (routine and nonroutine), and external factors that might impact the process. These considerations assist in determining the hazards and potential failure points or failure modes in a process" (p. 6412)[11] Moreover, in late September of 1992, OSHA released the Compliance Guidelines for Process Safety Management Standard, wherein, under the PHA section, in reference to human factors it states, "Such factors may include a review of the operator/process and operator/equipment interface, the number of tasks operators must perform and the frequency, the evaluation of extended or unusual work schedules, the clarity and simplicity of control displays, automatic instrumentation versus manual procedures, operators' feedback, clarity of signs and codes, etc."[12]

6.2.2 Human-organization-technology interactions

Stability, safety, and the efficient operation of technological systems, as well as their ability to tolerate environmental disturbances, are a function of the interactions among their *human* (i.e., personnel and organizational) and *engineered* (technological) subsystems. In other words, the survival of technological systems depends on the nature, formation, and interaction of their human, organizational, and technological (HOT) subsystems.[3,13,14] The connection of these three HOT subsystems, in the context of the total system, is represented in Fig. 6.1. This simplified and symbolic demonstration depicts only one critical system's reality—the role of each subsystem as a link in a chain—in the integrity of the whole system. It does not, of course, show all the needed subsystems' interactions and interrelationships.

Figure 6.1 Major subsystems of a technological system.

The chain metaphor is also helpful in understanding the effects of output or production load, produced by the system, on its individual subsystems. Any increase in the output level or the capacity-utilization rate imposes strain on *all* subsystems.

Obviously, the chain (system) will break down if any link fails. This may occur if all the links (subsystems) are not equally strong and designed for handling the additional load or if they are not adequately prepared and reinforced to carry the extra load in a sustainable fashion. Research has shown that a majority of the accidents in complex large-scale technological systems have been caused by breakdowns of the weakest links in this chain, most often the human or organizational subsystems.[14,15,16,17]

6.3 Human Factors and Ergonomics

Human factors, or *ergonomics,* is a scientific field concerned with improving the productivity, health, safety, and comfort of people, as well as the effective interaction between people, the technology they are using, and the environment in which both must operate. While both *human factors* and *ergonomics* are used interchangeably, the term *ergonomics* is used when focusing on how work affects people.[18] This concerns issues such as fatigue due to prolonged monitoring tasks, injuries due to unsafe workstations, and errors due to a confusing console layout. Because of the various facets covered by the science of ergonomics, it is considered interdisciplinary and draws from several fields: engineering, physiology, psychology, industrial design, biomechanics, anthropometrics, information technology, and industrial management.[19]

A straightforward justification for the need for ergonomic considerations is that technological systems are being controlled by humans; therefore, they should be designed with the human operator's physical and psychological needs, capabilities, and limitations in mind. Ergonomics can be divided into two related and complementary areas of concentration: microergonomics and macroergonomics. Micro- and macroergonomic approaches build on each other and concentrate on the introduction, integration, and use of technology and its interface with the end-user population. The overall objective is to improve the safety and efficiency of the intended technological system.[20]

6.3.1 Microergonomics

Microergonomics, also called *human engineering,* addresses the relationship between humans, equipment, and the physical environment. It is focused on the human-machine system level and is, for example, concerned with the design of individual workstations, work methods, tools, control panels, and displays. Microergonomics includes studies of human body sizes, known as *anthropometrics,* physical and psychological abilities and limitations, information processing, and human decision making and error. It is noteworthy that according to studies of control room design of nuclear power plants: "The Human Error Probability (HEP) will be reduced by factors of 2 to 10 if the workstations (display and controls) are improved by the incorporation of standard human engineering concepts."[21]

Microergonomics aims to reduce incompatibilities between operator abilities and system requirements. The following list represents additional areas of microergonomics consideration:

- *Materials handling.* The materials-handling function includes the methods, equipment, and paths by which raw materials, work-in-progress, finished products, and process materials are moved into, within, and out of a facility. Materials handling should be evaluated from both the user's point of view and the safety of others in the facility. Examples (and areas of consideration): workplace layout, mobile racks, mechanical lifting, handling without twisting, two-way transport, marked transport ways, and clear escape-ways.

- *Handtool design and use.* Handtool use is especially critical in maintenance and construction areas but should be considered throughout a facility. Attention should be directed at acute (single-occurrence) risks as well as chronic (long-term) risks and fatigue. Examples (and areas of considerations): locations of tools, pressure on joints or tissue, fatigue and soreness, pinch points, awkward hand positions, trays and carriers, special-purpose tools, safe power tools, hanging tools, hand support for precision, minimizing tool weight, handtool guards, tool vibration and noise, maintenance of tools, stable footing for power tool operators, insulation of handtools, handle design, switches, and stops.

- *Machinery design.* The interface between the operator and the machinery used is of prime importance. Effective displays can assist operators in determining action needs while contributing to their general facility knowledge. Ineffective machines and displays not only contribute to errors but do not provide essential operator feedback. Examples (and areas of considerations): mode of display, signal detection, auditory presentation, visual presentation, accidental activation, emergency controls, reaching controls, easy-to-distinguish foot pedals, easy-to-distinguish displays, legible labels and signs, markings on displays, easy-to-read symbols, warning signs, interlock barriers, feeding and ejection devices, enclosing moving parts, dial designs, control spacing, coding, resistance, and location.

- *Workstation design.* Workstation design involves the consideration of body measurements (anthropometrics) in the arrangement of equipment in the operator's immediate vicinity. Workstation design revolves around optimizing the physical interface between operator and workstation through comfort, body posture, reach, and sight. Examples (and areas of considerations): video display unit design, viewing angles, eye height, eyeglasses, elbow height, work reach consideration for smaller workers, space consideration for larger workers, objects within reach, sitting versus standing surfaces, adjustable chairs, adjustable work surfaces, adjustable terminals, platforms, steps, mechanical lifts, footrests, and armrests.

- *Workplace environment.* Workplace environment considerations include those physical aspects of the immediate environment which contribute to the workers' comfort and ability to perform their jobs without excess physical exertion or discomfort. Discomfort and suboptimal environmental factors (such as lighting and temperature) interfere with the workers' ability to perform their job correctly and efficiently. Examples: use of daylight, wall/ceiling colors, brightness, sufficient lighting, glare prevention, visual task backgrounds, insulating hot surfaces, ventilation systems, reducing noise, sanitary facilities, break areas, reaches, and clearances.

For further information, design guidelines, and data on microergonomic considerations, see refs. 9, 18, and 22 through 32.

6.3.2 Macroergonomics

Ergonomics at the macro level, *macroergonomics,* is focused on the overall people-technology system level and is concerned with the impact of technological systems on organizational, managerial, and personnel (sub-) systems. Macroergonomics includes such areas as training, management, the planning process, information systems, internal review/inspection programs, performance measurement systems, reward structure, initial employee qualifications assessments, and personnel selection criteria.[33] Additional areas on which macroergonomics focuses include

- *Job analysis.* Its purpose is to provide a description of what workers do on the job for which selection and training procedures are developed. The description should cover operations performed, equipment used, conditions of work, radiation, other hazards, and other special characteristics of the job; nature and amount of required basic, classroom, and on-the-job training; opportunities for transfer; and relation to other jobs and other pertinent information.

- *Training.* Operators should receive initial/introductory training as well as refresher and continuing-education training. Examples: training-needs analyses based on inputs from job analysis, tool skills, machinery skills, workstations, involvement in improvements, worker rewards, and task combination.

- *Communications.* This area includes formal and informal communications between all levels of employees and contract workers. Communication requires participation by all who are involved and provides operators and management with better ideas of facility conditions and responses required. Examples: ensuring the compatibility of organizational communication and decision-making networks, information sharing, feedback, and instructions.

- *Policies and procedures.* This area is related to both training and communications. Policies and procedures provide an outline of how issues should be addressed. It is very important that different departments do not have conflicting procedures and that they are consistently followed. Examples: design of the standard operating procedures and emergency operating procedures.

- *Organizational design.* It is well known that the two major building blocks of any technological system are the physical engineered components and the human operators. The organization (and its structure) has an equally important supporting role, being perhaps analogous to the mortar—facilitating the interface, connecting and joining the blocks together. Example: design of the organizational structure of the control room crew of dynamic technological systems. Sometimes when complex technological systems, such as nuclear power plants, move from routine to nonroutine (normal to emergency) operation, the control operators need to dynamically match the new systems requirements. This requires the organizational reconfiguration of the operators' team and leads to some changes in team (organizational) communications.

6.3.3 Incorporation of ergonomic considerations

In order to prevent accidents in industrial facilities, an integrated approach to design and operation should be taken that is as attentive to human factors as it is to technical elements.[13,16] This approach should be based on a systems-oriented and integrated analysis of the processes, operations, procedures, workstations, management, organizational, and supervisory systems.

Recommendations for design. In order to ensure the relative safety of future (to-be-designed) large-scale technological systems, such as processing plants and refineries, a holistic, totally integrated, and multidisciplinary approach to system design, construction, staffing, and operation, based on sound scientific studies and human factors guidelines, is recommended. The *total system design* (TSD) constitutes such an approach. The TSD, according to Baily,[34] is a developmental approach that is based on a series of clearly defined development stages. TSD, which has been used extensively for computer-based systems development at AT&T Bell Laboratories, implies that, from the inception of the plan, *equal* and *adequate* consideration should be given to all major system components (i.e., human, organizational, and technological). The system-development process, therefore, is partitioned into a series of meaningfully related groups of activities called *stages,* each of which contains a set of design and accompanying human factors activities.

The early participation of all related and needed disciplines, including human factors, in plant system design and development is also strongly recommended. This mandates and encourages interdisciplinary dialogue among engineers, managers, human factors experts, and safety specialists. A recent joint publication by AT&T and the U.S. Navy[35] has attempted to operationalize some of these problems, labeled *latent design defects,* at the boundaries of systems. This approach to the integration of design and manufacturing is in accordance with what is proposed by Davidow and Malone as engineering design in *The Virtual Corporation:* "Everyone affected by design decisions becomes involved in the design process to make sure that the multiplicity of downstream needs (manufacturability, serviceability, market demand, and so on) are met."[36]

In addition to independent and isolated problems at the workstation (interface), job (task), and organizational (communication) levels, there was a serious lack of cohesive processes of data collection, integration, and coordination (as was demonstrated by many complex technological systems accidents). Logically, information is gathered from the inter- faces (at the *workstation* site), analyzed according to the operators' stipulated job descriptions (at the *job* level), and passed through orga- nizational communication network (according to the *organizational* structure) to the appropriate team members responsible for decision making. Thus this continuous process in the control rooms of large-scale technological systems must include[16]

1. A cohesive and integrated framework for data gathering from the interfaces (at the workstation site)

2. Displays, decision aids, and reference information to permit opera- tor comprehension, analysis, and response (at the job level, as stip- ulated in the job descriptions)

3. A communication network for the passage of information (accord- ing to the organizational structure) to and from the appropriate decision makers

The design effort will be more effective if the design team understands and anticipates the micro- and macroergonomic considerations of plant operation.

Operating considerations. The first priority of operating management should be the close examination of human operators' physical and psy- chological needs, capabilities, and limitations in the context of plant oper- ation during normal and emergency conditions. This also should be coupled with thorough analyses of critical workstations, panels, control rooms, and their design features; control room procedures and emergency situations; task-loading factors, job demands, and operators' mental workloads (during normal as well as emergency situations); emergency response system; organizational and administrative factors such as structure and hierarchy, communication, decision latitude, performance indicators, and rewards; managerial practices and supervisory styles; work and shift schedules; and training needs, programs, and methods.

In order to produce and maintain a better motivated, more flexible, safety conscious, and higher-skilled workforce, it is recommended that petrochemical plants implement the "skill-based pay system." This is fundamentally different from the conventional system of job-based pay, where employees are paid for the particular jobs they are performing, not for their ability to perform other tasks. In the skill-based pay system, operators are rewarded for both the skill and the knowledge they apply at work and their individual performance and contribution to team goals.[37] Moreover, this pay system will further foster and reward the formation of self-organized teams of operators which, as past experience also has shown, are critical in safe handling of emergency situations.

A summary of the proposed micro- and macroergonomic considerations for integration into the design and operation of industrial facilities is presented below.

1. Microergonomic-related areas

    - Workstation, control panels, and control room design
    - Physical layout of the process in the plant and its required controls
    - Control room procedures and emergency situations
    - Human-computer (user) interface design-related issues
    - Potential for "procedural traps"
    - Annunciators and emergency notification and response systems
    - Mental and physical workload (during normal as well as emergency situations)
    - Potential for distraction, unexpected interruptions, preoccupation, and premature exits during normal situations
    - Occupational stress analysis
    - Motivational factors
    - Anthropometric considerations
    - Human (physical and psychological) needs, limitations, and capabilities
    - Human decision-making and information processing
    - Causes of human errors
    - Potential for systematic human error
    - Job design and task loading factors
    - Rationale for prioritization of inputs to operators and their activities
    - Shift duration and rotation schedule

2. Macroergonomic-related areas

- Safety culture
- Organizational structures
- Policies and standard operating procedures
- Management of change
- Management activities and capabilities
- Management information systems and reporting structure
- Internal review/inspection programs
- Compliance with reviews and corrective actions
- Selection and development of training programs
- Qualifications and training of instructors
- Definition and evaluation of skills and knowledge (for personnel training)
- Ongoing performance and refresher training
- Operating and maintenance procedures
- Initial employee qualifications assessments
- Performance measurement systems and their effectiveness
- Records management

6.4 Lack of Human Factors Considerations: A Case Study of a Chemical Plant Accident

6.4.1 Background and introduction

In this case study, micro- and macroergonomic analyses have been used postmortem to identify hazards associated with human actions (routine and nonroutine) in a chemical plant. This chemical plant accident occurred in 1992 and caused major losses. About 280 operators, supervisors, and other employees lost their jobs. The plant, which was valued at around $20 million with revenues of $17 to $21 million a year, had to be closed. The mishap at this chemical plant was caused by a chain of events and problems that collectively contributed to a major accident. It has been concluded that both equipment failure (possibly caused by maintenance problems) and lack of human factors considerations, which are discussed below, caused this accident.

6.4.2 Facts and observations

The accident occurred in the chlorination area. The morning operator had informed the afternoon operator and his supervisor that the previous load from reactor 3 had been produced faster than normal (17 hours instead of 23 to 25 hours, which is the normal cycle). The morning operator left reactor 3 with a new load.

- Operators did not take any further action on this information.
- Supervisors did not take any action because they were not properly informed about the characteristics of the specific equipment.

The afternoon operator left his workstation to repair a fume tower, an action that he considered very important because it could prevent a "backup" of fumes and major problems later on. He closed all the chlorine valves in order to stop the plant process and prevent other accidents.

- The operator did not have a communication system with the supervisor or maintenance crew.
- As a result, the operator had to repair the tower himself instead of having the maintenance people take care of the problem.

The operator was informed that the load from reactor 2 was ready for transfer. While transferring the load, the operator felt air leaking from the pneumatic line that connects the temperature sensor on the reactor to the graphic display. From this line ran the signals to the control valve of the automatic cooling system.

- The automatic cooling system should have had its own temperature sensor instead of relying on information from the graphic display.
- The operator did not check the air pressure, which had to be 62 kPa (9 lb/in^2) for the pneumatic system to work properly.

When another operator patched a hole in the pneumatic signal line, the graphic display from reactor 3 increased drastically from 71°C (160°F) to 100°C (212°F). The reactor operator checked the display gauge, which showed the reactor temperature to be 75°C (167°F).

- The operator assumed that the 71°C and 75°C measurements were correct.
- Both the graphic and display gauges were showing incorrect temperatures.
- The supervisor approved the operator's assessment without any analysis.

After observing that all temperatures and pressures were "normal," the operator went back to the fume tower to continue repairs. During these repairs, the operator heard a rupture disk break; he started the gas observation pump and then monitored the reactors' temperatures and pressures. He saw that they were all correct but, upon leaning against reactor 3, discovered that it was extremely hot.

- The operator did not know which rupture disk broke, because after the rupture disk on reactor 3 burst, the pressure in the reactor went down into the normal (nearly atmospheric) range.
- The design did not include the typical alarms for high pressure.

At this point, the operator blocked the transfer of chlorine vapors between reactors 3 and 4 in order to stop the rise in temperature. While he was doing this, he heard a pounding at the water exit pipe. Thinking that cooling water was going into the reactor (a very volatile situation), he proceeded to shut down the cooling water for the whole system.

- Just before he heard the pounding, the operator's assessment of the situation was accurate. He thought that the automatic cooling valve did not work, and he was about to take the correct action, which was to open the water bypass valve. Instead, he aggravated the problem by shutting off the water.
- The operator had to rely solely on his previous experience in order to make a decision.

After closing the water valve, the operator thought that the problem was solved. He went and closed the chlorine valve from the storage tanks. Since the contents of reactor 3 were still getting hotter, thermal expansion of the liquid caused the level to reach the pipe for the rupture disk; this pipe was made of PVC, which melted and caused a spill. At the same time, the contents also reached the expansion tank, which contained nitrobenzene. This caused a reaction that produced a large amount of gas.

- The expansion tank should not have contained any material. On this occasion it was being used as a transfer tank.

At this time, supervisors started the emergency procedures, called the fire department, and evacuated the plant.

6.4.3 Summary of the critical events and actions

The mishap at this chemical plant was caused by a chain of events and problems that collectively contributed to a major accident. Three factors collectively caused this accident: *equipment failure* (possibly caused by maintenance problems), *lack of human factors considerations,* and *organizational factors.*

1. *On the role of equipment failure*

   a. The fume tower was not working properly. This caused the operator to leave his work area.
   b. The pneumatic line for the graphic display was leaking. This deprived the operator of accurate measurements.
   c. The display thermometer did not work properly. The operator could not have verified the correct temperature in relation to the graphic display.
   d. The design lacked an integrated alarm system for various elements of the process.

2. *On the role of human factors considerations*

   a. The operator had to rely too much on previous experience with the process (operating in normal regimes).
   b. There was a lack of training for emergency situations, both for operators and for supervisors.
   c. There were too many required decisions for one operator. There was a lack of decision aids for helping the operator in the decision-making process.
   d. Gauges were not located at a centralized place where the operator could stay and obtain all the necessary information.
   e. The use of an expansion tank for the storage of nitrobenzene was not the correct procedure. This action exacerbated damages caused by the accident.

3. *On the role of organizational factors:* No action was taken regarding the previous load, which was produced abnormally fast. This could be caused only by two factors: either an added amount of reactant or a rise in the reactor internal temperature. In the case of this process, the operator did not add any extra reactant, and therefore, from the posterior results, we can surely assume that the problem was caused by improper cooling of the reactor. This, in turn, was the cause for the temperature rise in the next load, which resulted in the accident. A careful analysis of these factors could have prevented this accident.

6.4.4 Analysis

As mentioned before, shutting off the main cooling water of the system was probably the most important error made by the operator. This systematic error occurred because the operator "heard a pounding at the water exit pipe and thought that the cooling water was going into the reactor." In his judgment, the operator was trying to follow the common wisdom and procedures to prevent "a very volatile situation."

An important category of errors within the context of monitoring and supervisory tasks in chemical plants (in which the operators typically have to respond to changes in system operation by corrective actions) is called *systematic error.* Also in this context, two causes of systematic errors seem to be important and should be considered; they are excessive workload and design traps.

Excessive workload. Research has shown that operators' responses to changes in a technological system will be systematically wrong if task demands exceed the limits of capability. In the case of the operator's job, demands and capability may conflict with several aspects of a task such as the time required, availability of needed information, and background knowledge on system functioning.

The physical and mental workload in an industrial plant is highly variable and sometimes could reach high levels. This is synonymous with having or lacking balance between task demands and an operator's capabilities. According to Tikhomirov,[38] high or unbalanced mental workload causes

- Narrowing span of attention
- Inadequate distribution and switching of attention
- Forgetting the proper sequence of actions
- Incorrect evaluation of solutions
- Slowness in arriving at decisions

Design traps. In addition to occasional unbalanced workloads, human factors–related problems of the workstation are a major cause of errors in plants. These types of errors, called *design-induced* or *system-induced errors,* are forced on operators.

Systematic operator error may be caused by several kinds of "procedural traps."[39] During normal working conditions, human operators are generally extremely efficient because of very effective adaptation to convenient representative signs and signals that they receive from the system. This is a very effective and mentally economical strategy during normal and familiar periods, but it leads the operator into traps when changes in system conditions are not adequately reflected in displays. Such mental traps often significantly contribute to the operator's misidentification of unfamiliar and complex system states. This misidentification, in turn, is usually caused by the activation of "strong but wrong" rules, where the "strength" is determined by the relative frequency of successful execution. When abnormal conditions demand countermeasures from the operator, a shift in the mental work strategies is needed. However, it is very likely that familiar associations based on representative but insufficient information will prevent the operator from realizing the need to analyze a complex and/or unique situation. The operator may more readily accept the improbable coincidence of several familiar faults in the system rather than the need to investigate one new and complex "fault of low probability." In this case, the efficiency of the human operator's internal mental model allows him or her to be selective and, therefore, to cope effectively with complex systems in familiar situations but at the same time may lead him or her into traps that are easily seen after the fact.

The importance of the different categories of error depends on the task conditions. It is suggested that repetitive routine tasks in the plant, which are preplanned, such as responding to alarms, errors caused by demands exceeding resource limits, and errors resulting from procedural traps should be thoroughly investigated and subsequently removed by redesign of the task.

6.4.5 Lessons

This accident caused major losses, as stated in the beginning of the case description. Although accidents are always tragic and can have devastating effects, there are many lessons that society and industry can learn from them. The most important one is that there is a great need for thorough analyses of equipment reliability and human factors in order to prevent other similar major losses.

Most accidents start with equipment malfunction, a process upset, or operator error, but they are aggravated and propagated through the system by a series of factors that could be attributed to bad design, inadequate training, and lack of preparation. Attributing accidents to the action of front-line operators is an oversimplification of the problem. As research has shown, in most cases, operator error is only one attribute of the whole technological (plant) system—a link in a chain of concatenated failures—that could result in accidents. In order to prevent accidents in chemical plants and other facilities, as demonstrated by this case study, an integrated approach to the design and operation, as attentive to human factors as to technical elements, should be taken.[13,40] This approach should be based on a thorough and integrated micro and macro human factors (ergonomic) analysis of the process workstations, procedures, management, and supervisory systems.

6.5 References

1. N. Meshkati, "Human Factors in Large-Scale Technological Systems' Accidents: Three Mile Island, Bhopal, Chernobyl," *Industrial Crisis Quarterly,* 5: 133–154, 1991.
2. N. Meshkati, "An Etiological Investigation of Micro- and Macroergonomic Factors in the Bhopal Disaster: Lessons for Industries of Both Industrialized and Developing Countries," *International Journal of Industrial Ergonomics,* 4: 161–175, 1989.

3. P. Shrivastava, *Bhopal: Anatomy of a Crisis,* 2d ed., Paul Chapman, London, 1992.
4. *New York Times,* March 25, 1993, p. A7.
5. *Occupational Hazards,* November 1991, p. 33.
6. *New York Times,* September 12, 1990.
7. *Los Angeles Times,* March 13, 1989.
8. R. Jenkins, "Bhopal: Five Years Later," *In These Times,* July 18, 1990, pp. 12–13.
9. *A Manager's Guide to Reducing Human Errors: Improving Human Performances in the Chemical Industry,* Chemical Manufacturers Association, Washington, 1990.
10. S. J. Ainsworth and D. J. Hanson, "Plant Disasters Fuel Industry, Government Concern Over Safety," *Chemical & Engineering News,* October 29, 1990, pp. 7–12.
11. OSHA 29 CFR Part 1910.119, "Process Safety Management of Highly Hazardous Chemicals," *Federal Register,* July 1, 1993, pp. 364–385.
12. OSHA Instruction CPL 2-2.45A, U.S. Occupational Safety and Health Administration, Washington, September 28, 1992, p. A-14.
13. N. Meshkati, *An Integrative Model for Designing Reliable Technological Organizations: The Role of Cultural Variables,* Position Statement for the World Bank Workshop on Safety Control and Risk Management in Large-Scale Technological Operations, World Bank, Washington, October 1988.
14. N. Meshkati, "Ergonomics of Large-Scale Technological Systems," *Impact of Science on Society* [The United Nations Educational, Scientific and Cultural Organization (UNESCO) Journal; published also in Arabic, Chinese, French, Portuguese, and Russian], 165: 87–97, 1992.
15. N. Meshkati, *A Framework for Risk Management of Petrochemical Plants in Developing Countries,* United Nations Industrial Development Organization (UNIDO), Vienna, Austria, IO.57 (Spec.) 92: 51858, March 1992.
16. N. Meshkati, "Integration of Workstation, Job, and Team Structure Design in Complex Human-Machine Systems: A Framework," *International Journal of Industrial Ergonomics,* 7: 111–122, 1991.
17. N. Meshkati, J. S. Garza, V. M. Morales, and A. del la Garza, "The Use of Human Factors Methodology in Process Hazards Analysis: A Case Study of a Chemical Plant Accident," *Proceedings of the American Institute of Chemical Engineers Summer National Meeting,* American Institute of Chemical Engineers, New York, August 1993.
18. Eastman Kodak Company, *Ergonomic Design for People at Work,* Vol. 2, Van Nostrand Reinhold, New York, 1986.
19. J. Dul and B. Weerdmeester, *Ergonomics for Beginners: A Quick Reference Guide,* Taylor & Francis, London, 1993.
20. N. Meshkati, "Critical Human and Organizational Factors Considerations in Design and Operation of Petrochemical Plants," *Proceedings of the First International Conference on Health, Safety and Environment in Oil and Gas Exploration and Production,* Vol. 1, Society of Petroleum Engineers, The Hague, Netherlands, November 1991, pp. 627–634.
21. A. D. Swain and H. E. Guttmann, *Handbook of Human Reliability Analysis with Emphasis on Nuclear Power Plant Applications,* NUREG/CR-1278, Final Report, U.S. Nuclear Regulatory Commission, Washington, June 1983, p. 11-5.
22. Air Force Systems Command, *Human Factors Engineering* (AFSC Design Handbook, DH 1-3), Wright-Patterson Air Force Base, Ohio, 1980.
23. K. R. Boff and J. E. Lincoln, *Engineering Data Compendium: Human Perception and Performance,* Vols. 1 to 3, AAMRL, Wright-Patterson Air Force Base, Ohio, 1988.
24. *A Manager's Guide to Ergonomics in the Chemical and Allied Industries,* Chemical Manufacturers Association, Washington, 1992.
25. Eastman Kodak Company, *Ergonomic Design for People at Work,* Vol. 1, Lifetime Learning Publications, Belmont, Calif., 1983.
26. *Human Factors Guide for Nuclear Power Plant Control Room Development,* EPRI NP-3659, Electric Power Research Institute, Palo Alto, Calif., 1984.
27. E. Grandjean, *Fitting the Task to the Man: A Textbook of Occupational Ergonomics,* 4th ed., Taylor & Francis, London, 1988.
28. *Improve Your Workplace: Ergonomic Checkpoints,* International Labour Office, Geneva, 1995.

29. *Man-Systems Integration Standards,* NASA-STD-3000, Vols. 1 and 2, U.S. National Aeronautics and Space Administration, Lyndon B. Johnson Space Center, Houston, 1989.
30. *Human Engineering Design Criteria for Military Systems, Equipment and Facilities,* MIL-STD-1472D, U.S. Department of Defense, Washington, 1989.
31. H. P. Van Cott and R. G. Kinkade (eds.), *Human Engineering Guide to Equipment Design,* sponsored by Joint Army-Navy-Air Force Steering Committee, U.S. Government Printing Office, Washington, 1972.
32. W. E. Woodson, B. Tillman, and P. Tillman, *Human Factors Design Handbook,* 2d ed., McGraw-Hill, New York, 1992.
33. H. W. Hendrick, "Macroergonomics: A Concept Whose Time Has Come," *Human Factors Society Bulletin,* 30(2): 1–3, 1987.
34. R. W. Baily, *Human Performance Engineering: Using Human Factors / Ergonomics to Achieve Computer System Usability,* 2d ed., Prentice-Hall, Englewood Cliffs, N.J., 1989.
35. AT&T, *Design to Reduce Technical Risk,* McGraw-Hill, New York, 1993.
36. W. H. Davidow and M. S. Malone, *The Virtual Corporation,* HarperCollins, New York, 1992, p. 88.
37. *The Economist,* July 13, 1991.
38. O. K. Tikhomirov, *The Structure of Human Thinking Activity,* translated from the 1969 Russian book, Moscow University Printing House, J.P.R.S. 52199, January 1971.
39. J. Rasmussen, "Notes on Human Error Analysis," in G. Apostolakis, S. Garribba, and G. Volta (eds.), *Synthesis and Analysis Methods for Safety and Reliability Studies,* Plenum, New York, 1980, pp. 357–389.
40. N. Meshkati, "Preventing Accidents at Oil and Chemical Plants," *Professional Safety,* 35(11): 15–18, 1990.
41. J. Reason, *Human Error,* Cambridge University Press, New York, 1992.

Consequence Analysis for Facility Design and Siting

Jatin N. Shah and Krishna S. Mudan
Four Elements

7.1 Introduction

Consequence analysis is an essential part of risk analysis that considers the physical effects of an event and the damage caused by the physical effects. Of all the components of risk analysis, the consequence-assessment portion is usually considered the most complex. It is conducted in order to form an opinion on the seriousness of potential hazards associated with accidents and their possible consequences. The purpose of consequence analysis, therefore, is to act as a tool in the process of decision making that includes

- Hazard identification
- Consequence assessment
- Assessment and comparison of risks
- Evaluation of accident-prevention options
- Evaluation of risk-mitigation techniques
- Emergency response planning

In the past decade, several comprehensive hazard-assessment techniques have been developed. The U.S. Coast Guard undertook the development of a Chemical Hazard Response Information System

(CHRIS) in the mid-1970s. The Office of Environmental and Scientific Affairs of the World Bank developed a *Manual of Industrial Hazard Assessment Techniques* and an associated computer program package (WHAZAN). Under the sponsorship of the Dutch government, the state agency TNO developed a complex hazard-assessment module called *EFFECTS*. The U.S. Environmental Protection Agency (EPA) and National Oceanographic and Atmospheric Administration (NOAA) have developed real-time hazard-assessment and emergency response programs (ALOHA and CAMEO). There are scores of other computerized proprietary models to estimate consequences of hazardous materials releases (CHARM, Super-CHEMS, SAFER, PHAST, TRACE, FOCUS, and several others) that are specifically designed to address the issues of emergency planning.

However, many of these are not designed with the intention of evaluating the near-field hazards that are of particular interest to facility design and siting. Thus this chapter discusses the parameters needed to define near-field effects of hazardous materials release and demonstrates their usefulness in the design of facilities processing dangerous chemicals. Section 7.2 discusses defining the appropriate endpoint criteria for assessing these short-term hazards. The relevant parameters for consideration in consequence-assessment models are discussed in Sec. 7.3. The importance of these parameters is illustrated in Sec. 7.4 with various case studies involving fire hazard, explosion hazard, toxic dispersion hazard, and effectiveness of mitigation techniques.

7.2   Vulnerability Assessment

Estimating the appropriate hazard zones depends on the level of concern one is trying to investigate. This section presents a brief description of likely events that may follow the release of a hazardous material and the endpoint criteria (or level of concern) that are appropriate for defining the hazard zone for each particular type of hazard. The consequence models and the parameters affecting the modeling are discussed in the next section.

7.2.1   Endpoint criteria for consequence analysis

In establishing the endpoint criteria, it is recognized that different materials can exhibit different types and degrees of hazard. A chemical such as ethylene oxide may pose flammable, explosive, and/or toxic vapor exposure hazards. It is important to recognize that not all hazards can occur simultaneously. For example, a release of ethylene oxide followed by immediate ignition would lead to a fire hazard. A delayed ignition may lead to an explosion, while no ignition would result in a toxic hazard. Although these scenarios are likely to lead to different types of hazards, each requiring different endpoint criteria, a degree of consistency must be maintained by establishing the endpoint criteria based on an equivalent level of concern. It would be incorrect, for example, to use injury criteria for toxic exposure while using fatality criteria for flammable exposure.

7.2.2 Fire and flammability endpoint criteria

Thermal radiation from a fire can cause burns on bare skin if the radiation intensity is high enough and if the exposure is of sufficient duration. The experimental data[1] for significant injury threshold, 1 percent lethality, near 50 percent lethality, and near 100 percent lethality indicate a relationship between incident heat flux (thermal radiation) and exposure duration. The U.S. Federal Safety Standards for Liquefied Natural Gas Facilities (49 CFR Part 193) have specified levels of thermal radiation fluxes that are used in the layout of LNG facilities. The Health and Safety Executive (HSE) of the United Kingdom has the regulatory authority in the siting of hazardous materials facilities. The Major Hazards Assessment Unit of the HSE has established acceptable levels of thermal radiation flux surrounding LPG facilities.[2] These levels are used to determine a "consultation distance" that may be considered as a buffer zone surrounding a facility. The Risk Criteria for Land Use Planning in the state of New South Wales, Australia (1990), also identifies levels of thermal radiation and their associated hazards. Table 7.1 describes the damage expected for different thermal radiation levels.

7.2.3 Vapor cloud explosion (VCE) endpoint criteria

A flammable vapor cloud may lead to explosion hazards upon ignition. To determine the extent of the explosion hazard, a vapor cloud explosion (VCE) model can be used to compute the overpressure and impulse of an explosion. Based on a review of blast overpressure damage data, Eisenberg[3] estimated a threshold of 15 lb/in^2 (100 kPa) for causing biologic damage. However, severe structural damage could occur at much lower overpressures. Several case studies indicate that most injuries or fatalities in accidental explosions result from secondary effects caused by falling objects or flying debris due to structural damage rather than by direct biologic impact. Lees[4] described the damaging effect of overpressures on structures. Eisenberg used Lees' data to arrive at the following probability of structural damage for average process structures:

90 percent probability: 5.0 lb/in^2 (34 kPa)

50 percent probability: 3.0 lb/in^2 (21 kPa)

1 percent probability: 0.9 lb/in^2 (6 kPa)

The blast overpressure required to cause damage, however, varies considerably for different types of process equipment and buildings, as shown in Fig. 7.1. These variations should be taken into account when determining explosion endpoint criteria.

7.2.4 Toxic vapor exposure endpoint criteria

Hazardous materials could pose toxic effects via three primary routes of entry: inhalation, ingestion, or direct contact with eyes or skin. The extent of the danger zone for toxic exposure depends on the toxicity of the material that is released and its *mobility*. Therefore, releases of volatile toxic materials generally pose greater threats than do discharges of nonvolatile toxic materials.

TABLE 7.1 **Expected Damage for Various Thermal Radiation Levels**

Off-site target	Thermal radiation level (kW/m^2)		
	US DOT	UK HSE	New South Wales
1. Causes pain after 1 minute of exposure.	—	—	2.1
2. Will cause pain in 15–20 seconds and injury (second-degree burns) after 30 seconds.	5	6.3	4.7
3. Significant chance of fatality for extended exposure; high chance of injury after exposures of less than 30 seconds. Buildings made of cellulosic materials may suffer minor damage after prolonged exposure.	12.5	10	12.6
4. Extended exposure results in fatality; there is a chance of fatality for instantaneous exposure. Buildings made of cellulosic materials or not fire resistant will suffer damage after short exposures. Fire-resistant structures and metal may suffer damage after prolonged exposure.	21.0	—	23.0
5. Significant chance of fatality for people with instantaneous exposure. Fire-resistant structures suffer damage after short duration. Buildings of cellulosic materials ignite spontaneously. Metal fatigue after short to medium exposure.	31.5	—	35.0

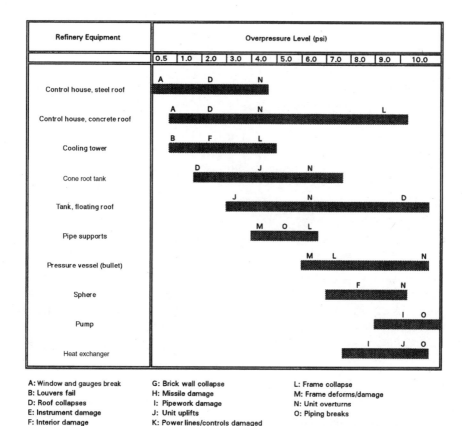

A: Window and gauges break
B: Louvers fail
D: Roof collapses
E: Instrument damage
F: Interior damage

G: Brick wall collapse
H: Missile damage
I: Pipework damage
J: Unit uplifts
K: Power lines/controls damaged

L: Frame collapse
M: Frame deforms/damage
N: Unit overturns
O: Piping breaks

Figure 7.1 Examples of overpressure effect on process equipment and buildings.

The measures of toxicity for various chemicals have been described in the literature and in standards promulgated by regulatory bodies. Many of the threshold limiting values (TLVs) consider chronic exposure to workers over several years and are not applicable for acute hazard determination. The three emergency response planning guidelines (ERPG1, ERPG2, and ERPG3) developed by the American Industrial Hygiene Association (if available) are for a 1-hour exposure and may be used for emergency response planning. ERPG3 values are generally used to determine hazards to individuals who require immediate attention, while ERPG2 and ERPG1 may be used for individuals who are not in immediate danger but may require eventual attention. In the absence of ERPGs, the immediately dangerous to life and health (IDLH) levels published by the National Institute of Occupational Safety and Health (NIOSH) and fractions thereof, as suggested by the EPA in its guidance document (1987), may be used in a similar manner.

Although concentration levels may be used for the determination of toxic vapor exposure hazards, it is better to use a dose level (the intensity of the hazard and the exposure duration) to determine the degree of injury or damage that can result. The method that is used increasingly is *probit analysis*. For toxic gas exposure, the probit (probability unit) is represented as follows:

$$Pr = A + B \ln (C^n t)$$

where Pr, the probit, is a measure of the percentage of the vulnerable resource that sustains fatality, injury, or damage, C is the concentration in parts per million, t is the exposure duration in minutes, and A, B, and n are empirically derived constants.

7.3 Consequence Assessment

To identify representative release scenarios for a consequence analysis, one may use formal hazard-identification techniques such as a HAZOP study or what-if analysis. To supplement formal hazard-identification techniques, one also may use typical historical accidents at petroleum refineries and processing facilities. The list, for example, may include the following:

- Total or partial pipe rupture, such as that due to mechanical impact or vibration
- Leak from a corrosion hole
- Flange leak
- Tank overfill
- Hose failure during transfer operations
- Activation of a rupture disk as a result of a runaway reaction or overpressurization
- Pump or compressor leak
- Vessel rupture due to overpressurization or material failure

Before selecting a consequence-assessment model, it is necessary to consider the outcomes that may follow a release of a given hazardous chemical. In general, a hazardous material release may exhibit one or more of the following three types of hazards:

- Flammable exposure (thermal radiation, impingement)
- Explosions (blast overpressures)
- Toxic exposure hazards

The types of parameters that are important for the evaluation of hazard zones vary by the type of hazard exhibited by a specific material. These parameters are discussed below in greater detail.

7.3.1 Factors affecting vapor dispersion

For toxic material dispersion and flammable material dispersion prior to ignition, one must be able to estimate the potential release rate of the hazardous vapor and its condition at the moment of release into the atmosphere. This step is followed by estimating the extent of the hazard zone. Several methods are available for the prediction of the source term and the hazard zone surrounding an accidental release of a toxic material. These methods vary in their degree of sophistication from simple rules of thumb to emergency response planning models such as ARCHIE (U.S. Federal Emergency Management Agency), EFFECTS (TNO, Holland), ALOHA (U.S. National Oceanographic and Atmospheric Administration), WHAZAN (World Bank), and CHEMS-PLUS (Arthur D. Little) to more accurate and mathematically demanding models such as DEGADIS (Gas Research Institute/University of Arkansas), HEGADAS (Shell), PHAST (DNV Technica), Super-CHEMS (Arthur D. Little), CHARM (Radian), SAFER (DuPont), FOCUS (Quest Consultants), and EHAP (Energy Analysts).

Simplified methods for evaluating the hazards presented by toxic materials at a facility include the ICI Mond Index and Dow's Chemical Exposure Index.[5] This Dow/Europe model is different from the Dow (AIChE) Index, which is designed to address the hazards of fires, explosions, and toxic gases released *only* as a result of fires and explosions.

For the accuracy levels needed in siting of industrial facilities, one can develop a set of tables, plots, or nomograms that will allow the user to determine quickly whether or not a problem exists. In such a case, a more elaborate calculation is required. Such an approach for screening incidents has already been suggested and used by one of the authors.[6]

Models are also available for predicting the concentration of a hazardous chemical inside a building engulfed by a toxic vapor cloud. These models take into consideration the number of air changes per hour and the duration of the release. When evaluating the downwind dispersion of a particular release, several factors influence the dispersion. These include, but are not limited to,

- Release quantity
- Release rate
- Prevailing atmospheric conditions
- Duration of release

- Limiting concentration
- Source elevation
- Surrounding terrain
- Source geometry
- Initial density of the release

Each of these parameters is discussed in greater detail below.

1. *Release quantity/release rate* refers to the quantity of (or the rate at which) hazardous chemical that has the potential to be released in the event of an accident. The quantity (or rate) is the single most important parameter in determining dispersion distances. In general, larger quantities lead to longer dispersion distances. However, the dispersion distance does not increase linearly with quantity or release rate. In fact, a factor of 100 increase in release rate may only lead to a factor of 20 increase in the dispersion distance. For gaseous and high-vapor-pressure liquid releases, the vapor release rate will be the same as the discharge rate. However, for liquids, the vapor release rate is governed by the specific characteristics of the liquid and the spill area and will always be less than the liquid release rate. In its proposed rule making, EPA gives credit only for passive mitigation systems, such as dikes surrounding a hazardous chemical process or storage equipment. Therefore, modeling the containment aspects is particularly important in estimating vulnerable zones.

2. *Prevailing atmospheric conditions* include a representative wind speed and an atmospheric stability class. In general, neutral (or typical) stability leads to shorter dispersion distances than stable weather. The wind speed affects the dispersion distance inversely. Since weather conditions at the time of an accident cannot be determined a priori, it is important to exercise the dispersion model for both typical and worst-case (stable) weather conditions. However, heavy gas dispersion does not follow the traditional neutral dispersion phenomena considered in many of the EPA and other models, and stable weather does not always lead to the longest downwind dispersion distance.

3. *Limiting concentration* affects the dispersion distance inversely. Lower concentrations lead to larger dispersion distances. As with release quantity/rate, the effect is not linear. In other words, a factor of 100 reduction in the limiting concentration may only result in a factor of 20 increase in the dispersion distance.

4. *Duration of release* is a parameter that is dependent on the release mode. For example, a safety-valve release may not last more than a few minutes, whereas a line rupture may continue to discharge for tens of minutes. For liquids forming evaporating pools, the duration

is dependent on the evaporation rate. Most dispersion models use one of the two extreme cases, i.e., continuous release or instantaneous release. In the case of instantaneous release, the duration of release is very short (e.g., pressurized storage tank rupture), and the total quantity of the chemical released during the accident contributes to the dispersion hazard. Further, the dispersion takes place in longitudinal (along wind), lateral (across wind), and vertical directions. In the case of a continuous release, the release lasts a relatively long time, and the release rate is the most important parameter. The dispersion is assumed to take place only in the lateral and vertical directions.

5. *Elevation of the source* may be attributed to its physical height (tall stack) or to the release mode and the properties of chemicals being released. For example, a high-speed jet issuing from a vent stack is likely to travel some distance in the vertical direction before it disperses in the direction of the wind. Similarly, a material whose density is less than that of surrounding air (buoyant) also will rise in the atmosphere before it disperses. In general, the effect of source height is to increase dispersion in the vertical direction and reduce the concentration at ground level. This results in shorter ground-level hazard distances.

6. *Surrounding terrain* affects the dispersion process greatly. For example, rough terrains involving trees, shrubs, buildings, and structures usually enhance dispersion. This leads to a shorter dispersion distance than predicted using a flat-terrain model. There may be localized regions, however, where concentrations may be higher than allowable limits.

7. *Source geometry* refers to the actual size and geometry of the source of emission. For example, a release from a safety valve may be modeled as a point source. However, an evaporating pool may be very large in area, which requires an area source model. The source-geometry effects are significant when considering near-field dispersion. For toxic substance releases, the dispersion hazard distances are usually large; therefore, source-geometry effects are not significant.

8. *Initial density of the release* affects the dispersion process in various ways. For releases at or near ground level, the initial density determines the initial spreading rate. This is particularly true for large releases of pressurized chemicals, where flashing of vapor and formation of liquid aerosols contribute to additional density differences. The research conducted on this topic alone can fill several books; special conferences are held to discuss the phenomenon of heavy gas dispersion.[7,8] The U.S. Coast Guard has sponsored a dense gas dispersion program under the direction of Professor J. Havens of the University of Arkansas. The U.S. Air Force and the Joint Industry Group have conducted experiments involving hydrogen fluoride, ammonia, and nitrogen tetroxide at

the Department of Energy's Liquefied Gaseous Fuel Facility located in Nevada. The Health and Safety Executive (HSE) of the United Kingdom has conducted a series of large-scale tests at its facility in Thorney Island. As indicated by the review of several dispersion models and field data,[9] the results of all these research programs are not conclusive by any means. However, they do indicate the importance of heavy gas dispersion in the area of chemical hazard assessment.

7.3.2   Factors affecting fire hazards

When considering large open hydrocarbon fires, the principal hazard is from thermal radiation. The primary concerns are personnel safety and potential damage to nearby equipment and facilities. Again, many of the models described earlier for vapor dispersion also calculate thermal radiation from pool and jet fires. Most of these models take into account the size of the pool, the type of material, prevailing atmospheric conditions, and the location of the target. However, most of these models do not consider some important factors, such as

- Flame geometry
- Flame drag
- Flame temperature and emissive power
- Smoke obscuration
- Atmospheric transmissivity
- Geometry of the receptor
- Receptor properties such as emissivity and absorptivity

Flame geometry, including the height, tilt, base shape (circular, square, rectangular), and base height, may not affect the thermal radiation levels at large distances from the fire surface but may have a significant impact on near-field effects important for facility design. When computing hazards from fires, it is important to consider the flame tilt and flame drag that are caused by wind because these two factors bring the flame front closer to the target.

Flame temperature and emissive power have direct effects on the amount of heat and thermal radiation transmitted. Atmospheric transmissivity depends on the ratio of flame and ambient temperatures, relative humidity and certain trace gases, and distance from the fire. It has a direct effect on the level of thermal radiation observed at a given distance from the fire.

For many hydrocarbons, such as hexane, gasoline, and JP-4, a considerable part of the luminous flame is covered with smoke, limiting the emissivity of the flame. Data on large-scale fires (10 to 80 m, or 30 to 300 ft) indicate that as much as 70 percent of the flame surface may be covered in smoke. Therefore, it is important to model the reduction of thermal radiation due to smoke obscuration.

Receptor geometry and properties affect the amount of heat flux absorbed. A good model will consider not only the distance from the fire but also the height and orientation of the target. A storage tank that is painted white will absorb less heat than a gray tank and thus will be able to withstand the thermal radiation for a longer duration. When one is attempting to accurately determine the safe separation distances between process units or tanks in a tank farm, all these parameters will influence the outcome and need to be considered.

7.3.3 Factors affecting explosion hazards

Vapor cloud explosion is probably the most difficult phenomenon to model. As in the case of toxic vapor clouds, there are several models for predicting the resulting overpressures from unconfined vapor cloud explosions. Again, these models vary from simplified approaches for quick hazard zone estimation, to a slightly better TNT-equivalent or fast-deflagration model, to multi–energy source models, to three-dimensional explosion models using computerized fluid dynamic (CFD) models such as FLACS by Christian Michelsen Institute, GASEX2 by the U.K. Safety and Reliability Directorate, and CHAOS by British Gas Corporation.

The ICI Mond Index and the Dow Index for fire and explosion may be used to qualitatively judge whether or not distances between buildings and the source are adequate. In the TNT-equivalent method, used in practically all commercially available hazard-prediction models, the energy present in the cloud is assumed to be centralized and represented by an equivalent mass of TNT. The *TNT equivalent* is defined as the ratio of the heat of combustion of the vapor cloud material to that of TNT, multiplied by an appropriate yield factor.

Another method that can be used is the fast-deflagration model, which looks at flame acceleration. However, flame speeds are not well defined, and as in the TNT model, they must be estimated. More recently, TNO of the Netherlands developed a multi–energy source model to assess flame acceleration and overpressure buildup. The multi–energy source method uses several smaller explosions centered around relatively high areas of congestion to simulate the effects of the vapor cloud explosion (VCE).

More recently, an explosion modeling methodology that eliminates most of the subjectivity associated with the prediction of VCE overpres-

TABLE 7.2   Current Status of Vapor Cloud Explosion Modeling

Parameter	Level of current knowledge			
	Virtually unknown ————————————————→			Scientifically known
Theoretical assessment of two-phase, flashing flow of hydrocarbons				x
Practical assessment, immediately following a release			x	
Composition of vapor cloud		x		
Cloud dimensions			x	
Cloud drift	x			
Ignition potential		x		
Explosion yield		x		
Flame acceleration		x		
Unconfined pressure field				
Completely confined pressure field				x
Partially confined pressure field	x			
Behavior of structures subjected to explosion load			x	

sure and impulse was presented at the 28th Annual Loss Prevention Symposium.[10] This method relies on the use of VCE blast curves developed by Strehlow and a correlation of maximum flame speed to confinement, obstacle density, and fuel reactivity.

Computational fluid dynamics (CFD) models are three-dimensional models that solve the theoretical equations to model the three-dimensional geometry. These models are very robust but require immense resources. For the types of calculations needed for most onshore facility siting purposes, it is generally not necessary to consider them. Table 7.2 summarizes the current state of explosion modeling.

The explosive effect that can be produced by ignition and reaction of flammable vapor clouds in air is one of the less frequent, but potentially the most severe consequence of spills. Some of the factors affecting blast overpressure hazard zones are

- Mass of fuel involved
- Degree of confinement
- Obstacle density
- Material reactivity

The mass of fuel is the flammable mass in the cloud that is available for explosion. In general, larger masses result in greater hazard zones. The fuel-mass basis used in the explosion model is very important in determining the explosion efficiency. Many models assume that all the flammable material in the cloud is available for combustion; however, some models take only the mass of the flammable portion of the cloud, which may be an order of magnitude less than the mass of the entire cloud. The basis of the fuel mass affects the explosion efficiency that is input to the model. For models that use the entire mass of the cloud, the explosion efficiency is rarely greater than 10 percent, and it is considerably higher for the models that use only the flammable mass of the cloud.

Classically, gas explosions have been categorized as either confined or unconfined. A typical example of a *confined* explosion may be ignition of a vapor cloud inside process equipment or a building. The flammable gas is completely surrounded by the building or the structure, and the combustion takes place inside the confinement. Confined explosions produce considerably higher overpressure per mass of fuel than do unconfined vapor cloud explosions. The term *unconfined vapor cloud explosion* (UVCE) is often wrongly used to describe an explosion that occurs in the absence of an obvious confining structure. In fact, if combustion occurs in a truly unconfined region, then significant explosive overpressure is not generated. Research has shown that even in modest-sized process plants, significant congestion due to process equipment and piping is common. Thus the so-called unconfined explosions are in reality due to either partial confinement within a dispersing vapor cloud or obstacles.

The degree of confinement has a profound effect on the blast overpressure. UVCE models predict a uniform attenuation of the overpressure with distance. Presence of buildings, structures, and process equipment alters the pressure field and usually leads to an acceleration of flow and hence an increase in overpressure.[11] Higher confinement leads to larger hazard zones due to more efficient combustion. Increased obstacle density results in greater turbulence intensity and, therefore, higher flame speeds and overpressure.

Explosion efficiency depends on the type of material (fuel), the degree of confinement, and the obstacle density. It has been generally accepted that it is conservative to assume a 10 percent explosion yield efficiency for hydrocarbon explosions. Recent results[12] have shown that the probability distribution of explosion efficiency has no distinct upper limit. Therefore, the explosion efficiency for use in the model ought to be carefully determined.

7.4   Case Studies

The best way to address the key modeling parameters discussed in the preceding section is to illustrate their effects with case studies. Two specific case studies are given to illustrate the importance of near-field parameters that should be taken into consideration for accurate portrayal of hazard zones.

7.4.1   Chlorine storage mitigation

This case study involves storage of chlorine at or near its atmospheric boiling point in a refrigerated container. Of particular importance to the study is the secondary containment (dike) constructed with concrete. The dike height, diameter, and construction material can be changed as long as the impoundment volume contains the 100-ton content of the tank. Other relevant parameters are assumed as follows: storage pressure, 34 kPa gauge (5 lb/in^2); storage temperature, 230 K ($-45°$F); and impoundment volume, 100 m^3 (3500 ft^3); the prevailing weather conditions are assumed to be Pasquill-Gifford D stability with 5 m/s (11 mi/h) wind speed. The ERPG3 for acute inhalation hazard for chlorine is 20 ppm, and dispersion distances were calculated for this concentration limit.

First, the dispersion distance was determined using EPA's 1987 guidance document model. Here, the release is assumed to last for 10 minutes, regardless of the physical state of the material. Application of this model to estimate the dispersion distance gives a vulnerable zone of over 10,400 m (6.5 mi). Next, the dispersion distance was calculated using the EPA-proposed RMP rule's current definition of the worst case, which would mean the release of 100 tons instantaneously. Application of a traditional dispersion model leads to a distance of over 16,000 m (9.9 mi) for the ERPG3 level of concern. EPA's proposed rule also requires the evaluation of more credible release scenarios and allows one to use all the passive mitigation in place for determining the dispersion hazard. This is the kind of scenario where a more detailed analysis can be of significant assistance. Four passive mitigation options are postulated, and the corresponding reductions in dispersion distance are given below. For sake of comparison, assume a complete rupture of the largest line that leads to a flashing liquid release of 58 kg/s (130 lb/s). The adiabatic flashing fraction is about 2.4 percent, and the remaining liquid is allowed to collect and evaporate from the substrate.

Option 1. Effect of dike area on source term: The dike diameter is assumed to be 11.6 m (38 ft), and the dike material is assumed to be structural concrete. This computation usually involves calculation of time-dependent pool size, heat transfer from the substrate to the liquid pool, and convection and radiation effects. Several of the advanced models do take these parameters into account and compute the steady-state (time-averaged) or time-dependent source release rate. This source term is the input to the dispersion model. The maximum evaporation rate is the same as the total release rate of 58 kg/s (130 lb/s), but it does decrease with time due to cooling of the substrate.

Option 2. Effect of dike volume on source term: In reality, the primary objective of an impoundment is to provide secondary containment for the hazardous substance. For large, cryogenic storage of chemicals, this provides a variety of benefits. Apart from containing the spill, the dike floor and walls cool rapidly and reduce conductive heat transfer to the cold liquid. Further, the heavy chlorine vapor stays inside the impoundment until the volume of liquid and vapor exceeds the dike volume. The vaporization or the source term at the time of dike overflow depends on the heat transfer at the time of overflow and can be substantially less than the initial heat transfer rate. These are precisely the parameters specified in Department of Transportation 49 CFR 193.2059 for siting of liquefied natural gas facilities, and the models can be adapted easily for addressing the hazards of other chemicals stored under refrigerated conditions. For example, in the present case, with a dike height of 1 m (3.3 ft) for the same 11.6-m (38-ft) diameter, taking the heat transfer from walls and the impoundment capacity of the dike leads to an overflow time of 18 seconds. The maximum overflow rate at the instant of overflow is reduced to 11.1 kg/s (25 lb/s).

Option 3. Effect of reduced dike area with same dike volume: Since the EPA's primary objective is to address mitigation of hazards, design changes should be evaluated in the consequence assessment. In the preceding case, if the dike diameter is reduced to 6.7 m (22 ft) and the height is increased to 3 m (10 ft) to maintain the same impoundment volume, the effect on the source release rate is dramatic. The analysis indicates that the overflow time is increased to about 82 seconds and the maximum source release rate is about 3.2 kg/s (7.1 lb/s).

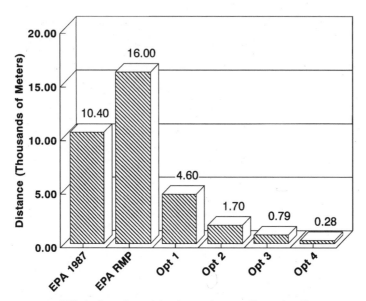

Figure 7.2 Effect of passive mitigation options on dispersion distance.

Option 4.   Effect of reduced ullage pressure and insulated concrete: The reduction of pressure inside the storage tank will help in maintaining chlorine closer to its atmospheric boiling point, thereby reducing the adiabatic flash fraction considerably. For example, reduction of the ullage pressure from 34 to 3.4 kPa gauge (0.5 lb/in^2) will reduce the flashing fraction from 2.4 to 0.27 percent. The insulated concrete reduces the amount of heat transferred from the surroundings, which increases the time required for the vapor to overflow the dike to about 15 minutes from 82 seconds. This results in a maximum overflow rate of about 0.34 kg/s (0.75 lb/s).

The effect of the mitigation options on the dispersion distance to ERPG3 is shown in Fig. 7.2. As can be seen, models that take into account the detailed design enhancements (mitigation options) can help to estimate the difference in hazard zones with a greater degree of confidence. In this particular case, by choosing the appropriate passive mitigation systems, it is possible to contain the vulnerable zone well within the plant fence line.

7.4.2 Flammable liquid storage tank farm

A key concern in the storage of flammable liquids in American Petroleum Institute (API) type atmospheric storage tanks is the spread of fire from one tank to its neighbor. The National Fire Protection

Association (NFPA) and the API have established guidelines on safe separation distances for storing flammable liquids. Many of the flame radiation models use simplistic point sources or circular flame bases to compute the heat flux at various locations. These approximations are usually sufficient to estimate the distances that cause public concern. However, they are not appropriate to compute the flame radiation accurately for siting purposes. As mentioned in Sec. 7.3.2, the facility siting model should consider the detailed flame geometry, emissive characteristics, atmospheric transmissivity, receptor orientation, and receptor absorption characteristics.

The importance of these parameters can be illustrated with a case study. Let us consider the refined product storage tank farm at a large refinery. About 950 m³ (250,000 gal) of product (say, gasoline) may be stored in a 12-m-diameter (40-ft) cone-roof tank of about 10-m (33-ft) height. The surrounding dike should have 125 percent capacity and will be about 35 m (120 ft) square. A large release from the tank followed by ignition could lead to a pool fire in the dike.

Figure 7.3 shows the computed heat fluxes using an equivalent circular base model without smoke obscuration (used in most software programs) and a square base pool fire model with all the parameters discussed in Sec. 7.3.2 taken into account.

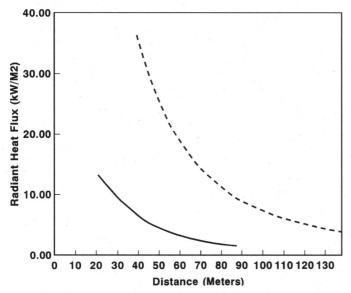

Figure 7.3 Distance versus thermal radiation for typical and rigorous models. The solid-line curve indicates the rigorous, and the broken-line curve the conservative, option.

The typical design heat flux for construction-grade steel is about 12.5 kW/m^2. As can be seen from Fig. 7.3, the distances at which each one of these models gives this flux level varies considerably. Being conservative in the estimation of hazards to the public is often desirable, and most of the simpler models are sufficient for this purpose. However, for facility siting, safety and operability are the primary concern, along with the most effective use of existing real estate. The conservative model usage would require almost 1000 percent more real estate for siting of adjacent tanks, and for a refinery with about 40 storage tanks, the additional space required would be almost 77,000 m^2 (19 acres).

7.5 Summary

Consequence assessment is an integral part of process risk management. The current OSHA regulations require facilities processing hazardous chemicals to consider facility siting as an important aspect of overall safety management. The proposed EPA Risk Management Program requires facilities to consider all passive mitigation systems in assessing public hazards. In addressing these requirements, it is important to use quantitative consequence models because they provide an objective basis for comparison. Most integrated consequence models do not have the necessary flexibility to address near-term consequence effects or accurately model design/mitigation options. However, most stand-alone models consider appropriate parameters necessary to model near-field phenomena and the effects of mitigation measures. Therefore, it is equally important to select consequence models that consider the necessary details to make prudent engineering and management decisions.

7.6 References

1. G. Mixter, "The Empirical Relation Between Time and Intensity of Applied Thermal Energy in Production of 2 + Burns in Pigs," Report No. UR-316, Contract W-1041-Eng-49, University of Rochester, 1954.
2. P. J. Crossthwaite, "Development Control in the Vicinity of Certain LPG Installations," *Proceedings of GASTECH '85*, Gastech Ltd., Herts, U.K., 1985, pp. 128–132.
3. N. A. Eisenberg et al., *Vulnerability Model: A Simulation System for Assessing Damage Resulting from Marine Spills*, AD-AO15-245, NTIS, Springfield, Va., 1975.
4. F. P. Lees, *Loss Prevention in the Process Industries*, Butterworth, London, 1980.
5. E. L. Graaf, "Chemical Exposure Index," *Proceedings of the Sixth International Symposium on Loss Prevention and Safety Promotion in the Process Industries*, Norwegian Society of Chartered Engineers, Oslo, June 1989.
6. K. S. Mudan, "FIRST Hazard Ranking for Chemical Process Facilities," ASME Winter Annual Meeting, New York, December 1987.
7. S. Hartwig (ed.), *Heavy Gas and Risk Assessment*, Vols. 1 to 3, D. Reidel Publishing, Dordrecht, Germany, 1984.
8. G. Ooms and H. Tennekes (eds.), *Atmospheric Dispersion of Heavy Gases and Small Particles*, Springer-Verlag GmbH & Co. KG, Berlin, 1983.

9. S. R. Hanna, D. G. Strimaits, and J. C. Chang, "Evaluation of Fourteen Hazardous Gas Models with Ammonia, and Hydrogen Fluoride Field Data," *Journal of Hazardous Materials,* Elsevier, Amsterdam, pp. 159–186, 1991.

10. Q. A. Baker et al., "Vapor Cloud Explosion Analysis," *Proceedings of the 28th Annual Loss Prevention Symposium,* American Institute of Chemical Engineers, New York, 1994.

11. K. S. Mudan, "Blast Waves in Partially Confined Regions: A Numerical Simulation Model," *Heavy Gas and Risk Assessment Conference,* D. Reidel, Dordrecht, Germany, 1984.

12. J. E. Shepherd, G. A. Melhem, and P. A. Athens, "Unconfined Vapor Cloud Explosions: A New Perspective," *Proceedings of the International Conference and Workshop on Modeling and Mitigating the Consequences of Accidental Releases of Hazardous Materials,* American Institute of Chemical Engineers, New York, 1991.

8

Frequency Evaluation

Lisa M. Bendixen and Michael Kalfopoulos
Arthur D. Little, Inc.

8.1 Introduction

8.1.1 Purpose of chapter

In almost any industry, there are safety concerns that corporations must be aware of and must address. Frequency evaluation is one of the tools that can be used to help understand and address such concerns by determining the likelihood of unwanted events.

The intent of frequency evaluation is to measure the likelihood of occurrence of various events or failures. This is both an acceptable and a necessary part of reliability studies, and it helps tie together data on historical occurrence with predictive analysis for particular situations. Ideally, it also should help identify where in a given system or facility the largest contributions to overall risk levels are made. Moreover, one can determine if overall procedures or practices are having an impact on multiple areas. For example, too long inspection intervals, insufficient preventive maintenance, or inadequate staffing can all affect many aspects of one facility. The primary outcome of frequency evaluation should be a set of cost-effective mitigation measures that are targeted at the significant sources of risk or an understanding that risks are adequately controlled and do not require such measures.

The potential problems associated with frequency evaluation are incompleteness and uncertainty. Only those risks which have been identified can be quantified, and the hazard identification will only be as good as the experience, knowledge, and intuition of those performing it. However, this does not mean to invalidate the concept; rather, this suggests that a good, solid team be employed instead of just one or two individuals.

With regard to the accuracy of the quantification, only an actual assessment can reflect the idiosyncrasies of one plant as compared with industry averages. Therefore, frequency evaluation is at least as accurate as any other approach. Since the most important contributor to uncertainty is events that are not identified, additional effort generally should be spent on hazard identification rather than on minor improvements to databases.

The benefits of frequency evaluation can be enhanced by proceeding with consequence modeling and risk evaluation (which determines the number of individuals adversely affected by a given event or the associated damages and downtime, as well as the likelihood of such impacts). This is usually an iterative process that shows the effectiveness of design or procedural changes. A full risk assessment that includes these steps can show a complete distribution of risks and allows specific mitigation measures to be developed and applied. It is also valuable in interpreting the results and making risk-management decisions.

Frequency evaluation determines the significance of residual hazards, allows hazards requiring mitigation to be prioritized for more cost-effective results, and helps develop mitigation measures.

8.1.2 Matching to overall needs

One of the most important aspects of conducting an adequate frequency evaluation is to understand the overall study needs. Should the study just determine likelihood? Should both the likelihood and the consequences be determined? Should risk be determined? Are the results being used as a comparison with another design? These are the types of questions one must ask prior to initiating an evaluation.

These questions are very important for several reasons. First, different study needs require different levels of resources and data. A study to just determine the relative likelihood of an unwanted event requires much less time than a study that requires an absolute estimate or a risk assessment where consequences are also considered. Second, the appropriate approach for performing the frequency evaluation must be selected based on the study need. For example, a detailed quantitative approach is most suitable if one needs to perform a risk assessment. Third, the accuracy of results for each study need is different. For example, if an analyst is to compare the safety aspects of two designs by performing a frequency evaluation, the same unwanted event may be associated with each design. Because the event appears in both design variations and the study purpose is to compare the two designs, the failure rate may not have to be extremely accurate unless the design variations also influence the likelihood of the event. Often the design variations will affect only certain hazards, and these may not be the critical or significant hazards.

8.1.3 Organization of chapter

The remainder of this chapter is divided into four sections. Section 8.2 discusses the available methodologies used in frequency evaluation. A brief overview of the available methodologies is given, followed by a more detailed description of each methodology. The strengths and weaknesses of each technique are presented, as well as appropriate situations for using the methodologies.

Section 8.3 addresses some of the data sources available for frequency evaluation and their use. This includes discussions concerning data review and collection efforts, a summary of key data sources, the limitations in using reliability data from the sources, the selection and use of reliability data, and references to other sources for discussions of using failure-rate distributions, bayesian analysis, uncertainty, and so forth.

Section 8.4 provides actual frequency-evaluation examples for the fault-tree and event-tree methodologies and a semiquantitative example. The final section provides a list of references.

8.2 Available Methods

Various methodologies are available that can be used to perform hazard quantification. The use of these methodologies may differ depending on the nature of the particular frequency evaluation being undertaken. One case may only require that the overall failure of each piece of equipment be evaluated, while another also may require the identification of individual component failures causing the equipment failure.

Three main approaches are used to perform frequency evaluations. The first approach is qualitative and very simplistic. In short, rough qualitative comparisons of failure rates are made for pieces of equipment or human activities. For example, suppose the frequency of failure must be determined for a system comprising a pump and associated piping. Using the qualitative approach, the analyst knows that the pumps are more likely to fail than the piping; i.e., the pumps have a higher failure rate.

The semiquantitative approach is the second basic approach to frequency evaluation. The failure rate is estimated using order-of-magnitude ranges (10^{-1} to 10^{-2} per year, 10^{-3} to 10^{-4} per year). This approach does not actually assign a specific numerical value to the unwanted event but matches the failure rate to a category, which consists of a numerical range. The failure rates that are assigned by ranges of orders of magnitude are commonly used in matrix form so that another variable can also be addressed (such as consequence).

The last approach to frequency evaluation is the quantitative approach. This approach assigns numerical failure rates to unwanted events using data sources or other available information. Quantitative approaches can themselves be simplistic or very detailed. A simplistic approach assigns numerical failure rates, but the failure rates are usually addressed in orders of magnitude (10^{-1} per year, 10^{-2} per year, 10^{-3} per year) and are not determined in great detail. However, they may be assigned for many subevents and then combined to estimate the overall event's likelihood. A comparison of the frequency of failure for the unwanted events also can be performed before assigning a failure rate. For example, using the semiquantitative approach, suppose the frequency of failure must be determined for a system comprising a valve, a hose, and a vessel. Depending on the type of valve and the type of failure, the failure rate may vary between 10^{-1} per year and 10^{-2} per year. However, for the purpose of illustration, assume that the valve has a failure rate of approximately 10^{-2} per year. Hose failure rates can range from 10^{-2} per year to 10^{-3} per year. One might assume that the failure rate is 10^{-3} per year if the hose is considered less likely to fail than the valve. Finally, a failure rate of 10^{-5} per year for the vessel could be assigned to illustrate that its probability of failure is very unlikely.

A detailed quantitative approach involves in-depth quantification. The accuracy of determining the frequency of unwanted events is maximized, since the failure rates are more specific and are expressed in more detail than orders of magnitude. When performing a detailed quantification, failure rates can be specified to two or more significant digits using scientific notation (1.23×10^{-3} per year). This chapter presents techniques for all three types of analyses.

8.2.1   Overview of available methods

Some of the methodologies available for frequency evaluation include

- *Fault-tree analysis (FTA).* A methodology that graphically presents the sequences and combinations of failures that lead to a particular outcome. It utilizes a top-down approach that starts by identifying the effect and seeks the causes.

- *Event-tree analysis.* A methodology that identifies a component failure and graphically analyzes the potential outcomes or development of that failure. Event trees display the time sequence and likelihoods of the events that may occur.

- *Cause-consequence diagrams.* A methodology that is a combination of both fault trees and event trees. The fault tree is used to develop causes of a critical event, and the event tree displays its consequences.

- *Failure mode and effects analysis (FMEA) and failure mode, effects, and criticality analysis (FMECA).* Methodologies that analyze all the failure modes for each given item of a component for their effect on other components and the overall system. As opposed to the FTA methodology, these methods use a bottom-up approach that is very thorough, since all failure modes can be identified and subsequently quantified.

- *Historical data or epidemiologic approach.* An approach that applies the findings of a review of historical occurrences in the understanding of a particular system.

- *Preliminary hazard analysis (PHA)/semiquantitative approach.* A methodology that identifies potential hazard conditions within a system and subsequently assesses the relative significance or criticality of resulting accidents in terms of either public or employee safety.

- *Ranking/qualitative approach.* An approach that identifies failures for a particular scenario. The failures are then assigned failure rates qualitatively and ranked relative to one another, usually by orders of magnitude.

Other methodologies that can be used in frequency evaluation include the parts-count method, the simulation method, and reliability analysis. The *parts-count method* is a very simple technique that counts the number of parts by their type (such as pumps and valves), determines the failure rate of each type of part, multiplies the respective counts and failure rates, and then sums over all the components to arrive at an overall system failure rate. *Simulation methodologies* usually start with fault trees or some other model of the system along with a probability distribution for each event. *Reliability analysis* can cover a detailed study of system failures and associated downtime using a model facility and probability distributions or point estimates. In addition, it can be used to determine the effectiveness of a particular safety system for incorporation into one of the other methodologies.

8.2.2 Fault-tree analysis (FTA)

FTA starts with the effect and seeks the causes, unlike other methods, such as FMEA, which start with the failure of a component and seek the consequences. Although this technique analyzes the potential combinations or sequences of events, it does not cover all possible failures or all causes of system failure; instead, it focuses only on the most credible means by which an undesired event may occur. Fault trees can be used as an identification method if top events are selected based on experience, imagination, checklists, and historical occurrences; the pathways of events leading to each specified outcome (top events) are then identified. Alternatively, fault trees can be constructed for events identified by another method and used to verify the findings of that method. The latter approach is usually more efficient. Fault trees are generally used as a partial means of identification and for quantification.

To construct a fault tree, one assumes the state of the system or the undesired event and then repeatedly asks how that might come about until the basic causes or the lowest practical level of detail is achieved. The construction of the fault tree is the most critical step in FTA and involves elements of both art and science. A standard set of logic and event symbols facilitates construction, and a reduced/modified set makes fault trees more readily understood by nonexperts (see Fig. 8.1).

One of the most common mistakes in quantifying fault trees is to multiply two or more frequencies together. This yields meaningless results. Hence the symbols can be changed to clarify which events are given as frequencies and which are probabilities. (No more than one event leading into an AND gate may be a frequency, and all events leading into an OR gate must be in the same units.) A further degree of consistency is achieved by trying to ensure independence between events, particularly during quantification. By simplifying the presentation of the fault tree, there is a greater direct understanding of the effects of various mitigation measures from those not involved in fault-tree construction. Also, the fault trees are more useful as documentation.

Fault trees are time-consuming and require a thorough understanding of a system and its behavior in all operating modes. However, they also provide a systematic approach to identifying the weak or hazardous points in a system and a clear graphic record of the analysis process. FTA can consider effects of both human errors and equipment failures, as well as operating and maintenance procedures.[1]

FTA can be used at almost all stages of project development and can analyze a particular facility or evaluate alternative designs or procedures. Fault trees can handle large, complex systems; they are often received fairly well by plant engineers/designers because they can handle multiple failures, including situations that require more than engi-

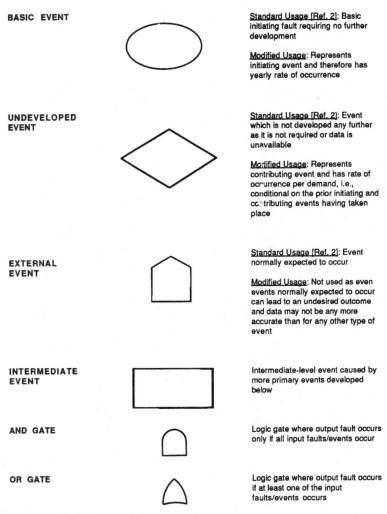

BASIC EVENT		Standard Usage [Ref. 2]: Basic initiating fault requiring no further development
		Modified Usage: Represents initiating event and therefore has yearly rate of occurrence
UNDEVELOPED EVENT		Standard Usage [Ref. 2]: Event which is not developed any further as it is not required or data is unavailable
		Modified Usage: Represents contributing event and has rate of occurrence per demand, i.e., conditional on the prior initiating and contributing events having taken place
EXTERNAL EVENT		Standard Usage [Ref. 2]: Event normally expected to occur
		Modified Usage: Not used as even events normally expected to occur can lead to an undesired outcome and data may not be any more accurate than for any other type of event
INTERMEDIATE EVENT		Intermediate-level event caused by more primary events developed below
AND GATE		Logic gate where output fault occurs only if all input faults/events occur
OR GATE		Logic gate where output fault occurs if at least one of the input faults/events occurs

Figure 8.1 Fault-tree symbols.

neering judgment alone. The level of detail to which a fault tree is developed depends on the purpose of the analysis, the present and future users of the report, and the level of data availability.

Absolute accuracy is generally secondary to identification of failure sequences and determination of the effectiveness of various mitigation measures, particularly in daily loss-prevention activities. FTA provides insight into failure sequences and serves as a guide for answering questions on which system is more likely to be a source of trouble. Fault trees display the relative significance of the cause of a particular event and the importance of one top event as opposed to others. The technique not only quantifies the likelihood of specific events at a particular facility—instead of using industry-wide averages—but also allows the frequency of events to be determined for complex systems where historical data are not available on a system level.

Quantification of a fault tree may be done by hand or using a computer model, depending on the accuracy desired and the complexity of the fault tree. However, the computational method is generally not as critical as the proper, logical construction of the fault tree and the identification of all significant causes. Numerous references are available on automated fault-tree construction and computational codes.[2-4]

8.2.3 Event-tree analysis

Event trees are very similar to FMEA or FMECA. Most applications of event-tree analysis drop branches that do not make engineering sense. The analysis starts by defining the initiating event and subsequently identifying and defining the safety systems that may come into play. It proceeds by ordering the events and system states in time and then finally by identifying any dependencies and removing nonsensical branches. The method has several advantages in that it

- Defines and organizes scenarios.

- Orders events in the time sequence in which they are expected to occur.

- Identifies top events for subsequent fault-tree analysis.

- Demonstrates the relationship between the functioning or failure of a safety system and the ultimate accident.

- Displays various consequences or outcomes that may result from a single initiating event.

With careful evaluation, it is possible to discover common-mode failures and redefine events (with a reanalysis of the event tree also) so that they properly represent common initiating events.[1,5]

The problems associated with event trees include the potential for a false sense of completeness (if all initiating events are not identified), the difficulty of handling more than two event states (i.e., failure and success can be handled, but a delayed success or partial failure cannot), and the need to use something like fault-tree analysis to develop the probabilities of many of the branches. If this is done for many branches, it may be difficult to identify common causes.[5]

Event trees are felt by some users to be best not for the analysis of system failures but rather in helping to examine the consequences of a failure and possibly showing the impact of operator intervention and various weather conditions.[6,7]

8.2.4 Cause-consequence diagrams

This methodology combines fault trees and event trees. The fault tree develops the causes of critical events, and the event tree displays the consequences. It is the most flexible of the methodologies and can handle external applied conditions and time delays. It offers a wide variety of logic gates and can be used for start-up and shutdown operations along with batch processes. Cause-consequence diagrams can deal with both hazards and system reliability problems.[7]

8.2.5 Failure mode and effects analysis (and FMECA)

Failure mode and effects analysis is equipment-oriented and is a bottom-up approach. The failure modes for each individual component are analyzed, and their effects on the other components and the overall system are evaluated. The actual steps involved in determining the consequences of the malfunction or failure of components[8] are to

- Identify and list all components.
- Identify all failure modes, considering all possible operating modes.
- Determine the effects of each failure on other components and the overall system.
- Calculate the probability of each failure mode.
- Evaluate the seriousness of each failure mode.

This process can be extremely time-consuming. Also, it does not provide any systematic approach for identifying failure modes or determining their effects. These segments of the analysis must be done totally from the basic material at hand and the knowledge and experience of the analysts. The format, however, does introduce some level of discipline.[7]

Typical column heads on FMEA worksheets would be component, failure probability, failure mode, percentage of failures by mode, and effects (may be broken down into critical and noncritical or any other category desired). It is possible to make the analysis more conservative by lumping many unlikely or unknown failure modes into one category called "other" and then assuming them all to be critical (i.e., causing system failure). Such a grouping also makes the thoroughness of identification somewhat less problematic.[2]

FMEA is system-oriented, not hazard-oriented, and embodies the concept of system failure resulting from "critical" component failures. It is not designed to treat combinations of failures or redundant components, although this can be done to a minimal extent. More important for the loss-prevention engineer concerned with daily operations of a plant, there is no real means for discriminating between alternate courses of improvement or mitigation.

Failure mode, effects, and criticality analysis is quite similar to FMEA except that it formally considers the criticality of a given failure in greater detail and looks at the system design aspects and controls that are intended to limit the chance of failure. As with FMEA, one must first identify the fault and then determine its effects. The remaining two steps are unique to FMECA and of particular interest to those concerned with safety or loss prevention. In these steps, means of control already present or proposed are determined and then the findings, such as the modified chance of failure and an indication of whether or not further control is necessary, are summarized.[2]

8.2.6   Epidemiologic approach

This approach reviews historical occurrences in the understanding of a particular system. It is a straightforward method that requires only two or three steps and can be performed relatively quickly. The first step is to acquire data on historical events, the second is to analyze the data for the system of concern, and the third is to modify the findings in light of trends that may have been uncovered or improvements that will be or have been made.[9] This technique will identify events that have already happened if the data sources are complete and can be applied in situations where all the details of a system are not yet known. However, this also means that hazards that are unique to a particular facility or system will not be identified. Adequate data also may be difficult to collect. This type of approach is often an input to a more detailed study.

8.2.7 Preliminary hazard analysis (PHA)/semiquantitative approach

This methodology identifies potential hazard conditions and assesses the criticality of resulting accidents in terms of public and/or employee safety. PHA historically has been carried out very early in the development of a facility, allowing both design changes and procedure development to control identified hazards cost-effectively. The first step in a PHA is to use engineering experience or judgment along with checklists to identify potential hazardous elements or components. Second, it must be determined which events would transform a hazardous condition into a potential accident and how serious the accident would be.[2]

PHA is a worksheet approach, much like FMEA and FMECA. The sheets generally have a minimum of four columns covering the component or subsystem of concern and its failure modes, the possible effects of a failure, the means of identifying or controlling the failures, and the overall findings or remarks. One report used

- Equipment
- Operating mode
- Failure mode
- Potential failure effect on functional area or system, facility, and personnel
- Severity level (from predefined categories)
- Probability level (from predefined categories)
- Critical item (yes or no)

Other categories also can be developed. Like many of the techniques mentioned earlier, the potential incompleteness of the failure mode identification (particularly for new equipment or processes) is one of the limiting aspects of a PHA, as is the difficulty in demonstrating the effects of mitigation.

8.2.8 Ranking/qualitative approach

In this approach, the failures are identified for a particular scenario. Each failure is then assigned a failure rate qualitatively and subsequently is ranked or prioritized relative to other failures or into predefined categories. The analyst can use the results to prioritize further study and/or to develop potential mitigation measures. Usually the ranking is performed by orders of magnitude. This approach is very simplistic and is not time-consuming. It can be used without knowing the details of the system, perhaps because data are not available in greater levels of detail. On the other hand, this approach only estimates failure rates. The estimates are not particularly accurate and cannot be used for absolute risk estimates or detailed risk assessments.

8.2.9 Other methods

As mentioned previously, the *parts-count method* counts the number of components in a particular system by type. The failure rates for each type of component are determined. Then the number of components by their type is multiplied by the respective failure rates to determine the overall failure rate of that type of component. The overall rate of the system is determined by summing over all types of components. Built into this approach is the assumption that any component failure is critical and will cause system failure. There is no such thing as an undetected failure, nor are there any redundant pieces of equipment. This leads to very conservative estimates for system failure and does not provide any real indication of the actual hazard associated with a failure. However, this method does cover the possibilities of both common-mode failures and dependent components.[2]

If a component or subsystem is not critical when analyzed by this approach, it is not likely to be critical when analyzed in greater detail. However, this conclusion is more applicable to reliability than to safety. A counterexample for a safety engineer would be a system that is insignificant when analyzed by a parts-count approach but whose failures always resulted in catastrophic consequences (such as a high-pressure pipeline carrying a toxic material) as opposed to a large, complex system that never or very rarely had major consequences (such as a highly automated, instrumented, and contained cylinder-filling operation). A slightly more realistic estimate might be obtained by distinguishing between critical and noncritical failures in the failure rates applied. This would use the concept of fail-to-danger without stating the specific failure mode that resulted in that state.

The *simulation method* associates a probability distribution for each event using models such as fault trees. It is flexible enough to vary input conditions and determine the effects on the overall system. The general steps involved are

- Develop a model of the system.
- Determine the probability/severity-of-failure distribution for each event or component in the model.
- Represent distributions as a set of discrete points.
- Run the model continuously until it generates a distribution for overall system failure/severity.

This can be costly and time-consuming, but it can lead to more realistic results than most other methods.[8] Such an approach is used on many military and space projects, where the consequences of failure can be devastating.

Reliability analysis can verify or define reliability levels and targets. Structural reliability analysis, on the other hand, uses nonlinear dynamic structural models or more simplified response models to evaluate the effects of extreme seismic, wind, or wave loadings on a structure such as an offshore rig or a storage tank. Design loads, safety factors, transient loads, and the nonlinearity of structural behavior must all be considered.[7]

8.3   Data Sources and Their Use

When performing a frequency evaluation, one of the most important aspects in determining the frequency of an event is to use data that are both appropriate and available. Many data sources are available to the analyst, including comprehensive handbooks, publications, journal articles, and equipment or site-specific data. Each source usually provides a specific subset of reliability data, such as data for specific types of equipment. For example, Lees[10] presents failure-rate data for control equipment such as measurement devices, control loops, and analyzers. Data sources also may provide specific frequency data on human error rates. Smith[11] provides specific error probabilities for various types of human activities; Swain and Guttmann[12] present even more.

There are many instances where several data sources contain information on the human errors and equipment failures of concern. A more accurate frequency evaluation usually can be performed when failure rates from various sources can be compared or double-checked. However, the reader is cautioned to verify the independence of the data sources, since many data sources share some of the same original sets of data.

8.3.1   Discussion of other data reviews

There are many cases where proven techniques are available to perform analyses; however, the system-specific information or data required to perform the analyses may be insufficient to generate accurate results. The Center for Chemical Process Safety (CCPS) developed a handbook that provides reliability data to designers, operators, and safety engineers who perform quantitative risk assessments. This handbook (included in the list in Sec. 8.3.3) is a compilation of data from many different public and private sources and, for the components included, is quite thorough in addressing various failure modes. It has attempted to bring together the data most often needed in frequency evaluations within the chemical process industry. CCPS also has developed a taxonomy to aid in the classification of equipment-failure data. It is intended that the taxonomy will be expanded, modified, and filled out as more equipment data are gathered from other companies who make their reliability data available. This will lead to a more comprehensive database for analysts to perform quantitative risk assessments and frequency evaluations.

8.3.2 Discussion of data-collection efforts

There are many cases where a risk analyst is unable to perform an adequate frequency evaluation on a process due to the lack of reliability data for specific pieces of equipment. To resolve this issue, some companies and industrial committees have developed specific databases to collect and record relevant reliability data for various pieces of equipment used in their operations.

Although reliability data for various types of equipment may be readily available, both the equipment operating environment and the process conditions may be very different from one application to another. Because of this difference, the failure rates can be much higher for more severe operating conditions. As a result, using reliability data based on pieces of equipment with very different operating, maintenance, or process conditions may be inappropriate. Therefore, in order to determine the reliability data for pieces of equipment in unique operational environments, data-collection efforts may be necessary to obtain more accurate reliability data for frequency evaluations.

8.3.3 Summary of key data sources

There are many different data sources available, including

- *Guidelines for Process Equipment Reliability Data with Data Tables,* prepared by the Center for Chemical Process Safety of the AIChE, 1989. Provides data on process systems and equipment.

- *Non-Electric Parts Reliability (NPRD-91),* Reliability Analysis Center, 1991. This report contains information on failure rates for valves, instruments, pumps, hardware, etc.

- *Failure Mode/Mechanism Distributions (FMD-91),* Reliability Analysis Center, 1991. This report contains information on the distribution of failure modes for valves, instruments, pumps, hardware, etc.

- OREDA, *Offshore Reliability Data Handbook,* 2d ed., published by the OREDA participants, Oslo, Norway, 1992. This project was undertaken to collect existing reliability data from several European oil companies who ran offshore platforms and summarize all the data into a reliability handbook. Compared with the 1984 edition, this second edition provides both more data and higher-quality data on equipment found on offshore platforms.

- S. H. Bush, "Statistics of Pressure Vessel and Piping Failures," *Journal of Pressure Vessel Technology,* 110:225–233, August 1988.

- D. J. Smith, *Reliability and Maintainability in Perspective,* Macmillan, New York, 1985.

- A. D. Swain and H. E. Guttmann, *Handbook of Human Reliability Analysis with Emphasis on Nuclear Power Plant Applications,* NUREG/CR-1278, U.S. Nuclear Regulatory Commission, Washington, October 1980.

- *Methodologies for Hazard Analysis and Risk Assessment in the Petroleum Refining and Storage Industry,* prepared by CONCAWE's Risk Assessment Ad-Hoc Group, Den Haag, Netherlands, December 1982. Provides failure rates for various human errors.

- D. W. Johnson and J. R. Welker, *Development of an Improved LNG Plant Failure Rate Data Base,* GRI-80/0093, Final Report, Gas Research Institute, Chicago, Ill., September 1981. This contains information on instrumentation as well as major equipment items.

- F. P. Lees, *Loss Prevention in the Process Industries,* Butterworths, London, 1980. This gives data on instrumentation and control devices, such as valves.

- "Report on Reliability Survey of Industrial Plants," Part I: "Reliability of Electrical Equipment," and Part III: "Causes and Types of Failures of Electrical Equipment, the Methods of Repair, and the Urgency of Repair," *IEEE Transactions on Industry Applications,* IA-10(2): 213–235, 242–252, 1974. These give information on circuit breakers, transformers, cables, and other electrical equipment.

- *Component Failure and Repair Data for Coal-Fired Power Units,* prepared by Fluor Power Services, Inc., EPRI AP-2071, RP239-2, Topical Report, Electric Power Research Institute, October 1981. This contains useful information on agitators, fans, and other large equipment items.

- *Reactor Safety Study,* Appendix III: "Failure Data," WASH-1400 (NUREG-75/014), United States Nuclear Regulatory Commission, Washington, October 1975. Provides data on human errors as well as equipment failures and is one of the most extensive sources of failure-on-demand estimates. (*Note:* Although objections have been raised regarding the WASH-1400 report, the source of disagreement or dissatisfaction is generally the treatment of uncertainty and not the methodology as a whole. The data set collected and compiled for the study is considered to be reliable and accurate, and it is not subject to the same criticisms as the overall study. The failure rates and probabilities given by the report are based on information from operating industrial facilities such as chemical plants, refineries, power plants, and manufacturing facilities.)

- *Annotated Bibliography of Reliability and Risk Data Sources,* NUREG/CR-5050, EG&G Idaho, Inc., Idaho Falls, March 1988. Many of the data sources in this bibliography can be used for facilities other than nuclear. Forty-nine accessible data sources are described in detail.

8.3.4 Limitations of data

When performing frequency evaluations, it is essential for the analyst to understand the definition of failure to reduce the likelihood of assigning an improper failure rate to the undesired event. If the analyst does not know the proper definition of the failure, the wrong failure rate may be assigned, and erroneous results for the total frequency of the scenario may be produced. For example, if the failure of concern is an external leak from a pump's casing, the failure rate will be much lower than for a failure of the pump to operate.

There are cases where an undesired event may be initiated by the failure of a piece of equipment that encompasses all its failure modes. In other cases, the undesired event may be initiated by a specific failure mode for the piece of equipment. For example, suppose that the hazard scenario to be quantified concerns itself with the release of a toxic chemical. It is determined by the plant engineer that a "valve failure" is one of the possibilities of initiating a toxic release. In analyzing the definition of a "valve failure," the analyst must question how a valve failure can cause a toxic chemical release. Certainly, internal leakage or bypassing will not cause a release unless there is another failure in the system. A plugged valve may only create a no-flow condition. However, it is possible that a "valve body failure" or "external valve leakage" will result in a toxic chemical release. The definition of failure has changed drastically from "valve failure" to "valve body failure" or "external valve leakage." The failure rate that must be assigned to the undesired event also will change. Rather than use the total failure rate, which encompasses all failure modes associated with a valve, only the specific failure mode of concern should be used. Depending on the type of equipment and failure mode to be quantified, it is possible to make an error of as much as three orders of magnitude if the definition of failure is not understood correctly.

Other situations where inconsistencies in the definition of failure may result in the improper assignment of failure rates are as follows:

- When assigning failure rates to pieces of equipment such as pipes or hoses, it is important to know whether the failure mode is a rupture or a leak. This can lead to an order-of-magnitude difference.

- Degraded-performance failures of equipment have very different failure rates from total or critical failures, where the equipment fails to function.

Not only is it important to ensure that the definition of a failure is properly specified, but it is also important to understand the distinction between a *failure* and a *release*. A *failure* can be defined as a condition that does not meet the desired design or process intended requirement. Both hardware anomalies and human errors fall within this definition. The occurrence of a failure condition usually generates an undesired event. One particular undesirable event that can be produced from a failure is a *release*. It is very easy to interpret a release of a hazardous substance as a failure of the process. However, most data sources include all types of failures. If the specific distribution among various failure modes is not given, another source or engineering judgment (not necessarily that of the analyst) may be required to determine the most applicable failure rate for the situation. Lees[10] has suggested a figure of one-third-to-danger when more specific information is unavailable.

The actual units in which the data are given also must be monitored carefully. Failure rates may be given as

- Failures per unit time (usually 1 million hours or a year)
- Failures per demand
- Failures per operating year
- Failures to danger per unit time
- Failures by specific failure mode per unit time

The analyst must ensure that all data are in the appropriate format and are consistent.

There are occasions when the analyst determines the failure rate using one data source, but due to the type of reliability data found within that data source, a second data source is needed to verify that the failure rate is appropriate. Verification of failure rates for one data source using a second data source may be adequate if each data source contains reliability information that is independent of the other. However, there are many sources that incorporate the data from other sources and may not therefore really be independent. If these data sources are used to verify a failure rate, it is possible that the analyst may select an improper failure rate or falsely believe that a rate has been verified by an independent source. When data appear in more than one source, the analyst must make a situation-specific assessment as to whether the available data should be averaged, a most representative value selected, or a value from the most representative end of the range of possible values selected. The choice will often depend on the comparability of the data to the situation at hand. Are the data from comparable environmental conditions? For equipment of a similar age? Has the design of this equipment changed over time?

8.3.5   Selecting and using data

As stated earlier, numerous methodologies can be used to perform a frequency evaluation. However, there are two types of frequency evaluations: *absolute frequency evaluations* and *relative frequency evaluations*. Some methodologies are inadequate for absolute frequency evaluations. Absolute frequency evaluations essentially provide the best estimate of the expected event and subevent frequencies of a specified scenario. The main purpose of performing an absolute frequency analysis is to identify the expected frequency of the undesired events and to determine where possible mitigative measures can be implemented. In addition, the total frequency of the event also can be used as an input into a quantitative risk assessment (QRA). The best (most representative and accurate) data available are needed in an absolute frequency evaluation.

On the other hand, the main purpose of performing a relative frequency evaluation is to provide a comparative analysis of the event or subevent frequencies for a given scenario using any of the methodologies in Sec. 8.2. The analysis of the absolute frequencies for each of the comparative scenarios is usually not required, since the analyst is more concerned with comparison of the frequencies between the scenarios.

A relative frequency evaluation can be used to perform a comparative analysis of events and subevents for scenarios in two different manners. First, it can be used to compare the scenario frequency using different design conditions. For example, a company may decide to implement a modified design to reduce the number of accidents or potential for fatalities within a working environment. A comparative analysis of the old and new system designs will enable the analyst to determine if a decrease in scenario frequency is achieved. Second, a relative frequency evaluation can be used to compare the frequency of two entirely different designs performing the same function. For example, a chemical manufacturer may use a comparative frequency evaluation to compare the frequency of release during transportation of a hazardous chemical by rail versus truck.

In such situations, it is easier to use estimated reliability data without degrading the integrity and quality of the results. Because a relative frequency evaluation involves a comparative analysis between two scenarios, the relative likelihoods of the events contained within each scenario are more important than their individual frequencies. In addition, many subevents may be the same between the two scenarios, further minimizing the significance of their frequencies.

Throughout this chapter, the terms *human error* and *equipment failure* have been used. When performing frequency evaluations, almost all events leading to hazardous scenarios are either equipment failures or human errors, although external events also may lead to a hazardous scenario. Equipment failure rates are usually time-related failure rates and are expressed as a frequency, i.e., per some time period (hourly or yearly). Equipment failures can be broken down into two types: passive failures and active failures. *Passive equipment failures* include failures occurring in pipes and vessels, i.e., equipment that is not actuated to perform a process function or equipment that is in a passive state during operation. The failure rates for passive equipment are generally determined using calendar time. *Active equipment failures* include failures occurring in pumps, compressors, and control valves, i.e., equipment that is in physical motion to perform a process function or equipment that is in an active state during operation. Passive equipment failures usually have lower failure rates than active equipment failures. The failure rates for active equipment are calculated using the operational, exposure, or functional time during a process.

If an equipment item is in use most of the time, the analyst may want to assume that it is in use for a full calendar year rather than just using operational time. This is particularly true if the data source does not indicate whether the failure rates are given on a calendar or operating year basis. There are some items of equipment that may always be at risk, even if they are not always in use.

One such example concerns loading arms and hoses. While these can cause releases only when they are in use, they may be subject to environmental stresses, impact, and stresses from improper stowing at any time. If they failed catastrophically when not in use, this would be very obvious at the time or when the operator next went to use them. Even if not observed, such failures would usually yield a (small) release before full flow was initiated. Hence ruptures are usually of concern only if they occur *during* loading operations.

An exception might be a very corrosive environment that would affect the integrity of the equipment, making it more susceptible to failure at its next full-pressure use. In this case, one would assume that the equipment is always at risk and would fail at next use. Leaks may occur at any time and are unlikely to be noticed until the next use. Therefore, they are generally quantified using calendar rather than operating time. The best solution would be historical data on failures per use.

Additionally, if equipment is normally designed for continuous use and is being used intermittently, it is possible that the additional starts and stops will increase the likelihood of failure even if the total number of operating hours is reduced.

Human errors are actions performed by operators, maintenance staff, and engineers that lead to or result in an undesired event. They are normally expressed as a per-demand failure rate. The failure rate for human errors represents the number of times an operator might make an error in performing a specific operation a certain number of times. For example, a human error rate of 10^{-3} translates into 1 error occurring every 1000 operations.

In many instances, both equipment failure rates and human errors (as well as external events) must be adjusted to meet the site-specific conditions. Data sources provide generic failure rates that are largely or completely derived from data tested under different operating conditions and designs as compared with the site. Adjustment factors are intended to recognize certain site-specific conditions and increase or decrease the failure rates as appropriate. They are largely based on the analyst's judgment and experience as well as that of personnel familiar with the site. When evaluating the applicability of databases and specific failure rate values, the following factors should be considered:

1. *Age.* Data sources usually provide long-term steady-state failure rates. If a piece of equipment is very old, it may be necessary to adjust the generic failure rate to more accurately reflect the increased failure rates typically associated with aged equipment.

2. *External environment.* The external environment of a site may be severe (corrosive atmosphere or extreme heat), thereby reducing the reliability and life of a piece of equipment.

3. *Materials of construction.* Generic equipment failure rates are determined using equipment manufactured with a specific material. If the site-specific equipment is manufactured with a different material and it is concluded that the material will affect equipment reliability, then the failure rate must be increased or decreased (depending on the type of material).

4. *Start-ups/shutdowns.* Sometimes equipment is subjected to frequent start-ups and shutdowns. Data sources usually calculate equipment failure rates while the piece of equipment is in continuous operation. Start-ups and shutdowns increase the wear on mechanical components and can drastically reduce the life of the equipment. In some cases, thermal stress or corrosion is more severe during shutdown or maintenance conditions. Therefore, the failure rate must increased to account for a piece of equipment subjected to frequent start-ups and shutdowns.

5. *Maintenance practices.* If sites have developed stringent maintenance practices (especially preventive maintenance) for equipment, the failure rates should be decreased, since a stringent maintenance program will likely maintain a piece of equipment in like-new condition or replace it before it fails. On the other hand, if the maintenance program is very relaxed, the failure rate may need to be increased.

6. *Operating practices.* If the process is operated at partial capacity rather than full capacity, the reliability of a piece of equipment should

increase, and hence the failure rate should be decreased. However, centrifugal pumps have increased stress and wear at reduced flow.

7. *Vibration.* Excessive vibration on a piece of equipment may result in an adjustment to increase the failure rate.

8. *Operating pressure and temperature.* Excessive operating pressures and temperatures may increase the failure rate for pieces of equipment. This is true for both high and low temperatures.

9. *Design.* If the design of a piece of equipment was enhanced as compared with the piece of equipment used to develop the generic failure rate, then the failure rate of the equipment should be decreased. On the other hand, if the equipment used on the site has an old design compared with that in the database, then the failure rate should be increased.

10. *Operator training.* This adjustment factor affects human errors. If the personnel on site are trained and retrained to perform their job assignments, then the human error rates will generally be better than average.

11. *Management systems.* Management systems include the enforcement of procedures, training and hiring practices, staffing levels, and so on. If the site has good management systems, then the human activities affected by the management systems may have lower than average error rates.

12. *Common causes.* Common causes of failure (common-mode failures) occur when two or more component failures result from a single cause. This topic is discussed more fully in Chap. 9. Examples of common causes of failure for a set of like or identical components include

- Shared components (like sensors) or utilities
- Design errors
- Manufacturing errors
- Installation errors
- Material flaws or incorrect selection
- Faulty or omitted maintenance
- Physical location

Reliability texts give guidance on addressing common mode failures rigorously. In general, they are handled by using multipliers to increase the individual failure rates.

The magnitudes of the adjustment factors can range from small percentage changes for individual factors to a factor of 10 or more for very significant features. If a data source contains the upper and lower ranges of the failure rate in addition to the median or mean failure rate values, then the upper and lower range bounds can be used. In addition, rather than developing a multiplier, adjustment factors can be applied to determine which end of a range of values is most appropriate.

As mentioned earlier, equipment failure rates are usually time-related, whereas human errors are usually demand-related. However, when using some of the methodologies for frequency evaluation, namely fault-tree analysis, equipment frequency data may need to be transformed into a probability on demand or probability of failure for the fault tree to have the proper logic. On the other hand, human error probabilities or equipment failures on demand may need to be transformed into frequencies to also ensure correct fault-tree logic.

There are two methods for transforming frequency data into probability on demand data. The first method uses inspection and maintenance information for specific pieces of equipment. The transformed probability is known as *fractional dead time* (FDT). FDT represents the fraction of time the equipment is in a failed state and thus the likelihood of it being unavailable on demand. (This assumes that the failure is not otherwise detectable.) The calculation of FDT requires information on how often the equipment is tested or inspected, used in routine operations, and used in a shutdown procedure (emergency or planned). The general expression for FDT is

FDT = (failure rate × 1/2 × 1/number of inspections per year) +
    (time unavailable during testing × total number of
    times equipment is unavailable per year)

The 1/2 recognizes that, on average, a failure would occur halfway through the inspection interval and would remain until the next inspection. Thus, if a malfunction/failure would be detected by a routine demand on the equipment or a shutdown, these demands effectively become inspections. The second term in the expression is used only if testing makes the equipment unavailable. FDT can be reduced by increasing the number of inspections/tests or decreasing the failure rate. However, the FDT is more properly a function of equipment unavailability due to failure, repair time, test duration, and human error in testing or repairing. As inspection frequency increases, these other factors can become more critical. In general, FDT is considered to have a lower limit of 10^{-4}, which is basically 1 hour per year. (The same value is often quoted for the lowest human error rate.) If two identical components are tested at the same time, the FDT is 1/3 (failure rate × test interval)^2. FDT is illustrated with the following example:

The failure rate of a relief valve to lift within 20 percent of its set pressure is given in one source as 0.01 per year. The relief valve is inspected annually (once per year) and takes 1 hour to replace. The FDT expression is as follows:

$$\text{FDT} = (0.01/\text{year} \times 1/2 \times 1/1 \text{ year}) + (1/8760 \times 1)$$

$$= 0.00511 \approx 0.005$$

Hence, if a piece of equipment has a short replacement period (hours), then the second term can be removed from the expression.

If the number of inspections for the relief valve was two per year, then the expression would be as follows:

$$\text{FDT} = (0.01/\text{year} \times 1/2 \times 1/2 \text{ year}) + (1/8760 \times 2)$$

$$\approx 0.0027$$

And the second term would be more significant.

Using the same example, suppose the testing of the relief valve takes 1 week instead of 1 hour. Because the relief valve is unavailable for 1 week on two different occasions, then the FDT expression is as follows:

$$\text{FDT} = (0.01/\text{year} \times 1/2 \times 1/2 \text{ year}) + (1/52 \times 2)$$

$$= 0.041$$

It should be noted that if the tank on which the relief valve is located is out of service during relief valve testing or the relief valve is still available during testing, then there is no risk and the second part of the FDT expression should not be added.

The second method to transform frequency data to probability on demand data is to distribute the equipment failures over the total number of demands per year. For example, suppose that the logic during fault-tree analysis requires a hose failure rate expressed as a failure probability on demand. To obtain this, the number of times the hose is used per year must be determined or estimated based on site experience. (The total number of uses should be estimated, not just those for that site, if the hose travels with the truck.)

When calculating FDT or determining the per-demand failure rate, there are several important questions the analyst should ask about the testing and operation of the equipment. Given below is a list of relevant questions:

1. Testing

   a. How often is it tested/inspected?
   b. How long is it out of service for testing?
   c. Is it operated during shutdown procedures? If so, how many planned or unplanned shutdowns are there per year?

  d. Are there routine demands on it? If so, how often? (Hoses may be tested every 2 years but used twice per week.)

2. Exposure and operating time

  a. How many exposures/operations per year?
  b. How long does each exposure/operation last?

  Probability on demand data also can be translated into frequency data. To perform this transformation, the probability on demand data must be multiplied by the number of demands per year. For example, suppose that a switch has a per-demand failure rate of 10^{-4}. If there are 100 demands on the switch per year, then the frequency of failure is calculated by multiplying the per-demand failure rate by the number of demands on the switch per year. Therefore, the frequency for switch failure is calculated to be 10^{-2} per year, or approximately once every 100 years.

  Regardless of how the data were developed or selected, it is very beneficial to review the predicted frequency of scenarios for realism. Plant personnel can be extremely helpful in checking event sequences and combinations (if any) and in reviewing assumptions such as the frequency of testing. Other analysts can provide a review for events that have not been identified and the credibility of individual data values as well as overall scenario likelihood based on previous experience/analyses. Lastly, the analyst can check overall scenario frequencies against historic data. Even if only incident counts are available (versus incident rates), the relative likelihood of various scenarios often can be cross-checked.

8.3.6   More advanced techniques

More rigorous techniques are available to allow consideration of failure rate distributions, to quantify uncertainty, to use bayesian analysis,

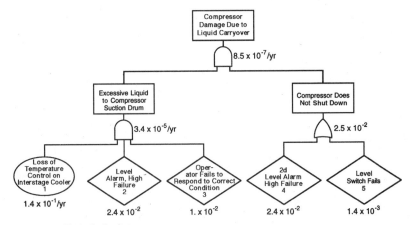

Figure 8.2 Sample fault tree.

TABLE 8.1   Explanation of Fault-Tree Quantification

Event	Frequency or probability	Source/discussion
1. Loss of temperature control on interstage cooler	1.4×10^{-1}/yr	Source A states a failure rate of 0.35/yr for temperature-measurement devices, with one-third failing to danger.
2. Level alarm high failure	2.4×10^{-2}	Source A states a failure rate of 1.7/yr for level measurement, with one-third failing to danger. For monthly inspection with failure occurring at the midpoint between inspections, this gives 2.4×10^{-2}.
3. Operator fails to respond to correct condition	1×10^{-2}	Source B states a probability of 1×10^{-2} for errors in routine operations where some care is required. (This is a common situation, and operators know how to respond to the condition.)
4. Second-level alarm high failure	2.4×10^{-2}	See event 2.
5. Level switch fails	1.4×10^{-3}	Source C states failure rates ranging from 0.053/yr to 0.53/yr for normal industrial level switches. A midpoint value of roughly 0.1/yr was used with one-third fail to danger. Monthly inspection with failure occurring at the midpoint between inspections yields 1.4×10^{-3}.

and so on. These topics are discussed briefly in Secs. 1.3.1 and 1.3.2. The reader is referred to other sources such as the *Fault Tree Handbook,*[2] advanced reliability tests,[13,14] and other books on frequency analysis.[15]

8.4   Frequency-Evaluation Examples

Several simple examples illustrating the results of a fault-tree analysis, an event-tree analysis, and a semiquantitative analysis are described below.

8.4.1   Fault-tree example

Figure 8.2 illustrates the construction and quantification of a fault tree for a top event of compressor damage due to liquid carryover. The assigned failure rates and probabilities are described in Table 8.1 and appear on the fault tree as well. The combined failure rates for each of the logic gates are also given on the fault tree.

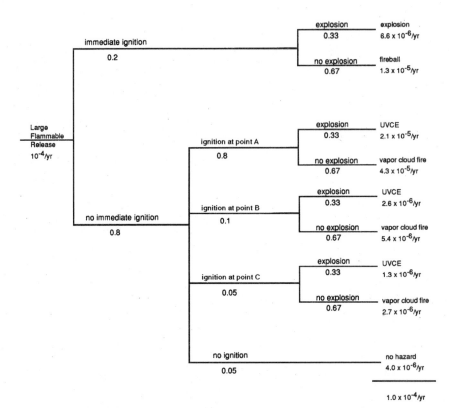

Figure 8.3 Sample event tree for a large flammable release from a pressurized storage tank.

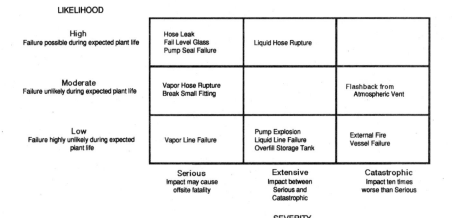

Figure 8.4 Semiquantitative evaluation of unloading/storage risks.

8.4.2   Event-tree example

Figure 8.3 gives an event tree depicting the potential outcomes of a release of a flammable material from a pressurized storage tank. The initial release frequency is also used, so the sum of the final event outcome frequencies must match this value, rather than 1.0. This event tree depicts a situation where only one meteorologic condition (such as D-stability with 5-m/s winds) is used. It could be expanded to address other meteorologic conditions. The likelihoods of ignition at points *A*, *B*, and *C* consider both the chance of ignition and the chance that the wind directs the release to that ignition source.

8.4.3   Semiquantitative example

A simple matrix is given in Fig. 8.4 along with a set of identified hazard scenarios. Each scenario has been evaluated in terms of both its expected likelihood or frequency and its potential severity or consequences. However, these evaluations have been based on experience and judgment rather than on rigorous analyses.

8.5   References

1. A. M. Schreiber, "Using Event Trees and Fault Trees," *Chem. Eng.*, 89(10):115, October 4, 1982.
2. W. Vesely et al., *Fault Tree Handbook*, NUREG-0492, U.S. Nuclear Regulatory Commission, Washington, 1981.
3. J. R. Taylor, "An Algorithm for Fault-Tree Construction," *IEEE Transactions on Reliability*, R-31 (22):137, June 1982.
4. L. Doelp et al., "Quantitative Fault Tree Analysis: Gate-by-Gate," *Plant / Operations Progress*, 3(4):227, October 1984.
5. R. A. Freeman, "The Use of Risk Assessment in the Chemical Industries," *Plant / Operations Progress*, 4(2):85, April 1985.
6. P. L. Holden, D. R. T. Lowe, and G. Opschoor, "Risk Analysis in the Process Industries: An ISGRA Update," *Plant / Operations Progress*, 4(2):63, April 1985.
7. D. H. Slater and R. A. Cox, "Methodologies for the Analysis of Safety and Reliability Problems in the Offshore Oil and Gas Industry," in *Application of Risk Analysis to Offshore Oil and Gas Operations: Proceedings of an International Workshop*, NBS Special Pub. 695, U.S. National Institute of Standards and Technology, Gaithersburg, Md., May 1985, p. 99.
8. *Methodologies for Hazard Analysis and Risk Assessment in the Petroleum Refining and Storage Industry*, CONCAWE Report No. 10/82, Den Haag, Netherlands, December 1982.
9. *Process Safety Management (Control of Acute Hazards)*, Chemical Manufacturers Association, Washington, May 1985.
10. F. P. Lees, *Loss Prevention in the Process Industries*, Butterworths, London, 1980.
11. D. J. Smith, *Reliability and Maintainability in Perspective*, Macmillan, New York, 1985.
12. A. D. Swain and H. E. Guttmann, *Handbook of Human Reliability Analysis with Emphasis on Nuclear Power Plant Applications*, NUREG/CR-1278, Final Report, U.S. Nuclear Regulatory Commission, Washington, June 1983.
13. R. Billinton and R. N. Allan, *Reliability Evaluation of Engineering Systems: Concepts and Techniques*, Plenum Press, New York, 1983.
14. H. F. Martz and R. A. Waller, *Bayesian Reliability Analysis*, Wiley, New York, 1982.
15. *Guidelines for Hazard Evaluation Procedures*, 2d ed., Center for Chemical Process Safety of the American Institute of Chemical Engineers, New York, 1992.

9

Common-Cause Failure Analysis

Gareth W. Parry
NUS

9.1 Introduction

One of the design principles that has been adopted commonly as a defense against undesirable consequences from facility accidents is that of redundancy. Use of redundant systems is intended to prevent single failures from becoming contributors to significant accidents. However, there is a class of failures, known as *common-cause failures,* that has the potential to cause the simultaneous failure of several redundant components. It is this potential to override the advantages of redundancy that makes common-cause failures such a concern. Because of this, the potential for common-cause failures should be analyzed for any facility design in which redundancy has been adopted as a defense against significant accident occurrence.

The approach to common-cause failure analysis discussed in this chapter focuses on the need to identify the plant-specific common-cause failure mechanisms and defenses. The chapter begins with a discussion of how common-cause failures (CCFs) may be classified as a subset of the more general class of dependent failures and continues with a description of an approach to CCF analysis that was developed for the nuclear industry but which can be used effectively on any type of facility. The method assumes that some form of logic model of overall system performance is to be constructed, provides approaches to screening for important CCF contributors, and finally addresses the quantification of

CCF probabilities. A quantitative example is provided. In addition, a qualitative approach to the review of defenses against CCFs is discussed, since this may be of particular value during the design stages.

9.2 Common-Cause Failures and Dependent Failures

When performing a *process hazards analysis* (PHA) or, as it is called in the nuclear power industry, a *probabilistic safety analysis* (PSA) using as a basis logic models such as event trees and fault trees, it is essential that any dependencies between the basic events of the model be recognized and accounted for. When constructing the logic models, i.e., the fault trees, reliability block diagrams, or event trees, many types of dependent failures may be explicitly included in the structure of the model. For example, the failure of a motor-operated pump can be modeled with one event representing failures of the pump itself and another representing failures of the power from the bus that supplies the motor. Furthermore, if the pump is such that it requires seal, bearing, or room cooling, events representing failures of the cooling systems may be included as contributors to failures of the pump. In this way a model can be constructed that reflects explicitly the hard-wired functional dependencies between the various components and support systems of the plant. The so-called external events[1] or hazards, such as earthquakes or fires, that have the potential for causing failures of multiple and diverse components are addressed by performing specific analyses that explicitly recognize the dependent nature of the hazards. Failures resulting from human error, such as failure to restore a system to its correct configuration following maintenance, may be explicitly represented. Furthermore, *cascade,* or *knock-on, failures,* where the failure of one component causes failure of another, will be modeled when the dependency is recognized. Thus many of the major sources of dependency can be and are best treated explicitly in the logic model structure. For a further discussion of the categorization of dependencies, see, for example, the *PRA Procedures Guide.*[1]

A typical plant logic model, constructed in such a way, has as its elementary constituents basic events that represent particular failure modes of the components. Examples of such basic events are pump A fails to start when demanded because of local faults and diesel generator D fails to run for 6 hours because of local faults. In order to produce quantitative results, the logic model is used as a basis for a probability model. First, the probability of each basic event must be estimated, preferably on the basis of some historical experience. The final stage in creating the quantification model is to specify the rules for combining the basic event probabilities and initiating event frequencies to obtain the accident sequence frequencies and system unavailabilities. Given that the identified sources of dependency have been explicitly modeled, the assumption of statistical independence of the basic events is not an unreasonable one. However, experience with collecting data on component failures, particularly those components in redundant systems, has shown that the number of multiple coincidental failures of like components is higher than would be expected on the basis of that independence assumption. Hence the concept of a common-cause failure model has been introduced to correct for this statistical dependence between the basic events. New, common-cause failure basic events are introduced into the logic structure to account for the expected excess number of multiple-component failures.

The reason for this residual dependency can be understood by recognizing that a single component/failure mode basic event contains contributions from all the causes that would result in that failure. As long as some of these failure causes have a higher propensity than others for failing a second or third component simultaneously with the first, it is clear that there will be a statistical dependence between the events representing the failures of these components. Dörre[2] has shown this clearly in the case of a model in which the increased propensity results from an increased failure rate for a given subset of the failure mechanisms, even though failures are independent at the level of the subset. The statistical dependence between the basic events arises because the probability of a basic event, taken by itself, characterizes average behavior, the average being taken over the failure causes contributing to that event.

Thus common-cause failure models are introduced into system models essentially to account for the fact that the logic models are not developed down to the level of causes. The need to consider common-cause failures (CCFs) in system models has been recognized for a considerable time. See, for example, Edwards and Watson,[3] who list a large number of potential causes of multiple-component failures, e.g., design and construction errors, abnormal environmental influences such as vibration or dust, and faulty maintenance. It is the realization that it is impractical to try to construct models that explicitly address all these causes that leads to the need to adopt the common-cause failure approach described here.

9.3 Definition of a Common-Cause Failure

From the discussion in the preceding section, it is clear that the CCF events incorporated into the logic structure are only necessary to account for those statistical dependencies which arise from mechanisms that are clearly not explicitly modeled. In the CCF procedures guide,[4] published jointly by the U.S. Nuclear Regulatory Commission and the Electric Power Research Institute, a *common-cause failure basic event* is defined in the following way:

> In the context of system modeling, common-cause (basic) events represent the impact of that subset of dependent events in which two or more component fault states exist at the same time, or in a short time interval, and are a direct result of a shared cause. It is also implied that the shared cause is not another component state because such cascading of component states is normally due to a functional coupling mechanism. Such functional dependencies are normally modeled explicitly in systems models without the need for special common cause event models.

This definition is written in such a way as to enable an analyst to establish a correspondence between a historical event and the logic model element of which that historical event is an example. This definition suggests that the analyst should not classify as (historical) common-cause events those events whose causes would be modeled explicitly in the logic model. It is therefore clear that what is meant by a common-cause event, in the terminology adopted in this report, is exclusive of what is being modeled explicitly. This semantic distinction is important when analyzing data for CCF probability-estimation purposes to avoid double counting the impact of the failure mechanisms that are explicitly modeled.

9.4   Requirements for a CCF Analysis

There is as much emphasis on the use of risk-assessment techniques for purposes such as risk management and maintenance program optimization as there is for the numerical evaluation of risk or accident frequency. Therefore, it is highly desirable that a CCF analysis should meet two major requirements:

1. The analysis should produce a quantitative assessment or prioritization of the impact of CCFs on risk that is reproducible and can be subjected to a third-party review. This implies that the approach be well defined and well documented, and that the assumptions made be clearly specified.

2. In addition, the analysis should provide the analyst with the means to identify those common-cause failure mechanisms which have the potential to be most significant for the plant of interest and to formulate corrective actions should they be assessed to be necessary.

9.5   An Overview of an Approach to CCF Analysis

The nuclear industry in particular has invested significant effort into developing methods to analyze the impact of common-cause failures on the availability of redundant systems. This is largely because nuclear power plant design makes significant use of redundancy, in addition to diversity, in providing defense in depth against accidents and because common-cause failures have the primary effect of reducing the increase in availability theoretically provided by the redundancy. An integrated framework that addresses qualitative and quantitative issues is reported in NUREG/CR-4780.[4] This framework consists of four major stages, each of which contains a number of steps (Fig. 9.1). This section provides a brief description of the framework.

Stage 1: System logic model development.   This stage is included in the framework essentially to emphasize the point that the starting point of a CCF analysis is a logic model that identifies the combination of component states that leads to the undesired system state. For the common-cause failure analyst, the emphasis in this stage is to review the system model to identify those elements of design, operation, and maintenance and test procedures which could influence the chance of multiple-component failures. The information collected in this step is essential input to the screening phases of the analysis (steps 2.1 and 2.2). In addition, those root causes of dependency which are explicitly modeled are identified. Examples of causes that are frequently modeled explicitly were given in Sec. 9.2. This stage therefore defines the scope of the common-cause failure analysis. It cannot be overemphasized that extra care is needed in the application of parametric common-cause models in order not to double count causes that are explicitly modeled.

Stage 2: Identification of common-cause component groups.   The objectives of this stage, which is essentially a screening analysis, include

- Identifying the groups of system components to be included in or eliminated from the CCF analysis.

- Prioritizing the groups of system components identified for further analysis so that time and resources can be best allocated during the CCF analysis.

- Providing engineering arguments to aid in the data-analysis step (step 3.3).

```
┌─────────────────────────────────────────────┐
│       Stage 1 - System Logic Model Development│
│                                               │
│                    Steps                      │
│                                               │
│      1.1  System Familiarization              │
│      1.2  Problem Definition                  │
│      1.3  Logic Model Development             │
│                                               │
└─────────────────────────────────────────────┘
```

```
┌─────────────────────────────────────────────┐
│              Stage 2 - Identification of      │
│           Common Cause Component Groups       │
│                                               │
│                    Steps                      │
│                                               │
│      2.1  Qualitative Analysis                │
│      2.2  Quantitative Screening              │
│                                               │
└─────────────────────────────────────────────┘
```

```
┌─────────────────────────────────────────────┐
│           Stage 3 - Common Cause Modeling     │
│                  and Data Analysis            │
│                                               │
│                    Steps                      │
│                                               │
│      3.1   Definition of Common Cause Basic Events │
│      3.2   Selection of Probability Models for Common │
│            Cause Basic Events                 │
│      3.3   Data Classification and Screening  │
│      3.4   Parameter Estimation               │
│                                               │
└─────────────────────────────────────────────┘
```

```
┌─────────────────────────────────────────────┐
│        Stage 4 - System Quantification and    │
│              Interpretation of Results        │
│                                               │
│                    Steps                      │
│                                               │
│      4.1   Quantification                     │
│      4.2   Results Evaluation and Sensitivity Analysis │
│      4.3   Reporting                          │
└─────────────────────────────────────────────┘
```

Figure 9.1 Procedural framework for common-cause analysis.

■ Providing engineering insights for later formulation of defense alternatives and stipulation of recommendations in stage 4 (quantification and interpretation of results) of the CCF analysis.

These objectives are accomplished through the qualitative analysis and quantitative screening steps. These two steps are presented separately, because they are generally performed at different times in the analysis, step 2.2 generally being performed after initiation of stage 3.

Step 2.1: Qualitative analysis. The qualitative analysis consists of a search for common attributes of components and of mechanisms of failure that could lead to common-cause failures. Past experience and understanding of the engineering environment are used to identify indications of potential dependence among redundant components. Also, this experience is used to identify the effectiveness of those defenses which may exist to preclude or reduce the probability of the occurrence of certain CCF events. The result of this step is an identification of groups of system components that should be included in the analysis as being susceptible to common-cause failures.

Step 2.2: Quantitative screening. In this step, conservative values are assigned to the probabilities of each CCF basic event included in the model following step 3.1, and the risk analysis is performed using these conservative values. In this way, the dominant contributors to the system risk are identified, and it is on these dominant contributors that resources should be concentrated in stage 3, steps 3.3 and 3.4.

Stage 3: Common-cause modeling and data analysis. At the completion of step 2.1, the analyst has developed a component-level logic model of the system and has defined the scope of the common-cause analysis in terms of the common-cause component groups. The purpose of stage 3 is to modify the logic model to incorporate common-cause events, to establish probability models for these events, and when possible, to analyze experience data or use judgment to estimate the parameters of this model.

Step 3.1: Definition of common-cause basic events. As discussed earlier, it is convenient to define common-cause failure basic events, i.e., basic events that represent multiple failures of components from shared root causes. This leads to a redefinition of the already existing single-component basic events. Incorporating the new basic events is achieved by redefining the structure of the logic model. For example, if the common-cause component group has three components *A, B,* and *C,* then the original basic event representing failure of event *A* is replaced by four events as shown in Fig. 9.2, with equivalent replacements for the basic events for *B* and *C.* While in the original model event *A* represented a

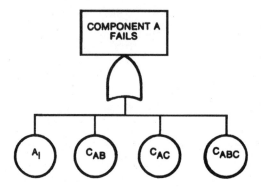

Figure 9.2 Substitution for basic events to incorporate CCF events. The events C_{AB}, C_{AC}, and C_{ABC} are the CCF basic events, where C_{AB} represents failure of components A and B (and not component C) from common causes, C_{AC} represents failure of components A and C (and not component B) from common causes, and C_{ABC} represents failure of components A, B, and C from common causes.

failure of component A, without specifying the status of components B and C, the new event A_I represents failure of component A alone.

Step 3.2: Selection of probability models for common-cause basic events. The objective of this step is to provide a transition from the logic model in step 3.1 to a model that can be quantified. This is done by associating a probability model, such as the constant failure rate model or the constant probability of failure on demand model, with each basic event, including both common-cause and independent failure basic events. For a discussion of these failure models, see, for example, refs. 5 and 6.

The set of basic event probability models associated with a CCF component group is often called a *common-cause failure model*. The literature contains a large number of common-cause failure models. Reference 4 categorizes them into two groups: nonshock models and shock models. The *nonshock models* can be characterized as variants of the so-called basic parameter model.[4] This model essentially treats each of the CCF basic events in the same way as the original single failure basic events; i.e., each of these basic events is associated with a simple probability model that has a parameter that is usually either a failure on demand or a failure rate.

Historically, the first and still the most widely used of these models is the *beta-factor model*.[7] A variant of this model, the *C-factor method*,[8] had the same mathematical structure but proposed a way to estimate the parameter that is, in some ways, similar to the method now described in ref. 4. These models are one-parameter models that effectively set the probabilities of events that represent multiple failures of fewer than the full complement of redundant components to zero. In the example given in Fig. 9.2, the probabilities of C_{AB} and C_{AC} are set to zero, and only A_I and C_{ABC} have nonzero probabilities. The multiple-Greek-letter[9] and alpha-factor[10] methods were developed to introduce more generality into the models so that nonzero probabilities could be included for all the CCF basic events, in the current example, the C_{AB} and C_{BC} terms.

The *shock models* are typified by the binomial failure rate model.[11] The binomial failure rate model is based on an underlying causal structure in that it proposes a mechanism in which certain agents called *shocks* affect all components in this group. Shocks are classified as lethal, in which case all components fail, or nonlethal, in which case the number of failed components are distributed according to a binomial distribution. The probabilities of multiple failures are prescribed on the basis of the frequencies of the two types of shocks, the binomial parameter, and the independent failure probability. The model has, at most, four parameters. It has been used in several probability safety analyses (PSAs), including the German risk study, phase B.[12] The multinominal failure rate model[13] also uses the concepts of independent and shock-related failures, but the probabilities of multiple failure events, given a shock, are essentially free parameters, and so it has elements of both a shock model and a nonshock model.

Other CCF models that are variants or developments of the BFR model have been proposed. They have not, however, been used in risk or hazards analyses. They include the common-load model (CLM),[14] the distributed failure probability (DFP) method of Hughes,[15] the stochastic reliability model failure of Dörre,[2] and the random probability shock model.[16] The extended common-load model[14] and the DFP method[15] have both been proposed as methods to deal with problems of highly redundant systems, such as the overpressure protection system in a boiling water reactor where the number of redundant safety relief valves may be as high as 16.

The nonshock models are not intended as models of underlying processes, and thus to call them *models* is a misnomer. They are really mathematical constructs to help partition data and facilitate quantification of the logic models. In use of these "models," the physical interpretation of failure causes or mechanisms is considered only when the data analysis is performed, as discussed later.

Step 3.3: Data classification and screening. The purpose of this step is to evaluate and classify event reports to provide input to parameter estimation. As mentioned previously, it is necessary to take care to distinguish between events whose causes are explicitly modeled and those which are to be included in the residual common-cause event models.

The sources of data available to an analyst are failure event reports on both single and multiple equipment failures. Since plant-specific data on multiple equipment failures are rare, it is necessary to extend the search to other plants. However, since other plants, even if they are similar in purpose, may be designed or operated differently, events that occur at one plant may not be possible at another. Thus the data cannot be used blindly but should be reviewed carefully for its applicability. This review should address root causes and coupling mechanisms, as well as the defensive strategies in place at both the plant of interest and the plant where the event occurred to determine whether the event could occur at the plant of interest and to assess what its impact would have been had it occurred there (see Sec. 9.8). Since event reports, even in a highly regulated industry, such as the nuclear power industry, are seldom as detailed as an analyst would need to make definitive decisions, analysis of the raw data requires a great deal of judgment; a systematic approach to this screening is essential for scrutability and reproducibility of the analysis. Reference 17 provides guidance on this issue. The result of this step is the creation of a pseudo-plant-specific CCF database giving numbers of events resulting in one-, two-, three-, and multiple-component failures.

Step 3.4: Parameter estimation.   The purpose of this step is to use the database created in step 3.3 to estimate the parameters of the common-cause probability models. There are several sources of uncertainty, including interpretation of the data to elicit causal mechanisms, assessment of their impact at the plant being modeled, and uncertainty about how the data were obtained. Consequently, it is essential not only to provide a point estimate but also to characterize this uncertainty numerically. In the case event data are not available, step 3.3 is bypassed, and the parameters must be estimated judgmentally.

Stage 4: System quantification and interpretation of results.   The purpose of this stage is to synthesize the key output of the previous stages to effect a quantification of system failure frequency, the performance of sensitivity analyses, and the interpretation of results.

9.6   Resource Needs and Value of Quantitative Analysis

To apply the full quantitative approach described above is very time consuming and requires data that are very detailed. NUREG/CR-5471[18] describes the data needed to perform a detailed CCF analysis. One of the key pieces of information is a clear and extensive presentation that describes the chain of events leading to the failure, a determination of the root cause, and an assessment of the inadequacy of defenses. It is also important to have specific information on the particular approach to operations, maintenance, and surveillance testing in existence at the plant when the event took place. This information is necessary for single failure events as well as for multiple failure events. Such detailed information is rarely available, however. Thus the quantitative approach of step 3.3 can rarely be achieved to the analyst's satisfaction.

Even if good-quality data are available, one of the questions often asked is, "Is it worth going through all the effort when the CCF probability may change only by a relatively small factor, if at all, particularly given the large uncertainty in the estimate?" Experience has shown that factors of improvement as high as two or three over the generic values obtained from a data source such as EPRI NP-3967[19] are difficult to justify. If the measures of risk (core damage frequency is a typical measure used for nuclear power plants) obtained using generic values are acceptable and meet a numerical safety goal, for example, then it is hard to argue that a detailed analysis must be done solely for the purpose of "improving the numbers." However, perhaps the most compelling reason for performing a detailed data analysis, even if the data are limited, is that it provides the analyst with insights into those features of plant design or operation which might be improved to prevent CCFs. Thus the value of a quantitative analysis is as much for qualitative as for quantitative reasons. However, even if adequate data are available, the data reviews are resource-intensive. Therefore, there is significant value in performing a quantitative screening analysis to achieve a cost-effective application of the method. An example of an application to the PSA of a nuclear power plant is discussed in the next section.

9.7   A Quantitative Example Application

Detailed quantitative common-cause failure analyses have been performed in a large number of probabilistic safety assessments (PSAs) of nuclear power plants. This section presents a summary of one such analysis, highlighting the areas where decisions were made to make the analysis as practical as possible. In this way, some of the commonly accepted practices are highlighted.

Stage 1: System logic model development. The starting point for the analysis is an existing PSA in which all the functional, intersystem, and human interaction dependencies are modeled explicitly. Nuclear power plant design makes considerable use of redundancy to improve system availability, so many of the systems are multitrain redundant systems. This particular example is of a boiling water reactor (BWR).

Stage 2: Identification of common-cause component groups. The first task for the CCF analyst was to identify the CCF component groups. It is a common practice to adopt a component-based rather than a cause-based screening.[4] Component-based screening depends on identification of groups of components with similar attributes (coupling factors) that might lead to a common susceptibility to failure. The partial list of attributes given in ref. 4 is

- Component type (e.g., motor-operated valve, swing check valve), including any special design or construction characteristics (e.g., component size, material)

- Component use (e.g., system isolation, flow modulation, parameter sensing, motive force)

- Component manufacturer

- Component internal conditions (e.g., absolute or differential pressure range, temperature range, normal flow rate, chemistry parameter ranges, power requirements)

- Component external environmental conditions (e.g., temperature range, humidity range, barometric pressure range, atmospheric particulate content and concentration)

- Component location

- Component initial conditions (e.g., normally closed, normally open, energized, deenergized) and operating characteristics (e.g., normally running, standby)

- Component testing procedures and characteristics (e.g., test interval, test configuration or lineup, effect on system operation)

- Component maintenance procedures and characteristics (e.g., planned and/or preventive maintenance frequency, maintenance configuration or lineup, effect of maintenance on system operation)

Using these attributes as criteria essentially results in identifying each group of redundant components within a system as being a CCF group. However, it is also generally accepted (see, for example, the results of the European benchmark on CCF analyses[20]) that the most significant failures are those of active components and, in particular, that passive failure modes need not be addressed. Even applying these conditions, this can still lead to a large number of potential CCF groups. The number of groups increases with the level of detail in the fault-tree models, since it is determined by the component boundaries. Those CCF groups for which a detailed analysis is necessary or desirable can be identified by quantitative screening.

The approach to quantitative screening adopted in the example study was to use the beta-factor model, with a beta-factor value of 0.1 for all the CCF groups regardless of the degree of redundancy. Use of 0.1 for the beta factor is generally accepted in the nuclear industry as being a reasonably conservative number except for some exceptional circumstances. It also has been recommended for use in the chemical process industry.[21] Therefore, for a group of four components, each of which had an unavailability P, the system fault tree for a system with a success criterion of 1 of 4 was modified by adding a single CCF cutset with value $0.1P$. The PSA model was quantified, and those CCF events which contributed more than 1 percent to the core damage frequency, as measured by their Fussel-Vesely importance,[22] were identified for detailed analysis.

As a result of this quantitative screening, only three CCF terms were found to be significant, those involving the service water pumps that supply cooling water to the emergency diesel generators among other components, the diesel generators themselves, and the ventilation relief dampers in the diesel generator rooms. These are all CCFs of support system components. That these should be the most important is not surprising, since boiling water reactors have several (diverse) systems for providing cooling water and decay heat removal, but they are all supported by the same systems and in particular, for a long-term loss of off-site power, they are dependent on the emergency ac power system.

Stage 3: Common-cause modeling and data analysis. For two of these components, the service water pumps and the diesel generators, data were available on a generic basis, i.e., data from the nuclear industry. After a detailed analysis, following the guidance given in ref. 17, the data were reduced to provide the following pseudo–plant-specific data:

Component type	Total number of failure events of i components N^i			
	$i = 1$	$i = 2$	$i = 3$	$i = 4$
Diesel generators	230.7	3.179	0.761	0.174
Service water pumps	15.08	0.204	0.013	0.003

The fractional numbers of failures are a result of the subjective assessment of the applicability of observed failure events and particularly of observed degraded states to the plant in question.

These data were used to estimate the parameters of the basic parameter model[4] using as a basis the estimate of the unavailability of a single diesel generator to start and run. This value was 2.83×10^{-2} per demand. In the basic parameter model, with the assumption of non-staggered testing, the unavailabilities Q_i are estimated as

$$Q_i = \frac{N^i}{\binom{m}{i} N_D}$$

where N_i is the number of events with i components failed, m is the size of the common-cause group, and N_D is the number of system tests, and

$$\binom{m}{i} = \frac{m!}{i!(m-i)!}$$

Equating 2.83×10^{-2} to Q_1 gives an estimate of N_D of $230.7/[(4)(2.826 \times 10^{-2})] = 2041$, resulting in the following estimates

$$Q_2 = 2.6 \times 10^{-4}$$

$$Q_3 = 9.32 \times 10^{-5}$$

$$Q_4 = 8.53 \times 10^{-5}$$

The use of four digits does not imply a high degree of accuracy but simply results from the arithmetic and is included to provide traceability.

While ref. 4 presents formal expressions for estimating uncertainty bands on these values, they are statistical uncertainty bounds but do not address the major source of uncertainty, i.e., that associated with the interpretation of the data. Consequently, the uncertainty range was established judgmentally by varying the assumptions used in analyzing the data.

The major effort in this particular study, however, was in trying to understand the engineering aspects of the CCF failures rather than in establishing "accurate" numbers, and it was the process of data analysis, rather than the numbers it produced, that was the greatest value.

Stage 4: System quantification and interpretation of results. Substituting the improved values for the CCF basic events resulted in these support system contributors still being significant contributors, but less so than with the conservative screening values. The core damage frequency was sufficiently low that no corrective action was taken with respect to the common-cause failure events.

9.8 Qualitative Approaches

Data that are detailed enough to complete a quantitative approach are very scarce. Therefore, as an alternative, it is advantageous to discuss qualitative approaches that aim to understand why common-cause failures arise and how they can be prevented.

The cause-coupling-defense view of common-cause failures. To understand common-cause failures, it is essential to understand how components can fail and why more than one component can be simultaneously susceptible to the same failure cause. In NUREG/CR-4780,[4] the model of a CCF comprised a root cause and a coupling mechanism (i.e., a means by which the root cause is more likely to affect a number of components simultaneously) and involved an implied failure of the defenses against such multiple failures. The description of the failure mechanism in terms of a single root cause is, in reality, too simplistic, as discussed below.

When viewed from the point of view of defenses in particular, it is useful to think of different types of common-cause failure events. First, consider causes of failure. While a "root cause" of failure taken, for example, from one of the many root cause classification schemes in the literature may provide a characterization of the ultimate condition that led to the failure, it does not in itself necessarily provide a full understanding of why the failure occurred. For example, it may be possible to identify that a pump failed because of high humidity, but if we are interested in a detailed understanding of the potential for multiple failures, we need to understand why the humidity was high, how it affected the pump, and whether it could affect other pumps. This understanding opens the doors to different approaches to defending against multiple failures.

To understand the characteristics of the failure, the following concepts are helpful: A *conditioning event* predisposes a component to failure but does not itself cause failure. For example, failing to provide adequate protection against high-humidity conditions a component to increased chance of failure should a trigger event that leads to high humidity occur. A *trigger event* is one that initiates the transition to a failed state. A trigger event may be an event internal or external to the component it affects. An event that leads to high humidity in a room and, as a result of conditioning events having occurred, a subsequent failure of a component would be an external trigger event. An internal event that causes a short circuit in a component would be an example of an internal trigger event. It is not always necessary or even possible to uniquely define a conditioning event and a trigger event for every type of failure. Conceptually, it is useful, however, to focus on identifying the immediate cause (trigger) and those factors (conditioning events) which leave the component in question susceptible to the trigger.

Another useful concept in discussing failures, and particularly defenses against them, is the speed of the failure mechanisms. This is a measure of the time between the occurrence of the trigger event and the occurrence of the actual failure. For the case of impulsive (i.e., fast-acting) triggers, such as missile strikes, the time scale is small. On the other hand, the time scale for the development of degradation to the point of failure for the persistent (i.e., slow-acting) triggers, such as aging or corrosion, may be large. This is important from the point of view of detection. Defects that develop slowly, and for which evidence of degradation is available, have a greater chance of being discovered before they result in failure.

For failures to become multiple failures, the conditions have to be conducive to the trigger event and the conditioning event(s) affecting all the components simultaneously. The first step in discussing this is the identification of *coupling factors*. A coupling factor is a property of a group of components or piece parts that makes them potentially susceptible to the same cause of failure. Such factors include similarities in design, environment, maintenance, and test procedures. To understand how common-cause failures can arise, it is important to understand how this common susceptibility is enhanced or activated, resulting in multiple failures. It also must be kept in mind that the coupling factors are different for different causes, conditioning events, and trigger events. The strength of the coupling is an important factor. Empirically, it can be measured by the time between successive failures of the redundant components relative to their individual mean time between failures (MTBF). A strong coupling means that the redundant component failures are virtually certain to occur almost simultaneously. A weak coupling means only that there is an increased chance of simultaneous failure over the chance of purely independent failures. The strength of the coupling, therefore, is a measure of the likelihood of the conditioning and trigger events affecting the redundant components simultaneously.

Of course, most systems are built with some sort of defense against multiple failures. EPRI NP-5777[23] proposes a classification for *defensive tactics* that can be used to minimize the effects of CCFs. These include barriers, personnel training, quality control, redundancy, preventive maintenance, monitoring, surveillance testing, inspection, procedures review, and diversity. Defenses against CCFs can be effective in two major ways. For example, they can prevent the cause. An example would be to protect motor control centers (MCCs) against humidity by sealing them (not sealing the MCCs is a conditioning event). This is equivalent to hardening the component, and the defense acts against the conditioning event. Another example is the training of maintenance staff to ensure correct interpretation of procedures. This prevents potential trigger events due to misapplication of procedures. A CCF defense also can act by decoupling failures in different components by effectively decreasing the similarity of components or the environments to which they are exposed and thereby preventing a particular type of root cause from affecting all components simultaneously. This allows more opportunity for detecting failures before they appear in all components of the group.

A cause-defense approach to CCF analysis.   Based on the discussion in the preceding section, it is clear that CCFs can be prevented or mitigated by design and procedural defenses. From this it follows that reliability and safety analyses that properly address CCF events can aid in designing defenses to prevent or mitigate the occurrence of these events. The objective of developing a cause-defense approach is to extend the state of the art of plant-specific analysis by providing enough detail in reliability and safety analysis to (1) establish and assess plant-specific defense alternatives against CCF and (2) improve the accuracy of plant-specific CCF analyses. NUREG/CR-5460[24] suggests an approach that involves developing matrices that show either the qualitative or the quantitative impact of different plant-specific defenses on different categories of causes and the degree of coupling associated with CCF events. Reference 24 has identified categories of potential root causes, the associated coupling factors, possible defenses, and characteristics of the matrices. It is suggested that separate matrices be developed for defenses that act primarily against the cause itself (and hence reduce independent failure frequencies) and for those which act to decouple failures in the common-cause group defined by the coupling factors. Some example qualitative matrices for diesel generators (Figs. 9.3 and 9.4) and batteries have been developed. The causes of failure, such as internal faults, are listed on the left side of the matrix. Across the top, selected defenses, such as inspection and testing, are listed. At the intersection of each cause and defense, the impact of the defense on the cause or coupling is specified and characterized as being weak (open circle) or strong (solid square). The items in the matrix can be broken down so that the analysis can be done in as much detail as necessary. Once developed and reviewed, the matrices could be used by analysts to perform comprehensive analyses of CCFs for any plant. The matrices also could be useful to plant designers, inspectors, and operators.

IEEE Standard 352[25] also has discussed a cause-defense approach, although the discussion is less extensive than that given in ref. 24.

The initial results from the cause-defense methodology[24] have shown that the matrices must be fairly detailed to allow for CCF analyses that truly account for design features and operational and maintenance policies. Therefore, the matrices should be developed for each component type and should account for design variations as well as the way the equipment is tested, maintained, and operated. The cause-defense matrices must be developed by experienced CCF analysts and reviewed by experts in design, operations, and maintenance of equipment. The matrices would then reflect the consensus of the people involved in developing and reviewing them, which is particularly desirable in areas where data are sparse.

Selected Failure Mechanisms for Diesel Generators	General Administrative/Procedural Controls				Specific Maintenance/Operation Practices				Design Features			
	Configuration Control	Maintenance Procedures	Operating Procedures	Test Procedures	Governor Overhaul	Drain Water and Sediment from Fuel Tanks	Corrosion Inhibitor in Coolant	Service Water Chemistry Control	Air Dryers on Air Start Compressors	Dust Covers with Seals on Relay Cabinets	Fuel Tank Drains	Room Coolers
Corrosion products in air start system	—	O	—	O	—	—	—	—	■	—	—	—
Dust on relay contacts	—	O	—	O	—	—	—	—	—	■	—	—
Governor out of adjustment	—	O	—	O	■	—	—	—	—	—	—	—
Water/sediment in fuel	—	O	—	■	—	■	—	—	—	—	■	—
Corrosion in jacket cooling system	—	O	—	—	—	—	■	—	—	—	—	—
Improper lineup of cooling water valves	■	O	—	O	—	—	—	—	—	—	—	—
Aquatic organisms in service water	—	■	■	—	—	—	—	■	—	—	—	—
High room temperature	—	O	—	O	—	—	—	—	—	—	—	■
Improper lube oil pressure trip setpoint	—	O	—	O	—	—	—	—	—	—	—	—
Air start system valved out	■	O	—	O	—	—	—	—	—	—	—	—
Fuel supply valves left closed	■	O	—	O	—	—	—	—	—	—	—	—
Fuel line blockage	—	—	—	O	—	—	—	—	—	—	—	—
Air start receiver leakage	—	—	—	—	—	—	—	—	O	—	—	—
Corrective maintenance on wrong diesel generator	■	■	—	—	—	—	—	—	—	—	—	—

Selected Defenses against Root Causes

Legend: ■ strong defense   O weak defense   — no defense

Figure 9.3 Assumed impact of selected defenses against root causes of diesel generator failures.

Selected Failure Mechanism for Diesel Generators	Selected Defenses against Coupling						
	Diversity			Barrier		Testing and Maintenance Policy	
	Functional	Equipment	Staff	Spatial Separation	Removal of Cross-ties (or Implementation of Administrative Controls)	Staggered Testing	Staggered Maintenance
Corrosion products in air start system	■	—	—	—	—	—	O
Dust on relay contacts	—	—	—	O	—	O	O
Governor out of adjustment	—	O	O	—	—	—	O
Water/sediment in fuel	■	—	—	—	O	—	—
Corrosion in jacket cooling system	■	—	—	—	—	—	—
Improper lineup of cooling water valves	■	—	■	O	O	■	■
Aquatic organisms in service water	■	—	—	O	O	—	O
High room temperature	—	—	—	O	—	—	■
Improper lube oil pressure trip setpoint	■	■	■	O	—	■	■
Air start system valved out	■	—	■	O	—	■	■
Fuel supply valves left closed	■	—	■	O	—	■	■
Fuel line blockage	■	—	■	—	—	—	—
Air start receiver leakage	■	—	—	—	■	—	—
Corrective maintenance on wrong diesel generator	■	O	■	O	—	O	—

Legend: ■ strong defense   O weak defense   — no defense

Figure 9.4 Assumed impact of selected defenses against coupling associated with diesel generator failures.

A procedure for CCF review based on defenses. Another suggestion given in ref. 24 is that of developing a procedure for performing a review of plant design and operations that is focused on identifying potential common-cause failure mechanisms. The overall philosophy proposed is to structure the review around a generic class of defensive tactics against equipment unavailability. These defenses can be argued to be present in some form or other at all plants. Since it is the role of defenses in inhibiting the CCFs that is of primary interest, the objective of the review is to identify particular weaknesses in the application of these defenses that could allow simultaneous multiple failures.

The reason for attacking the problem from the point of view of the defenses is that it can be argued that a good defense can prevent a whole class of common-cause failures for many types of components, irrespective of the details of the failure mechanisms. Thus identification of the existence of particular strengths in the defenses can lead to increased assurance that certain types of CCFs are unlikely to occur. The identification of weaknesses leads to an identification of the types of mechanisms for which a more detailed analysis is warranted. The first level of the review, therefore, is a high-level screening analysis.

Because of the emphasis on common-cause failures, a major requirement for a review is that it should provide a means to assess the adequacy of the overall defensive strategy being applied at a plant as a means of maintaining independence between redundant components with respect to the occurrence of failure causes. However, it should not be forgotten that an equally good strategy is to prevent CCFs by preventing the failure mechanisms themselves. Thus a review of the defensive strategy that is focused on the assurance of a low probability of common-cause failures cannot be divorced from one that is designed to minimize unavailability or maximize reliability of individual components.

In order to structure the review, it is necessary first to understand how each identified defensive tactic can help prevent CCFs. This can be used to define a requirement or set of requirements for the successful implementation of that tactic. Further, it will help to define the information that will be necessary to assess the quality of the implementation. An essential part of the review process will be the establishment of methods for determining the significance of any observed weaknesses. It is at this stage that an appreciation of individual failure mechanisms becomes more important.

As an example of the approach, consider the role of barriers as a defensive tactic. Given that the concern in this book is with design, barriers, in the most general sense of the word, are probably the most effective defense against CCFs in redundant systems. For other potential defenses, a corresponding set of requirements and review guidelines must be established.

Definition of requirements. Barriers are effective as defenses against common-cause failures resulting from environmental, or external, agents if they

- Create separate environments for redundant components and therefore reduce the susceptibility of components to a single trigger event that affects the quality of the environment.

- Shield some or all of the components from potential trigger events.

The barriers may separate redundant components, separate the trigger source from one or more components, or be local, at the component, and thus relate to the quality of the effectiveness of component design against prevailing or abnormal environmental conditions. Barriers are designed primarily to protect against internal or external environmental disturbances that are harmful to the components. (The internal environment is the fluid for fluid systems and the electric current for electrical systems. A barrier for the fluid system can be the provision of a separate water supply, for example. A fuse or protective relay acts as a barrier in an electrical system.) The specific characteristics of the barriers are different for different classes of environmental disturbance.

Review guidelines. For the purpose of review, it is initially sufficient to identify the potential types of environmental disturbances and their domain of impact, which will generally depend on the type of environmental disturbance. The disturbance type can be equated to the proximate cause, which is the agent causing failure, e.g., humidity or smoke. Thus a review of the effectiveness of barriers should include identification of the type, location, and purpose of barriers, the type of disturbance to which a barrier is impermeable, the quality of its installation, and the quality of administrative controls that maintain its integrity, coupled with an identification of potential sources for trigger events for the various environmental disturbances in terms of their location and severity. It should be noted that barriers are not the only defenses against environmental disturbances. Surveillance tests, monitoring, and preventive maintenance also can be effective against those agents whose effects result in measurable degradation of performance before leading to failure.

A review process for identifying potential locations of concern has been developed for dealing with fires and floods. It can be adapted to cover other types of environmental disturbance by following the steps below for each disturbance in turn:

1. Identify the location of the components of interest.

2. Identify the piece parts of the components that are susceptible to each disturbance.

3. Identify the locations of the barriers against the disturbance, and divide the plant into nominally independent zones.

4. Identify potential sources of significant environmental disturbances.

5. Identify those zones which contain more than one component, or vulnerable piece parts of more than one component, and a source or sources.

6. Identify potential pathways between zones containing components or vulnerable piece parts and/or sources via penetrations/connections or defective barriers.

The process identifies the zones, or groups of zones, on a qualitative basis and does not require a detailed analysis of the specific failure mechanisms. This constitutes a coarse screening analysis. It may be refined further, following again the examples of fire and flood analysis.

The adequacy of a design with barriers that have allowed a zone identified in step 5 to contain vulnerable piece parts of more than one redundant component and a potential source of a trigger event has to be assessed against the likelihood of the occurrence of the trigger affecting the component group. This type of analysis is done routinely in fire and flood risk analysis. The factors taken into account include the relative locations of the source(s) and the vulnerable component piece parts, the magnitude of the disturbance (as a function of frequency), the potential for propagation of the disturbance within the zone, and the possibility of early detection and mitigation of the disturbance and is thus dependent on a more detailed assessment of failure mechanisms.

For the groups of zones identified in step 6, the primary review should be directed toward establishing the adequacy of the barrier, since its existence implies that it is believed to be necessary. The barrier has to be investigated for its design adequacy, its installation, and the adequacy of and adherence to administrative controls designed to maintain the integrity of the barrier.

The example just discussed is relatively well developed conceptually because such a procedure has been used in PRAs to model the effects of fires and floods (see, for example, ref. 1). Development of detailed guidelines for other defenses will require substantial effort. It is relatively straightforward to define general requirements for and general characteristics of a good defensive strategy, which can be used as a tool for screening analysis, but developing guidelines for a more detailed analysis is more complicated. For example, setting criteria for measurement of the quality of operating procedures, which also might be regarded as part of the plant design, is not a trivial task. In addition, the qualities of the defenses are not independent. For example, the quality of the preventive maintenance program can be influenced by that of the in-service inspection (ISI) program and the quality of the training program by that of the procedures review. It is clear that the establishment of guidelines and their application in a review will be multidisciplinary and involve design engineers, operating staff, and human factors specialists.

Nevertheless, the idea of basing a review on the analysis of the quality of the defensive strategy seems to have considerable merit, particularly as a complement to a review against historically occurring events. It is of particular value because it approaches the problem from a different direction, thus increasing the scope of the review. The increased appreciation of the role of defenses provides input to the cause-defense matrices introduced in the preceding subsection, and it is also essential for the plant-specific quantification of CCF probabilities, as discussed earlier.

9.9 Recommendations

In a risk assessment of an industrial facility, it is essential to consider the impact of dependent failures and, in particular, when redundant systems are employed, common-cause failures. As a framework for the analysis, that described in ref. 4 is recommended. A recent publication[26] provides a summary of the approach and some of the more recent work on event interpretation and qualitative analyses that many readers may find more approachable. As a first approximation, the qualitative screening guidelines proposed in ref. 4 for identifying CCF component groups should be used. It has been argued that use of these guidelines captures the groups of components with the highest susceptibility. Since a comprehensive quantitative analysis is hampered for most facilities by the lack of an adequate database, it is recommended that simple parameterization of the CCF probabilities such as that afforded by the beta-factor model be used, employing conservative parameter values. This is similar to the recommendation in ref. 21. This will allow the most numerically significant common-cause terms to be identified. If an adequate database exists, refinement of the probabilities can be performed, but it should be performed in a consistent manner, and establishing guidelines for event interpretation is an important task. However, in any case, a qualitative investigation of failure causes and an assessment of defensive tactics in place at the plant are highly recommended. While a formal procedure for a detailed qualitative analysis does not yet exist in the literature, some guidance can be found in refs. 24 and 25.

9.10 References

1. *PRA Procedures Guide: A Guide to Performance of Probabilistic Risk Assessment for Nuclear Power Plants,* NUREG/CR-2300, Vols. 1 and 2, U.S. Nuclear Regulatory Commission, Washington, 1988.
2. P. Dörre, "Basic Aspects of Stochastic Reliability Analysis for Redundancy Systems," *Reliability Engineering and System Safety,* 24: 351–375, 1984.
3. G. T. Edwards and I. A. Watson, "A Study of Common-Mode Failures," UKAEA Report SRD R146, United Kingdom Atomic Energy Authority, Warrington, U.K., July 1979.
4. A. Mosleh et al., *Procedures for Treating Common Cause Failures in Safety and Reliability Studies,* NUREG/CR-4780 (EPRI NP-5613), U.S. Nuclear Regulatory Commission, Washington, Vol. 1, January 1988, Vol. 2, January 1989.
5. E. J. Henley and H. Kumamoto, *Reliability and Engineering Assessment,* Prentice-Hall, Englewood Cliffs, N.J., 1981.
6. T. Morgan, G. W. Parry, and C. Schwan, *Nuclear Plant Reliability: Data Collection and Usage Guide,* EPRI TR-100381, Electric Power Research Institute, Palo Alto, Calif., April 1992.
7. K. N. Fleming, "A Reliability Model for Common Mode Failure in Redundant Safety Systems," *Proceedings of the Sixth Annual Pittsburgh Conference on Modeling and Simulation* (General Atomic Report GA-A13284), April 1975.
8. G. W. Parry, "Incompleteness in Data Bases: Impact on Parameter Estimation Uncertainty," *SRA 1984 Annual Meeting,* Society for Risk Analysis, McLean, Va., 1984.
9. K. N. Fleming, and A. M. Kalinowski, *An Extension of the Beta Factor Method to Systems with High Levels of Redundancy,* PLG-0289, Pickard, Lowe and Garrick, Inc., Newport Beach, Calif., June 1983.
10. A. Mosleh, and N. O. Siu, "A Multi-Parameter, Event-Based Common-Cause Failure Model," Paper M7/3, *Proceedings of the Ninth International Conference on Structural Mechanics in Reactor Technology, Lausanne, Switzerland,* A. A. Balhema, Rotterdam/ Boston, August 1987.
11. C. L. Atwood, *Estimators for the Binomial Failure Rate Common Cause Model,* NUREG/CR-1401, U.S. Nuclear Regulatory Commission, Washington, April 1980.
12. *German Risk Study, Phase B,* Verlag Tüv Rheinland, Cologne, Germany, 1960.
13. G. Apostolakis and P. Moieni, "On the Correlation of Failure Rates," *Proceedings of the Fifth EUREDATA Conference, Heidelberg, Germany, April 9–11, 1986,* Springer-Verlag, Berlin, 1986.
14. T. Mankamo and M. Kosonen, "Dependent Failure Modeling in Highly Redundant Structures," *Scandinavian Reliability Engineers Symposium, Vasteras, Sweden, October 1988.*
15. R. P. Hughes, "The Distributed Failure Probability Method for Dependent Failure Analysis," *Proceedings of the International Topical Meeting, PSA 89, Pittsburgh, April 1989,* American Nuclear Society, La Grange Park, Illinois.
16. P. Horstad, "A Shock Model for Common-Cause Failures," *Reliability Engineering and System Safety,* 23: 127–145, 1988.
17. A. Mosleh, G. W. Parry, and A. F. Zikria, "An Approach to the Analysis of Common Cause Failure Data for Plant Specific Application," *Nuclear Engineering and Design,* 23:25–47, 1994.
18. D. W. Whitehead, H. M. Paula, G. W. Parry, and D. M. Rasmuson, *Enhancements to Data Collection and Reporting of Single and Multiple Failure Events,* NUREG/CR-5471, U.S. Nuclear Regulatory Commission, Washington, March 1993.
19. K. N. Fleming and A. Mosleh, *Classification and Analysis of Reactor Operating Experience Involving Dependent Events,* EPRI NP-3967, Electric Power Research Institute, Palo Alto, Calif., February 1985.
20. A. Poucet, A. Amendola, and P. C. Cacciabue, *CCF-RBE, Common Cause Failure Reliability Benchmark Exercise: Final Report,* EVR 11054 EN, Commission of the European Communities, Ispra, Italy.
21. *Guidelines for Chemical Process Quantitative Risk Analysis,* Center for Chemical Process Safety, American Institute of Chemical Engineers, New York, 1989.
22. W. E. Vesely et al., *Measures of Risk Importance and Their Applications,* NUREG/CR-3385, U.S. Nuclear Regulatory Commission, Washington, July 1983.

23. A. M. Smith et al., *Defensive Strategies for Reducing Susceptibility to Common Cause Failures*, Vol. 1, *Defensive Strategies*. EPRI NP-5777, Electric Power Research Institute, Palo Alto, Calif., June 1988.

24. H. M. Paula and G. W. Parry, *A Cause-Defense Approach to Understanding and Analysis of Common Cause Failures*, NUREG/CR-5460, U.S. Nuclear Regulatory Commission, Washington, March 1990.

25. *General Principles of Reliability Analysis of Nuclear Power Generating Station Safety Systems*, ANSI/IEEE, Std. 352, Institute of Electrical and Electronics Engineers, New York, 1987.

26. A. Mosleh, *Procedure for Analysis of Common-Cause Failures in Probabilistic Safety Analysis*, NUREG/CR-5801, U.S. Nuclear Regulatory Commission, Washington, April 1993.

Cost-Effective Application of Risk-Analysis Techniques in Facility Design: How the Pieces Fit

Philip M. Myers and Thomas C. McKelvey
Four Elements

10.1 Introduction

Experience has been gained in using risk-analysis techniques throughout the world for assisting in making key decisions for all types of facilities involving hazardous materials. When addressing cost-effectiveness, several different issues must be considered. The first is the cost-effectiveness of the analyses—that is, the studies must produce useful information for decision making in a resource-effective manner. Next, the analyses must develop and evaluate practical solutions that are cost-effective for a facility to implement and maintain. Of course, the risk-analysis process must be integrated with and meet the project design schedule. The clear intent of industry, regulators, and practitioners is that risk analysis be cost-effective. In the strategic management of assets, risks, and technologies, many different factors and techniques are part of the facility design equation.

During the early stages in the facility siting and design process, all pertinent regulations must be reviewed. These regulations may, in some cases, prescribe exactly what the design must include or which types of analyses are acceptable. Other regulations may be performance standards that allow the facility management more flexibility in exactly *how* the standards are met. Unfortunately, in some cases, public agencies require that certain assumptions be made that bias the outcome of a technical study before it is even undertaken and reinforce the agency's own policies.

The Superfund Amendments and Reauthorization Act (SARA) Title III regulations in the United States established the general duty for facilities to identify and mitigate hazards and to maintain safe operations. More recent legislation of particular relevance includes the Occupational Safety and Health Administration's (OSHA) process safety management regulation[1] and the Environmental Protection Agency's (EPA) risk-management programs for chemical accidental release prevention.[2] Each of these requires the use of risk-analysis techniques, in the broadest sense, to satisfy the legal requirements for new and existing covered facilities. In fact, as a result of work carried out by Federal Focus, Inc., for the EPA, quantitative risk analysis (QRA) was nearly made a mandatory requirement in the EPA rule.[3]

Certainly, codes and design standards or engineering guides can provide a useful starting point for facility design. Since codes and engineering guides are based on a consensus of individuals and their relative experiences, they may not adequately address the specific needs of a particular circumstance and often represent the minimum level of protection or design agreeable to the entire group. Many companies exceed the minimum design standards set in codes and engineering guides because it is strategically advantageous or in some cases because it is simply the right thing to do. Effective use of risk-analysis techniques can provide essential insights and additional information for the design, layout, and operation of a facility. Risk-analysis techniques are currently being used throughout industries handling hazardous materials to meet the letter and spirit of governmental regulations, for the evaluation of business opportunities, and for the management of risks.

10.2 The Decision-Making Process and Inherent Uncertainties

Determining the study scope and objectives and understanding the decision-making process are integral parts of carrying out any type of risk analysis. Only with a clear definition of the information needed for decision making and the scope of the analysis (at the onset of a project) can any analyst carry out a cost-effective study. Once the expectations of the analysis are understood, it is important to develop a work plan that will meet or exceed them. The work plan can be reviewed with the client (internal or external) to verify that it will indeed provide the necessary information within the proposed schedule. It is essential that key decision makers and the risk-analysis project team be involved in the study from the start. Many individuals in industry are not familiar with risk-analysis techniques. Therefore, even before starting any analysis, it is often beneficial to present to the decision makers basic information on the merits and weaknesses of various risk-analysis techniques, the relative level of effort required, the type of study results that can be obtained, and the level of uncertainty associated with those results.

Managers have sometimes been reluctant to use risk-analysis techniques because of the uncertainties associated with the results. Yet there are uncertainties inherent in almost every decision made at facilities handling hazardous materials. There are often uncertainties in opinions presented to management based on an individual's (or a group's) experiences—only the uncertainties may not be stated, or the importance explored. The quality of any decision-making process is highly dependent on the expert experience and judgment upon which the study is based. Decision makers routinely have to make decisions based on imperfect information. In the decision-making process, it is important to understand the degree of uncertainty in using the results of a risk analysis, to include other political and social factors, and to make the value judgment. It is important that decision makers be made aware of the degree of uncertainty in information presented to them.

Through a structured approach, the focus can be placed on the most important sources of uncertainty in the analysis, and often, personal biases and agendas can be discovered and resolved through the technical analysis. Further, sensitivity analysis can be carried out for the key sources of uncertainty to bound the study results. When the uncertainty is not presented openly, the credibility of any study can be severely undermined if a parameter change results in a different conclusion.

10.3 The "Smoking Gun"

At least one reason for underutilization of risk-analysis techniques (especially quantitative ones) in the United States is the concern over documentation of risks to workers and the public.[4] The legal climate in the United States, especially toward the process and hazardous chemical industries, is unfriendly at best. Much of the corporate uneasiness has been fueled by megaverdicts and the adverse publicity that follows.[5] Management at numerous companies now must face the issue of documenting the possibility of causing injuries or fatalities from an accidental chemical release. Common questions asked by managers and decision makers include: Is this information discoverable, and can it be used against us in a court of law following an accidental release? Does this knowledge make us more liable? Should we focus on global consistency or address local issues?

In the case of an accidental release, the operating company will be held liable for harm inflicted. What the management team can do is to make the best use of all appropriate tools available for identifying and evaluating the likelihood, magnitude, and potential impacts of the release of hazardous materials. By using such tools, management can decide how best to manage the risks. If the necessary information is not produced or made available to management, the best and most cost-effective solutions may never surface. Through complete understanding of the risks, management can limit the liability for the plant, operation, or corporation and protect both workers and the public through a comprehensive risk-management program. In addition, management also can minimize punitive damages arising from hazardous material incidents by demonstrating corporate concern for the environment, health, and safety.

The trend toward increasing documentation is also clear, as can be seen in the EPA requirements for risk-management plans (RMPs).[2] The regulations will require documentation of the hazards and preventive and mitigatory steps taken by the operator of the fixed facility for each regulated chemical. This information is to be documented in the RMP and provided to several agencies and the local emergency planning committee (LEPC). The decision maker's task is not to convince others that there are no hazards associated with the facility or that there is no uncertainty in the decision process. Rather, the decision maker should convey factors included in the decision-making process, including technical and nontechnical issues important to the stakeholders. In addition, it should be made clear that the best-available experts, techniques, and information have been used in the process.

10.4 How Much Review or Analysis Is Enough?

To a large extent, the answer to this question may depend on the judgment and foresight of an experienced risk analyst and the decision makers. Risk-analysis techniques can be used at preliminary (coarse) or detailed levels. There are also a variety of techniques and applications that can be used throughout the stages of a facility life from project conceptualization through to decommissioning.[6] The key is to let the study objectives and client needs determine both the technique to be used and the level of detail chosen.

For the risk analysis to be cost-effective, the scope, techniques, level of detail, and assumptions should be chosen to provide the necessary information to support decision making. In certain cases, when the study will undergo agency and/or public review, or if there is strong opposition to facility projects, it may be advantageous to conduct a more detailed study than is necessary for making internal business decisions.

Without selective quantitative evaluation, the analysis approach can result in subjective decision making and potentially unnecessary investments being made. It is possible to evaluate a problem at a superficial level below the point of emerging returns or to an overly detailed level beyond diminishing returns. An analysis can be so coarse that while it does generate results or numbers, the uncertainties are so high (or the methodology so simple) that the results do not provide a sound basis for decision making. It is also possible to spend an inordinate amount of resources for the design being studied. The latter condition may be easily tracked and diagnosed, while the former is insidious. The risk-analysis experience and credibility of the analyst are important in determining and conveying to others the scope and level of detail needed. It is the responsibility of the analyst to notify the decision makers of either extreme in the depth of study.

Typical project constraints include available data, economics, schedule, and uncertainties. An experienced analyst is needed to meet client requirements and expectations within the project constraints. An inexperienced analyst may not be aware of all the associated nuances of the problem or may not be fully versed in the possible analysis techniques, either of which may result in misinformation and a study that is not cost-effective.

The success of a particular approach depends on many factors, including the hazards, the environment surrounding the facility, the layout, the complexity of the design, and the design documentation available. Therefore, it is essential that the risk-analysis team have experience in using a variety of analysis techniques, from which the most appropriate techniques can be recommended. While the conclusions or lessons learned from the analysis of one facility may be helpful when considering similar facilities, the conclusions may not apply in general due to variations in design, surrounding environment, company culture, and other factors.

It is important in determining how much analysis is necessary to consider the informational requirements for decision making. The analyst and design team also must ensure that the analysis techniques and level of detail are proportional to the hazards and financial investments involved. Various risk survey and screening techniques can be helpful in determining the appropriate techniques and level of effort required for various aspects of facility design.

10.5   Risk Survey and Screening Techniques

The objective of an initial risk survey is to prioritize the order and relative level of analysis and assessment for various aspects of the facility design. Use of a risk survey facilitates cost-effective utilization of resources in the analysis and facility design. A risk survey considers the potential consequences, the system hierarchy, failure history, and process complexity in determining the relative importance of risks associated with the facility design. It is vital that the designers have access to previous company accident and incident histories and that they use this information in the design of new facilities and processes.

There are a number of simple screening techniques that can be used to qualitatively or semiquantitatively evaluate and prioritize various aspects of the facility design. Several examples of these techniques include the Dow Fire and Explosion Index, the Chemical and Exposure Index, the ICI Mond Index, and other simple consequence-estimation techniques. Of course, qualitative or semiquantitative frequency estimation techniques also can be used to assist in prioritization. These techniques are best applied by experienced risk analysts and provide "order of magnitude" likelihoods of occurrence.

The product of a risk survey and/or risk screening is a list of critical design items, prioritization of systems for analysis, and an indication of the best-suited techniques and level of detail required to meet the facility project needs.

10.6 Hazard Identification

Hazard identification is the key element in all risk-management and legislative actions worldwide. Only events that have been identified as posing acute, chronic, environmental, or financial hazards can be further analyzed. The EPA rule considers hazard identification (or process hazards analysis) to be the "critical element" of a risk-management program and the risk-management plan.[2] The process hazards analysis (PHA) is also central to the OSHA process safety management regulation.[1]

A number of techniques are used for hazard identification. These include a hazards and operability (HAZOP) study, a failure mode and effects analysis (FMEA/FMECA), what-if analysis, checklists, what-if checklists, fault-tree analysis (FTA), and other equivalent methodologies such as hybrid techniques. In practice, there is a great variation in the scope and level of detail used in hazard identification. This results in a great disparity in the quality of these studies. The type and number of recommendations generated also vary significantly—some studies have few recommendations, while others have a recommendation for every adverse consequence.

A number of factors can increase the quality of the hazard-identification study and its cost-effectiveness. Of great importance is the hazard-identification team leader. Preferably, the leader should have experience in all or most of the hazard-identification techniques. With this experience, the leader can aid in choosing the most appropriate and cost-effec-tive technique for the process or systems under study, the schedule, and the documentation and resources available. In addition, it is essential that the scope, objectives, and ground rules for the analysis be deter-mined and communicated before the hazard-identification study begins. The hazard-identification study leader also should make clear what con-stitutes a safeguard for the study documentation. Through preplanning, initial node selection, highlighting of drawings, and so on, the study tech-niques can be made more cost-effective. For hazard identification to be effective, it also must be clear that the study team has the authority for decision making and therefore need not use *consider* before each and every recommendation agreed on by the team. In situations where the team really is uncertain about a given action, the use of language such as *study, recommend, and implement as appropriate* is preferred in the study documentation. A useful tool in hazard identification is a chemical interaction matrix—this is sometimes supplied as part of the process safety information package to study team members. For changes at existing facilities, the hazard-identification study can be made more cost-effective by ensuring that a tour of the site facilities being redesigned or evaluated takes place immediately preceding the study.

To be cost-effective, team hazard-identification studies should make use of a technical recorder (engineer) and computer to fully document the proceedings and recommendations. These studies are brainstorm-ing sessions where team members quickly voice their ideas. It is not rea-sonable to assume that the leader will be able to thoroughly document the team ideas and proceedings and provide active and attentive lead-ership. By using both a team leader and a technical recorder, the brain-storming sessions can be thoroughly and quickly documented without slowing the team progress. In addition, the leader can focus efforts on team leadership. Of course, the alternative is to assign responsibility for team leadership and study documentation to one individual. While this initially has the appearance of being cost-effective, longer team sessions may result, full documentation of the proceedings may not be possible, and the leader may not be able to concentrate on team leadership, all of which lead to studies that are not cost-effective in the short or long term. Particularly if only recording by exception is used in the sessions, the costs will be greater for future periodic revalidation of the hazard-identification study because nonhazardous or minor scenarios will like-ly be fully discussed again.

Often, hybrid hazard-identification techniques provide the most cost-effective and highest-quality alternative early in facility design—at this stage, sufficient information is probably not even available for use of the HAZOP technique. Structured what-if checklist techniques provide a structured agenda for the study and can use team knowledge that is not yet formally documented. If limited information is available, the team of experts can define the process and analyze the potential hazards by developing lists of expected safety features on the subsystems. Next, they can systematically consider failures, identify potential hazards, and specify upgraded design and safety features. Finally, these new specifications can be documented and included in the piping and instrumentation drawings (P&IDs).

A further measure of cost-effectiveness can be achieved in hazard-identification studies by documenting the necessary information for consequence modeling of a range of scenarios. These scenarios can then be included in risk-management and emergency response plans.

10.7   Frequency, Common-Cause Failure, and Consequence Analysis

A variety of techniques can be used to qualitatively, semiquantitatively, or quantitatively estimate the likelihood of undesirable events. The primary techniques for quantitative frequency evaluation are the use of historical data with any applicable modification factors, fault-tree analysis, and event-tree analysis. Further, bayesian analysis can be used to incorporate limited plant- or facility-specific data with historical data to provide a more representative frequency estimate. One of the most critical problems associated with frequency analysis is omission of hazards or the causes of them.

There are a number of data sources available for historical plant and facility equipment failures and for human errors in a variety of circumstances. One of the common errors in the use of historical data is its misapplication. The analyst should understand the database used, the sources of the data, the service environment, and so on prior to application of data to a particular facility. A novice analyst could make a significant error in frequency estimation if the definition of the failure in the database is not recognized (e.g., fail to danger, total failures) and incorrect data are used inadvertently.

In fault-tree analysis, the most common serious errors include omission of entire branches of the tree and misapplication of the numerical data used. Yet fault trees are able to account for site-specific design factors, procedures, and practices and can include human errors explicitly. Fault trees also can be used to generate estimates for events where historical data are not available or applicable. To ensure that a sound basis is provided for decision making and the activity is cost-effective, fault trees should be constructed and reviewed by experienced analysts. It is very easy for novices to make errors in the use of fault-tree technique. A reality check of the results by other qualified analysts is always prudent.

Event trees incorporate factors such as the probability that protective systems are successful, the likelihood that human actions avert dangerous conditions, the probability of various weather conditions, and other postincident event probabilities (ignition, explosion, fireball). Event trees can be used effectively and in some cases are sufficient to show the differences between alternative designs.

In addition, risk analysis should address common-cause failures—those failures which can defeat protective systems by simultaneously disabling otherwise independent components. Typical common-cause failures that should be considered for process facilities include items such as loss of plant utilities (such as power, air, cooling water, and nitrogen), external events (e.g., earthquakes, tsunamis, tornadoes, hurricanes, flooding), and domino effects from accidents such as fires and explosions. Atypical common causes that are often of greater significance include such things as plugging from polymer formation, scaling or fouling, or extreme temperatures, which can disable or impair the functioning of critical sensors and protective systems by conditions within the process itself. Often, complex designs or equipment can mask hidden common-cause failures that are not known to exist. Common-cause failures can be identified, quantified, and systematically eliminated or reduced depending on their importance and the level of study detail.

Consequence analysis also plays an important role in facility design and layout. Consequence and risk analyses have been used by many operators and technology licensors to evaluate current designs and to develop low-risk alternatives. There are many factors that are important to consequence analysis. The most important of these are the choice of appropriate models and damage criteria or physical effects endpoints used in the analyses. Many consequence models do not contain sufficient theoretical development to evaluate near-field effects important to facility design and siting, such as from domino events. Even many "sophisticated" and expensive consequence models incorporate simplifying assumptions that may be acceptable in determining off-site effects but which prevent accurate determination of near-field effects. In fact, the Hanna study[7] indicates that for even far-field effects, the most expensive software programs do not necessarily provide the best match with experimental and field test data. There is a need for the models to be flexible and detailed enough to allow for evaluation of various mitigation options. This is of particular concern for fire and explosion models. Many existing models are overly conservative in estimating near-field fire and explosion hazards. A number of detailed, high-quality fire radiation models are available. The theoretical basis for several excellent fire models is provided in the Society of Fire Protection Engineers' *Fire Protection Engineering Handbook.*[8] Using overly conservative consequence models can result in equipment and tankage spacing that is simply impossible at many facilities. When good near-field consequence models are used in facility design and layout, valuable information can be obtained to address issues such as spacing and fire protection. In addition, these consequence models provide a good check for existing internal codes and standards.

As for other risk-analysis techniques, the most appropriate frequency estimation technique and consequence models for the particular study needs should be utilized. This ensures a measure of confidence in the results and cost-effectiveness in the analysis. The level of detail and accuracy also should meet the study requirements.

10.8   Human Factors

It has been shown repeatedly that human factors play a significant role in nearly all hazardous facility incidents and accidents. Determining that operators are responsible for most accidents is an inaccurate interpretation of the data. Rather, the human errors (or operating errors) are often a symptom of greater problems, such as poor design, inadequate procedures, insufficient training, or organizational factors. It should be noted that the OSHA process safety management standard[1] explicitly requires that human factors be included in all PHAs. In the interaction between human and engineered systems, both microergonomics and safety management systems should be considered. Microergonomics includes the study of control rooms, workstations, local work environment, and so on. In contrast, the impact of safety management systems includes evaluation of company culture, personnel hiring criteria, reward systems, communication systems, training, management systems, and other performance-shaping factors. Recent research into accident case histories has shown that traditional safety measures such as preventing lost-time injuries does not affect the occurrence of catastrophic events.[9] As a result of this research, more emphasis is now placed on the evaluation and improvement of safety management systems.

10.9   Quantitative Risk-Analysis Techniques

Comprehensive quantitative risk analysis, cost-benefit analysis, and financial risk-analysis techniques have been used to determine risks (financial, environmental, acute, chronic), evaluate total liabilities, determine insurance needs, develop cost-effective mitigation strategies, assess business opportunities, and address regulatory requirements. QRAs are used in many countries to aid in decision making, by providing objective numerical and technical information regarding hazardous chemical operations and processes.[4] Government agencies in the United Kingdom, Australia, and several provinces in Canada have established risk criteria for land-use planning. The Netherlands, Hong Kong, and Switzerland all routinely use risk criteria in evaluating the level of risk posed to the public and in determining the merits and cost-effectiveness of prevention or mitigation options.

In the United States, risk analysis has been used by a number of companies (e.g., Rohm and Haas,[10] BP[11]) in addressing the overall risks posed to the public and for evaluation of risk-reduction alternatives. Currently, there is no federal requirement for formal risk analysis, although the EPA alludes to the concept of a risk-based decision process in the hydrogen fluoride study report.[12] The County of Santa Barbara in California also utilizes formal risk criteria for evaluating hazardous chemical facilities.[13] The county also has addressed the cost-effectiveness issue when reviewing potential implementation of various alternatives to improve safety or, conversely, to reduce the level of risk. The recently approved revision of the New Jersey Toxic Catastrophe Prevention Act (TCPA) also uses risk-based decision-making principles.[14] Still, the potential benefits of using QRA for decision making are largely unrealized in the United States.

Since the worst-case release (as defined by the EPA) must be included in the risk-management plan, it becomes more important to be able to base discussions and decisions on the risks posed, not just the worst possible consequence. Basing decisions regarding PHA recommendations solely on the consequences will lead to consequence management, not risk management.

Many companies have used risk matrices to aid in evaluating PHA recommendations. These risk matrices do play a part in evaluating recommendations and organizing the responses to them. Yet categorization and prioritization of PHA recommendations using such a matrix can be very subjective. Often, the PHA team members propose their best guess as to the likelihood and consequences of release scenarios based on their experience. This approach is a useful *first step* in prioritizing and analyzing PHA recommendations. It can help in categorizing the scenarios and resulting recommendations into areas of concern (e.g., health and safety, environment, procedures, drawings). Additionally, it may be obvious that some recommendations should be implemented because they significantly reduce the level of risk posed to workers or to the public and can be implemented for very little cost. Often, though, the resolution of PHA recommendations is not obvious, especially when hundreds or even thousands of recommendations result from PHAs of numerous processes or operations.

Some companies also include a cost factor in the risk matrix and recommendation prioritization system. The PHA team or another responsible party estimates an "order of magnitude" cost of implementing each recommendation, and this is factored into the decision-making process. This can provide useful additional information for prioritization of further study needs as well. Clearly, when considering implementation of PHA recommendations with significant associated costs, further refinement of the likelihood, consequence, and impact of the proposed scenario (with and without mitigation) is certainly warranted. This type of analysis also serves as an aid for management in determining which recommendations not to implement. On occasion, the investment required for implementing all PHA recommendations has actually exceeded the cost of the entire process unit. Consistency also becomes an important factor when considering implementation of recommendations developed by different PHA teams studying several different processes.

QRA has been applied by a number of leading companies in addressing PHA recommendations and other process engineering and design issues. These studies have included a wide range of hazardous chemicals, processes, and operations. QRA studies have been carried out for project phases as early as conceptual design and have ranged from coarse to very detailed analyses and assessments. Figure 10.1 shows an application of cost-benefit QRA techniques to one hydrogen fluoride alkylation unit located in an urban area.[15] Note that a cost-benefit ratio of less than 1 indicates that the measure is cost-effective. Alternatives

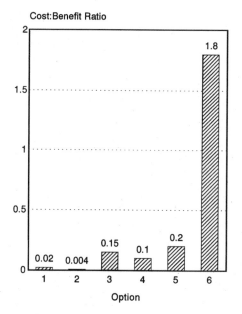

Figure 10.1 Hydrogen fluoride alkylation unit—urban setting.

with cost-benefit ratios slightly greater than 1 may be further evaluated and still considered for implementation, while those with higher ratios should be discarded. The risk-reduction options studied include (1) incorporation of remotely operated valves in key locations, (2) removal of the acid pump, (3) use of a vertical baffle in the acid settler to segregate the acid inventory, (4) use of an emergency acid dump system, (5) inclusion of measures 1, 3, and 4 in combination, and (6) implementation of the same basic features as in measure 5 but in a "gold-plated" system (where no expense is spared and all available features are included). The annualized costs for each mitigation measure were then compared with the net risk-reduction benefit. As can be seen from Fig. 10.1, the cost-benefit ratio ranges from 0.004 to 1.8. It shows that for this urban setting, implementation of measures 1 to 5 is worthy of consideration, while measure 6 is not as cost-effective.

A similarly designed process unit in a very rural setting also was studied.[16] The risk-reduction measures considered were (1) an extensive water spray system, (2) use of a vertical baffle in the acid settler to segregate the acid inventory, (3) use of an emergency acid dump system, and (4) measures 2 and 3 in combination. Application of cost-benefit techniques to this situation resulted in cost-benefit ratios of 20 to 675, as shown in Fig. 10.2. Therefore, in this environmental setting, none of the measures was considered cost-effective.

In the study of a different hydrogen fluoride alkylation unit design in another urban setting,[4] the risk-reduction measures considered included (1) use of an extensive water spray system, (2) use of a redesigned

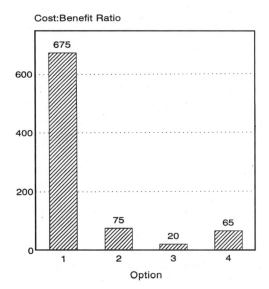

Figure 10.2 Hydrogen fluoride alkylation unit—rural setting.

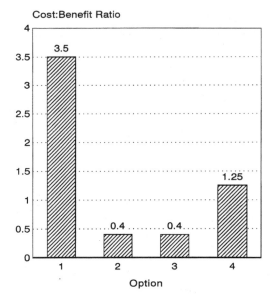

Figure 10.3 Hydrogen fluoride alkylation unit—another urban setting.

unit to reduce acid inventory, (3) a combination of measures covering improved detection, isolation, and mitigation systems, and (4) use of an additive to reduce acid aerosolization. Figure 10.3 shows that the initially planned water spray system (option 1) had a cost-benefit ratio of about 3.5. Therefore, other alternatives were studied in detail. Options 2 and 3 provided the best cost-benefit ratios, at about 0.4. Option 4 resulted in a cost-benefit ratio of about 1.25.

The results of such cost-benefit studies do not provide a definitive answer to decisions regarding PHA recommendation implementation. Other environmental or political factors may come into play as well. Yet the information from cost-benefit or cost-effectiveness studies can be a very helpful aid to the decision-making process. Of course, consequence or frequency analysis also can be utilized alone in cost-benefit analysis, but the level of uncertainty is greater than when QRA is used for decision making.

Various types of QRA studies can be carried out *cost-effectively* to provide decision aids for management. It is important that the scope, as well as the objectives of the study, be carefully defined. The study must quickly focus on those items or recommendations which significantly affect the risks. This can be achieved using screening techniques. As with most safety activities, it is often difficult to demonstrate the cost-effectiveness of the activity, since the intent is to prevent accidents from occurring. However, in several QRA studies, the circumstances made it

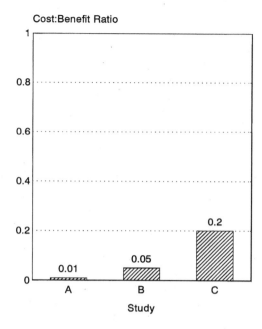

Figure 10.4 Cost-effective QRA studies.

easier to demonstrate the cost-effectiveness of the QRA studies themselves. In these cases, a capital budget and particular risk-reduction alternatives were agreed on and approved for implementation prior to the onset of the study and based on the experience of staff at the corporate and site levels. In each of the three cases presented here, the QRA study provided management with more effective and cost-effective solutions than those previously planned. This resulted in a savings of millions of dollars, in addition to a more effective risk-management plan. The cost-benefit ratio for each of these QRA studies is shown in Fig. 10.4. Note that the only benefits included in the calculations are the direct savings in planned expenditures.

10.10   Risk Communication

Often the results of quantitative risk analyses are used to communicate opinions regarding risk between opposing groups. One key factor to a successful facility project is involvement of all stakeholders early in the process. It is always important for decision makers to appreciate the public's viewpoints and concerns regarding the facility and the risk posed. Risks from high-consequence events (causing multiple injuries or fatalities or severe environmental damage) receive an inordinate amount of public attention and regulatory scrutiny, while those frequent but lower-consequence events almost go unnoticed. In addition, many people, including competent engineers, have difficulty in understanding and relating to the low probabilities or frequencies often found in risk analyses. A 1 in 1 million (or 1 in 10 million) event may not even seem that unlikely to members of the public—after all, many lottery tickets are purchased every week with similar odds of winning, and someone periodically wins. In addition, several people have even been hit by lighting two or more times! Therefore, the tendency is to focus on what they do clearly understand, the consequences and impacts of accidental release. It is vitally important to realize that, although various stakeholders may use the same words to express their opinions and concerns about risk, they often attach different meanings to these words. Misunderstandings can then occur without the individuals' realizing why.[17] As a result, communication of risks to the public becomes an even more difficult task, and it is the subject of many volumes of text. Critical to the risk-communication process is trust. This can be developed by open presentation and discussion of the study results, how the study influenced facility management decisions, and other factors of importance to the public, regulatory agencies, and opposing groups.

10.11 Summary

Environment, health, and safety dollars are an investment each company makes in its business and as such should be scrutinized to the same level of detail as other proposed capital investments or expenditures. Although other factors come into play when making decisions regarding environmental, health, or safety investments, it is critical that management have all the relevant technical information available to facilitate objective decision making. The integration of risk-analysis techniques and facility design results in implementation of the best and most cost-effective practical solutions.

It has been demonstrated through application of risk-analysis techniques to PHA recommendations, other process engineering changes, and hazardous material transportation issues that risk analysis can effectively facilitate management decision making. In fact, it also has been proven that such studies can be cost-effective and a wise company investment.

The use of quantitative risk analysis and assessment is essential for the development and implementation of a comprehensive and effective risk-management program. Decision makers also should be made aware of the complete impacts of alternative designs, including the tradeoffs among acute, chronic, environmental, and financial risks.

Many factors affect the cost-effectiveness of the studies, including experience of the analyst(s), choice of study technique and level of detail, choice of models, and development of practical and economical facility solutions, among others. Design engineers may have little training in risk-analysis techniques, and therefore, appropriate interfaces with the design team should be defined. In this way, the relevant risk-analysis expertise can be combined with design team efforts in a functional, cost-effective, and timely manner. The definition of these interfaces should be determined and developed for each company and its associated internal project stages and procedures.

A holistic management approach should be taken to facility design, incorporating factors affecting the environment, health, safety, and business throughout the life cycle of the facility.[18] As a result of this approach, risk analysis becomes an integral part of the total facility design project. Certainly, actions to improve facility or process design do not come without a price—but the use of risk-analysis techniques provides a sound basis for defining design features, determining what mitigation is necessary, and evaluating which solutions are the most cost-effective.

10.12 References

1. OSHA 29 CFR, Part 1910.119, "Process Safety Management of Highly Hazardous Chemicals, Explosives and Blasting Agents; Final Rule," *Federal Register*, July 1, 1993, pp. 364–385.
2. EPA 40 CFR, Part 68, "Risk Management Programs for Accidental Release Prevention; Proposed Rule," *Federal Register*, October 20, 1993, pp. 54190–54219.
3. Federal Focus, Inc., and The Institute for Regulatory Policy, *Toward Common Measures: Recommendations for a Presidential Executive Order on Environmental Risk Assessment and Risk Management Policy,* Federal Focus Inc. and the Institute for Regulatory Policy, Washington, D.C., June 1991.
4. P. M. Myers, "QRA as a Cost-Effective Management Decision Making Tool," *Proceedings of the 28th Annual Loss Prevention Symposium,* American Institute of Chemical Engineers, New York, 1994.
5. "Should Business Be Afraid of Juries?" *Business Week,* November 8, 1993, pp. 100–101.
6. M. D. LaGrega et al., *Hazardous Waste Management,* McGraw-Hill, New York, 1994.
7. S. R. Hanna, D. G. Strimaits, and J. C. Chang, *Hazard Response Modeling Uncertainty (A Quantitative Method),* Vol. 2: *Evaluation of Commonly-Used Hazardous Gas Dispersion Models,* Sigma Research Corporation for the Air Force Engineering and Services Center and the American Petroleum Institute, Washington, September 1991.
8. K. S. Mudan and P. A. Croce, "Fire Hazard Calculations for Large Open Hydrocarbon Fires," *Society of Fire Protection Engineers Handbook of Fire Protection Engineering,* National Fire Protection Association, Quincy, Mass., 1988, Chap. 2.
9. Four Elements, Ltd., "Further Development of an Audit Technique for the Evaluation and Management of Risk: Tasks 7 and 8, Analysis of Site Safety Performance Indicators," for the U.K. Health and Safety Executive, VROM, and Norsk Hydro, Columbus, Ohio, 1993.
10. F. M. Renshaw, "A Major Accident Prevention Program," *Plant / Operations Progress,* 9(3):194–197, July 1990.
11. A. B. Fleishman and M. S. Hogh, "The Development of Risk Acceptability Criteria for Worldwide Application: An International Energy Company View," *Third Conference of the Society for Risk Analysis—Europe,* Society for Risk Analysis, McLean, Va., 1991.
12. U.S. Environmental Protection Agency, *Hydrogen Fluoride Study: Draft Report,* U.S. Government Printing Office, Washington, May 1992.
13. D. Vrat and R. Almy, *Phased Engineering Developments and Multiple Agency Reviews of Public Safety Issues,* County of Santa Barbara, Calif., 1990.

14. State of New Jersey Department of Environmental Protection and Energy, *Toxic Catastrophe Prevention Act Program, Readoption with Amendments,* July 19, 1993.
15. P. M. Myers, K. S. Mudan, and H. Hachmuth, "The Risks of HF and Sulfuric Acid Alkylation," *Proceedings of the International Conference on Hazard Identification and Risk Analysis, Human Factors and Human Reliability in Process Safety,* American Institute of Chemical Engineers, New York, 1992.
16. P. M. Myers and J. N. Shah, "The Reduction of Chemical Process Risks," *AIChE Summer National Meeting,* American Institute of Chemical Engineers, New York, 1993.
17. R. H. Johnson, "What Are Your Chances of Communicating Effectively with Technical and Non-Technical Audiences?," *Society for Risk Analysis Annual Meeting,* Washington, 1982.
18. L. A. Rich, "The Sound of Both Hands Clapping," *Resources,* 15(5):3–5, December 1993.

11

Risk Reporting

Robert D. Zimmerman
Fluor Daniel, Inc.

11.1 The Challenge

The challenge for the analyst is in balancing the customer's needs and expectations regarding costs. A summary of ideas on how to report risks is contained in the CCPS book *Guidelines for Chemical Process Quantitative Risk Analysis*[1] and the CMA publication *Risk Communication, Risk Statistics, and Risk Comparisons: A Manual for Plant Managers.*[2] The regulatory requirements for risk reporting are discussed in Chap. 2 of this book. Although the approaches contained in these guidelines are adequate for communicating with technical people, the technical community is all too often surprised when it is challenged by skeptics at public hearings and in courtrooms. This chapter is dedicated to explaining how to incorporate some of the lessons learned by others.[1-12] The basic steps are to define the hazards, develop risk estimates and approaches for risk management, select the approach that meets internal criteria, involve public agencies and stakeholders (members of the public who have an interest to protect), and then listen carefully before making your decision. Risk reporting requires addressing concerns and resolving issues. You will not answer

The cocontributer for Section 11.7, "Example: Risk Analysis for a Gaseous Centrifuge Uranium Enrichment Facility," was Peter LeRoy of Duke Engineering and Services.

others' concerns until they have an opportunity to raise them, so the sooner they can raise their concerns, the better.

The first step in preparing a cost-effective report is understanding the purpose, intended use (internal, public relations, permit or license application), available data, and budget constraints in order to develop work plans. The second step is to divide the report into a series of activities that can be developed independently of each other. This prevents delays in any one area from stopping progress on the entire report. The authors also should make sure that the report includes a summary that explains the logic used to assess and manage risks with references to supporting information.

It is preferable to have a well-integrated multidisciplinary team write the report. If this is not possible, based on the customer's initial budget, extensive rewriting should be expected during the review cycles. Keep in mind, however, that it is easy to review the material that is there; it is not so easy to identify errors of omission. Just as important, your customer should understand both the limitations and the risks of the approach you are taking. Otherwise, the customer may be surprised during the licensing or permitting process. Failure of interested parties to satisfactorily support issues raised during the hearing process can lead to dismissal of claims or status as a recognized stakeholder in legal proceedings. Failure of applicants to resolve issues that have been raised by regulators or accepted into the proceedings can lead to costly delays, design changes, or even disapproval of a pending licensing or permit application.

To be of value, the analysis must communicate the results to the decision makers. The purpose of risk analysis is to gain insight into the relative significance of various risks to allow better decisions to be made concerning the design or operation of hazardous facilities. To be credible, a risk report must provide a perspective on the uncertainties, if not recommendations on how to reduce them. Normally, technically trained risk managers prefer quantitative risk estimates; nontechnical managers may place more emphasis on checklists and qualitative assessments.[12] Common sense and two-way communication are essential to cost-effectiveness. Often there is not enough information to generate statistically meaningful confidence limits around the results. Normally, it is possible, however, to express the sources of uncertainty and relative effects on the risk estimate in terms that provide decision makers with a perspective on how the uncertainties affect the results. The customer is motivated to balance costs, business risks, and regulatory constraints. The regulatory agency that has the general responsibility for making politically acceptable risk decisions often must interpret vague legislative objectives and coordinate with other government agencies and the public. Other institutional uses of risk reports include insurance rating and court cases related to negligence, liability, and nuisance.[14] In the final analysis, the cost of preparing the risk report has to be compared against other needs.

Internal technology evaluations and risk assessments can be used very effectively to demonstrate the safety of the technology, the company's ability to operate it safely, and the project's good-faith attempt at resolving local concerns.[5] The analyst can defuse misinformation and maintain credibility by acknowledging differences of opinion and uncertainty and by addressing prior incidents. It is also important to avoid going overboard in one area at the expense of others. Most severe accidents occurred because no one thought of the conditions that facilitated the propagation of unsafe conditions into an accident.[6] Typically, facilities that suffer major accidents have undergone several modifications.

11.2 Gaining Community Acceptance

Defusing the NIMBY ("not in my backyard") syndrome requires building trust and understanding. Risk reports are the mechanism for jointly solving problems and resolving conflicts among various vested interests. One report will not do that. Dissemination of individual reports through the appropriate reviews will help establish credibility and make for excellent reference material. The biggest credibility issues arise because a report did not cover an issue that did not seem important up to that point in the approval process but just happens to be a "hot button" for an influential individual or stakeholder who was not involved up to that point. This happens most frequently when siting a new facility. Find out what stakeholders think early, rather than just guessing and getting embarrassed later on.

The most cost-effective approach for obtaining public acceptance is to involve stakeholders early during the decision-making period. Putting the public debate *before* the decision is announced reduces not only the amount of money spent on design changes that might have to be made when the issue is resolved but also the time and effort required to receive construction and operating permits, as illustrated in Sec. 11.7 and discussed in more detail in ref. 5.

Some projects have immovable public opinion against them and will never be accepted by local or state government officials. It is better for project sponsors to uncover this early, before spending much money on design and licensing at that location. On the other hand, using the "decide, announce, and defend" approach usually raises suspicion and frequently results in controversy, needless litigation, and regulatory opposition. Careful library and opinion research and informal contacts with stakeholders (adjoining landowners, politicians, fire department, highway department, police, schools, and utility companies) and members of community groups (environmental, public service, religious) may work well on small projects. Bigger projects usually require formal applications to local planning agencies and professional public relations efforts, including citizen advisory groups and briefings for the media. We recommend identifying this activity as a separate step in your discussions with your customer and including a discussion of the approach in your risk report, even if the decision was to delay outside review of off-site constraints and impacts.

A carefully written risk analysis can become the cornerstone of successful permitting and public relations efforts. Preparing the risk analysis in a cost-effective manner requires careful planning and structuring of the effort to minimize errors and omissions that lead to costly rework and delay. The goal is to build trust in and understanding of the plant's safety and environmental management plan. Doing so requires two-way communication with both technical experts and the public, including the plant owners, workers, regulators, lenders and insurers, emergency responders, and special-interest groups. The public or special advocacy groups are likely to review the customer's operating record and community presence. Any analysis prepared by a single individual, corporation, or agency is likely to miss some important risk because that individual or agency was unfamiliar with it. For example, the frequency of severe fires and explosions has increased in the past decade, not because companies have become careless, but because the added complexity of interactions among petrochemical plants has increased the likelihood of common-cause failures and fault propagation.[5]

Reports written for external purposes should focus on addressing local community planning concerns and issues and should be written in simple terms, with reference to supporting technical reports. After all, the need for and financing of roads, water and sewer, emergency response, and worker and public safety are of the most interest to most of the readers, not the details of the plant or the correctness of a particular analysis. Reviewers will ask for the detail if they feel it is appropriate. The important message you want to convey to the public is that the claims, technical reports, and expert testimony given by project advocates were legitimized by the review process used to achieve agreements and commitments made during the regulatory process. Position the project as a responsible part of the community.

Specialists who study the problems associated with gaining public confidence have identified a number of suggestions.[5,7–10,13–15] Many of their observations can be summarized by stating that the report must demonstrate several attributes:

- The conclusion is logical and is supported by legitimate technical information that was validated by expert review.
- Individual readers' personal concerns were at least considered.
- A constructive interaction took place between proponents and people who represented citizen values and concerns.
- The claims are realistic.

There is general and understandable skepticism about claims that things will *always* work as designed. Poor implementation of the public process is the most common "failure mode" for projects. Examples of things that detract from report credibility are

- Ignoring or underestimating risk when the safety of children is involved.
- Lack of public confidence in the credibility and capability of the regulatory agencies.
- Statements of position without any consideration of the limits of science.
- Failure to evaluate and communicate risks in a meaningful, understandable form.
- Risk reports written without appropriately involving local people's concerns, or microenvironment, or addressing value differences.
- NIMBY ("not in my backyard") reactions resulting from antagonism and misunderstanding from contact with arrogant project proponents.
- Attempting to make social and political decisions for those most affected (those who will live with the risk).

Suggested practices for report formulation are

- Know your objective, audience, and their concerns: background for public relations, postincident fact sheets, OSHA compliance, EPA permit, license application, insurance rating, justifying or financing, future capital improvements.
- Describe the process used to reach the conclusion, recommendation, or decision.
- Describe who has the authority and responsibility for reviewing and approving the report, for operations, for utility upgrades, for emergency response, and for taking care of future liabilities.
- Do not omit significant issues or uncertainties.
- Describe who had input to the report.

- Avoid hidden agendas—be open and honest about your project, hazards, prior incidents, equipment performance, emergency response.
- Write in terms that are meaningful to nontechnical people.
- Acknowledge diversity of opinion (this is the real world).
- Create a mechanism for input and questions.
- Establish your staff's credibility (résumés, references).
- Identify expert reviewers and their qualifications.
- Do not ignore nontechnical concerns and issues.
- Provide access to scientific or technical expertise (such as professional societies, code committees, testing agencies).
- Seek and use existing expertise on risk communication and interaction (local governments, professional societies, and community groups).
- Do not alienate stakeholders by ignoring or insulting them.

The bottom line is to know your audience.

Public review and comment on risk assessments provide a mechanism for evaluating the technical features and risks, which is one of the means for cultivating trust.[2] Few plants get built where there is strong public opposition. Most individuals do not have the time or interest to learn about the nuances of risk assessment, plant designs, or technical issue resolution processes—they are, however, interested in how a proposed plant might affect their lives and, to a lesser extent, whether they think the plant will improve things in their community. Projects are often held up while community concerns and technical issues are discussed. The explanations used in the process should be kept in simple terms and should present the analysis in terms that demonstrate concern for the community. Avoiding issues or technical uncertainties can lead to public skepticism. Overly complex technical explanations are not readily understandable by nontechnical people and can make it appear that there is a great deal of risk or uncertainty when there is very little. Hidden agendas and errors of omission are worse; they destroy credibility.

Many researchers have concluded that public trust of social institutions has waned and that industry must restore its credibility by better understanding the stakeholders' view of the fairness of the firm's imposition of risks on their families.[5,7–10,13,14] Opinions vary as to the most cost-effective approach. Some risk managers recommend minimizing the level of risk reporting; others argue that the preferred approach is to achieve social legitimacy. Experience has shown that once the community is seriously aroused, attempts to resolve issues do not work because playing "hardball" has destroyed the firm's credibility.[3,5,12] The Chemical Manufacturers Association (CMA), which once promoted self-regulation through industry codes and standards, has initiated the "responsible care" concept as an attempt to counter alarmist claims and prevent the industry from being overtaken by overregulation.[12]

11.3 Getting Approval

Getting approval means negotiating authority and responsibility for decisions and developing a consensus about responsibility in the event of an accident. Although analysts and risk managers prefer to have clear criteria of acceptable risk, and there are some specific values that are used as threshold limits, societal values do not assign equal weights to risks. Voluntary risks are not viewed the same as involuntary risks, and risks to children are not perceived the same as risks to adults.[5-8] Community concerns and values also vary from location to location and are more involved with the risks and benefits of alternative uses of proposed facilities than with comparing complicated estimates. Individuals within any given community just may be risk-averse or may be culturally or morally averse to almost any hazard, even if there is no historical or scientific basis for their opposition. The best means for resolving conflicts is to facilitate communication by presenting all sides of the picture, including the sensitivity of the risk estimate to uncertainty in perceived health hazards, exposure pathways, and offsetting benefits. Approvals are achieved by reducing risk perceptions; acceptance is achieved by identifying win-win solutions. In the final analysis, the resolution of controversial technical issues will always be left to government regulatory agencies, with direct input by the applicant and some opportunity for review by stakeholders. This protects the rights of individuals, promotes fairness in the standards imposed on different industries, and is fundamental to the principle of checks and balances found in representative democracies such as the United States.

Public hearings can become highly polarized, with project sponsors and political advocacy groups presenting one-sided emotional appeals. Few outside the scientific community are going to favor or oppose a project based on the level of detail in a risk assessment or on the resolution of some abstract scientific issue. Risk assessment should help decision makers and the public understand the issues by defining the planned environmental and safety features, prudent community planning measures (fire protection, sewage treatment), and risks. Unfortunately, many experts in risk communication are coming to the conclusion that the risk-assessment experts are neither objective nor able to translate their results into meaningful estimates.[8,11,12] The high-level radioactive waste management program, which is discussed in Sec. 11.6, is but one example. Many others can be found.[9,14,15,18]

The regulatory agency's decision makers have no obligation or inclination to accept their technical staff's recommendations. The general public is often skeptical of regulatory agencies, knowing that they can be influenced by applicants and the knowledge that the regulators will not share in the risk if they are wrong. Industry is similarly skeptical, knowing that the agencies have no concern for cost or schedule and that the regulators can minimize personal risk to their own careers if they "just say no."

11.4   The Big Picture

While in practice the regulators may have both a duty and an economic interest in asking for more detail, the applicant may have little interest in doing more than is necessary to minimize his or her financial risk. This has resulted in tremendous industry-to-industry and area-to-area differences in both the level of detail and the benefits of risk analysis. The White House Office of Science and Technology and other administrative agencies periodically issue guidelines on risk assessment for federal agencies.[14,16,17] These guidelines have included consideration of costs and health and safety impacts of government-approved methods and regulatory standards. Unfortunately, the current methods used to estimate risks undermine both industry and public trust in the regulatory process.[15] The use of one-in-a-million risks distorts public health and regulatory priorities toward risks that are well studied but fails to address public concerns that *may be* well founded but have not been proven scientifically or dismissed.

Risk tolerance is very personal and depends on a multitude of factors such as individual benefits and risks.[12] The methods used to measure and estimate risks are complex and include a lot of technical judgments that are difficult for most people to grasp. All these factors set the stage for the political process, i.e., regulations, permit applications, independent reviews, and enforcement actions. For example, proposed changes to pesticide regulations include "sunsetting" approval of pesticide ingredients, preventing the economic benefits of pesticides from being considered in the approval process "except in exceptional cases involving significant disruption of the food supply," basing risk standards on children's tolerance levels rather than adults, and allowing citizen suit authority to sue private landowners on behalf of the government for alleged violations.[16]

The job of ensuring that the public gets good value is almost impossible to define; consequently, it is not included in the regulatory framework that most administrative agencies must comply with. Instead, it is relegated to periodic review by high-level oversight groups. Both the General Accounting Office and the Office of Management and Budget make periodic recommendations on how to make the regulatory process more cost-effective and fair.[2] The concept of fairness has many facets, including (1) uniform health and safety standards for workers, (2) community risks (food, water, recreation, health, and safety), (3) industry-to-industry regulatory costs and accident and injury rates, and (4) benefits (employment, taxes). The classic political debates about worker safety during the industrial revolution centered around whether it was fair to require guards around cutting blades, chains, and rotating equipment. Today, we debate the effectiveness of regulatory standards that set "zero accidents" as a goal versus performance standards of 10^{-6} health effects.[5,9–11,14]

Although technical analysis cannot resolve differences between cultural values and economic interests, it can help both sides sharpen their description of important issues, helping define politically acceptable solutions. The level of detail that does this should be cost-effective. To do more accomplishes less.[11] For example, ecological issues should be focused on major effects such as sustainable agriculture, drinking water, land use (emergency planning zones), social values (air pollution, endangered species, jobs, recreation, and money to build new support services), and flood control (minimize channelization and construction in flood zones and siltation behind dams). In today's world, the perception of fairness in the distribution of risk has become more critical than cost-effectiveness. Few communities will override the concerns of even a minority of its citizens if they feel that the minority is being subjected to risk and not deriving any benefits.[5–8,12] This includes cases where social costs for reducing the hypothetical risks of disposing spent nuclear fuel far exceed the nation's cost for occupational health and safety.[11]

Several administrations have initiated efforts to develop more cost-effective safety standards and regulations.[13] At the time this was written, the EPA, the Food and Drug Administration (FDA), and the Department of Agriculture (DOA) have drafted a proposal to replace the zero-risk provisions of the Delaney clause with a "negligible risk" standard. This approach would apply the same one-in-a-million cancer risk standard used in the nuclear industry for food and drugs. It also would make it easier for the FDA to review and approve or limit manufacture or use of pesticides, both improving food safety and reducing costs. This effort was resisted by consumer groups, who opposed the plan as being too lax because it legalized the small fraction of pesticides banned under the old standard, and by food industry lobbyists, who oppose restrictions on exports of pesticides outlawed in the United States.[16,17]

Therefore, it seems that consumer advocates need to be taught about acceptable risk, and industry will have to recognize that it needs to pay more attention to how it reports risk.[13–15,18] Until then, industry will be faced with ever-increasing restrictions and less effective use of its limited resources.

11.5 Summary

It is crucial that risk reports prevent the development of organized public opposition. This is best handled by eliciting the concerns of all stakeholders early so that the issues can be addressed in the report. The report must project technical competence and establish the credibility of the data and the logic. This is a tough assignment, given the wide variety of cultural standards and perceptions. It is counterproductive to view the public as irrational; a more accurate and productive approach is to recognize that "reality is in the eyes of the beholder" constrained by the assumptions, perspectives, and objectives of the writers. The most cost-effective approach to risk reporting is to manage internal risks and ensure that community expectations and guidelines have been met. If the report is planned properly, it will convey the perception that the analysis considered stakeholders' concerns about tangible or intangible risks that the project may impose on the community. This is not possible, however, unless the authors understand the community's concerns and perceptions.

The report should include a discussion of the process used up to that point to address local environmental conditions and individual concerns and describe any follow-up activities. It can be especially helpful to provide information on reviews completed or planned by independent agencies or groups. It is also important that the firms responsible for publishing the report validate the assumptions and commit to ensuring that the technical resources needed to meet stated risk-management goals and commitments made in the report will be implemented as promised. Finally, the report will not be credible if the conclusions contradict local experience or common sense. For example, there is widespread skepticism about claims that things will work as designed. This is especially true of individuals who will not receive benefits from the proposed facility. To be cost-effective, the report must be viewed as a communication tool helping the community understand the benefits, risks, and burdens the project may impose. It must be structured to build trust in negotiating community acceptance.

Risk practitioners should be conscious of the fact that biases built into their own background knowledge can and will establish blind spots in their approach to measuring and assessing risks. Occasionally, these biases are so deep-seated that they create distrust and political opposition. One example is the recent increase in major accidents after a long period where existing practices were considered adequate.[6,19] The result has been ever-increasing regulation.[5,12,14,20] A second example is the recent acknowledgment by the National Institutes of Health that prior research on common diseases systematically underrepresented women and children. This biased the collection of data to the point where it discredited the scientific credibility of the risk estimates.[13] Unfortunately, poor risk reporting in one area tarnishes the credibility of other work, but this can be overcome by acknowledging imperfection and being willing to accept challenge.

11.6   Example: High-Level Radioactive Waste Management

There are limits to everything, one of them being the effectiveness of technical-based risk assessment in public decision making. One notable example of this is the area of radioactive waste disposal. The decision-making process in this case is full of examples of what was done right, what was done wrong, and how far we have to go before risk reports can be an effective communication and decision-making tool. The opinions and observations in this section are based on the author's perspective as a participant in the program.

The nuclear industry was established by the federal government—first for national defense and second for peaceful uses such as power production. Nuclear power was promoted as being environmentally friendly and having the promise of being inexpensive. For the sake of expediency, the old Atomic Energy Commission had been exempted from administrative oversight by other agencies and from many federal and nearly all state and local regulations. This led to a number of cases where individual workers, private citizens, and state governments raised issues regarding abuses of power. In an attempt to correct these problems, Congress created a system of checks and balances between the Department of Energy (DOE), the Nuclear Regulatory Commission (NRC), the EPA, states, Indian tribes, and other public interests.[20] Congress also established a set of regulatory standards, some of which are very specific and others of which are quite vague. An example of the latter is the term *characterization*; how much characterization is enough to characterize a geologic repository? Unfortunately, experts pondering this question have fostered mistrust by the public and skepticism by the utilities. Meanwhile, the rest of the federal government has become increasingly critical of the cost-effectiveness and technical quality of DOE's risk reporting.[22-26] The utilities' response has been to get more actively involved in both the technical and the political aspects of nuclear waste disposal risk reporting.[27]

To give you a perspective, it is important to point out that DOE has a formidable task in effectively communicating risks about nuclear waste. First and foremost, it carries the burden that the general public lacks a benchmark for judging information about the nuclear industry at all. Few people have any education in the health and safety impacts of radiation, and fewer yet are familiar with nuclear facility work practices. Second, public communication and participation cannot make up for a general loss of public confidence in industry and government that has been fueled by the previous environmental, health, and safety practices.[24,25,28,29] Third, although one can identify sites where the local people would accept or even welcome the project, DOE must get approval from a large assortment of agencies, each of which is made up of many different individuals, and many of these people have proven to be averse to approving the project because that decision is politically unpopular with their agencies' hierarchy or because they fear that some future discovery or decision will put them in a bad position. Another problem is that the local benefits will be relatively small; most of the economic benefits will occur elsewhere in the country. The disruption and change will occur locally: road and rail construction and the burden of added traffic.

On the Civilian Radioactive Waste Management Program, the DOE went through a long and detailed process to evaluate candidate sites throughout the United States. Eventually, environmental assessments were prepared on nine candidate sites. The DOE went through the process of ranking various attributes of each site (current land use, impacts on nearby communities) and documented its recommendations regarding which sites met the siting requirements, making a recommendation regarding which would be its preferred sites in a report to Congress. After considerable debate, Congress enacted the Nuclear Waste Policy Amendments Act of 1987, which directed the DOE to concentrate its efforts on the Yucca Mountain site in Nevada. Considerable opposition developed in the state of Nevada, where opponents dubbed the 1987 Waste Policy Act the "Screw Nevada" law. Many feel that Nevada was selected because it had the least political clout, not because it had the best site.[30] The opposition gained political support as prior poor practices were disclosed. For example, the Oil, Chemical and Atomic Workers' Union won a court case that ruled that DOE had not complied with federal regulations for worker radiation exposure. This was compounded by the state's perception that the DOE did not live up to agreements to keep it involved in planning the site-characterization technical work. The state refused to approve the DOE's permit applications for activities that would allow site-characterization testing. This history of strained institutional relations is aggravated by many Nevadans' resentment over the degree of influence the federal government has in the state. On one hand, the DOE, the largest landowner in the state, is exempt from most state and federal laws; on the other hand, Nevadans find their lives more heavily regulated by federal than state laws. To put this in perspective, consider the casino industry, which has long been a target of federal investigators; it proved to be the strongest opponent of the project.[25] The result was major delays and further deterioration of public confidence in government institutions.

A significant problem for the technical community, which was attempting to demonstrate that the site would be safe and could be licensed, is that most of the public's concerns are nontechnical, while most of the licensing issues are highly technical as well as speculative and subjective. The project's advocates and opponents have very different perspectives about benefits and risks. Nevadans are generally very patriotic, have a favorable image of the test site, and accept the risks associated with defense-related nuclear waste. Many used to sit on lawn chairs and watch atmospheric testing of nuclear weapons and are not "antinuclear" per se. Like most of us, they want to protect their interests and do not want outsiders to turn the Nevada desert into the nation's dumping ground. They are just as opposed to accepting out-of-state hazardous wastes as they are to accepting spent nuclear fuel. They fear that doing so may, in fact, make the area less attractive to future tourists. They also do not want to be the ones who have to pay to improve the roads to keep the traffic flowing accident-free. These concerns are not within DOE's normal responsibility but are part of the planning and decision-making process that Congress included in the Waste Policy Act. To date, it has been impossible to resolve these issues with the casino industry, which has proven to be the project's most adamant and politically influential foe.[25] This type of issue demonstrates the limitations of risk reports: They cannot solve fundamental differences in values and interests.

The Yucca Mountain Project has had great difficulty in dealing with political opposition and technical uncertainty. The state's political leaders adopted a strongly held position of opposition to the project shortly after enactment of the Nuclear Waste Policy Amendments Act of 1987. Since that time, the state of Nevada has put into play every possible legal defense, from legal appeals all the way to the U.S. Supreme Court and the U.S. Congress to hearings and General Accounting Office (GAO) reports (such as ref. 22) that were highly critical of the project. The DOE's difficulties in responding to these attacks have been compounded by its difficulties in establishing a clear technical track for demonstrating that the Yucca Mountain site is a good site for the nation's first repository.

In the process leading to the final site-characterization plan, there was considerable lack of agreement, both within the DOE and in dialogue between the DOE and the NRC staff, concerning how much and what kind of technical work was necessary. Much of the discord within the technical community was motivated by visions of what might be done on the part of proponents of the various technical disciplines and was enabled by the lack of clear vision of what was required to comply with statutory and regulatory requirements.

The site-characterization plan that emerged from the process constitutes the formal basis for interaction between the DOE and the NRC and can only be revised during formal NRC staff reviews of DOE findings concerning site suitability. If the DOE stumbles in the procedural aspects of characterizing the site, the state will likely make additional legal challenges, further delaying the siting and licensing process. The high cost and delays in implementing the scope of work defined by the site-characterization plan have, however, aroused additional attention from Congress.[31]

The political, procedural, and technical contention has of course attracted considerable attention in the media and in the several hundred groups that count themselves as constituencies of the project. Their concerns include the risk that disposal cannot be accomplished safely at the Yucca Mountain site, risk that the DOE is technically weak, risk that the DOE is not an effective steward of its fiscal responsibilities, risk that the DOE may not be truthful in its communications, and risk that the DOE will not live up to its agreements and commitments with constituencies. Much of the media attention, most of which is focused on disagreements between agencies and experts, raises the perception of risk among the public.

Much has been written concerning these risks,[24,25,27,32,33] and more will undoubtedly be written in the future. Unfortunately, the DOE did not start to address stakeholders' risk perceptions until they were placed on the agenda by others. The DOE later refocused on conflict resolution and placed more emphasis on public information programs and site tours. Although these efforts had little impact on dedicated opponents, they were more effective with those who did not have nonnegotiable, emotionally charged positions. The ultimate resolution of the nuclear waste management problem, including the storage of spent nuclear fuel that is currently stored at nuclear reactor sites, will probably not be resolved until Congress modifies the current legislation. This is unlikely until Congress is satisfied that the critics' concerns have been fairly considered and that no one is subject to undue risk or loss of due process.

The following lists a few lessons learned by the DOE Office of Civilian Radioactive Waste Management:[23-25]

- The working relationships between project advocates, regulatory agencies, and local government agencies will work best when both sides live up to their agreements and commitments, whether they are formal or informal.

- Start trying to discuss ways to address concerns as soon as you can; they will not go away.

- Try finding mutually acceptable ways to measure and manage risks.

- Do not needlessly antagonize special-interest groups; that way, you will not needlessly alienate them.

- The analyst's economic incentives should emphasize conflict resolution and risk reduction.

- Providing preliminary information on risks and proposed solutions builds trust.

- Trying to perfect your report before you submit it for public review not only runs up the cost—it may foster the impression that you are trying to hide something while giving your opponents the opportunity to polarize concerned citizens.

The author wishes to acknowledge the insight gained on the problems associated with risk reporting and communications while working with former colleagues on the high-level radioactive waste management program and for the review comments and insight provided by John Bartlett, the former DOE program manager. Unfortunately, the political and technical issues associated with siting and licensing Yucca Mountain gave a false impression that the safe disposal of high-level radioactive waste is an intractable problem. Undoubtedly the need to compete in the marketplace was the force that caused the nuclear industry to refocus on cost-effectiveness in its approaches to risk reporting, conflict resolution, and the demonstration of regulatory compliance.[34]

11.7 Example: Risk Analysis for a Gaseous Centrifuge Uranium Enrichment Facility

A risk analysis was performed for Louisiana Energy Services' (LES) proposed Claiborne Enrichment Center. This facility was the first attempt to license a privately owned uranium enrichment facility in the United States. The purpose of the facility is to enrich natural uranium, in the form of uranium hexafluoride (UF_6), for use in commercial power reactors. This enrichment process is performed by using the gas centrifuge process. This would be the first application of this technology in commercial operation in the United States. Gaseous centrifuge enrichment plants have been operating in Europe for more than 20 years.

11.7.1 Licensing a UF_6 centrifuge enrichment process

In the centrifuge enrichment process, the uranium isotopes ^{235}U and ^{238}U are separated due to the difference in mass under influence of centrifugal forces in a fast-rotating cylinder (rotor). The feed, product, and tails are all in the form of uranium hexafluoride (UF_6), a compound that is well suited for the separation process because it is a gas at relatively low temperatures. Fluorine has only one stable isotope. No chemical or nuclear conversions take place.

The LES facility uses centrifugal enrichment because it (1) requires much less (approximately 5 percent) energy to produce separative work than competing technologies (e.g., gaseous diffusion enrichment methods) and (2) is easy to produce at high purity. The LES facility will produce UF_6 enriched in a range of 2 to 5 percent, ^{235}U. The feed material for the enrichment process at the LES facility has the same isotopic composition of ^{234}U, ^{235}U, and ^{238}U as mined ore. The raw ore is milled, purified, and converted to UF_6 before shipment to the enrichment process.

The design capacity of the LES facility is 1.5 million kilograms SWU per year. The SWU capacity defines the amount of work or energy needed to separate a quantity of feed material into an enriched fraction (product) and a depleted fraction (tails). This capacity represents approximately 15 percent of the annual U.S. commercial nuclear power plant requirements.

11.7.2 Hazards and exposures

Uranium hexafluoride (UF_6) is a hazardous material. First, a critical mass of enriched uranium could release intense radiation and thermal energy, which is called a *criticality*. Second, UF_6 reacts exothermally with moisture in the air to form uranyl fluoride (UO_2F_2) and hydrogen fluoride (HF). The hydrogen fluoride plume is visible, it resembles white smoke, and rises in the air until it cools, and the reaction products settle out of the air.

Hydrogen fluoride is a corrosive acid vapor that is very irritating and can damage the moist tissue of the lungs and other parts of the respiratory tract. The uranium in uranyl fluoride is a heavy metal, which can be toxic if it accumulates in body organs. The chemical hazards presented by UF_6 are more severe than the heavy metal or radiologic hazards presented by the uranium.

The NRC and American National Standards Institute (ANSI) standards specify design and procedural controls to prevent nuclear criticality. These controls include geometry, enrichment, and redundancy in the system and equipment designs to ensure that criticality safety is maintained even when two highly unlikely, independent failures occur concurrently.

The U.S. NRC has established in NUREG-1391, *Chemical Toxicity of Uranium Hexafluoride Compared to Acute Effects of Radiation,* the values for hydrogen fluoride and uranium that should be used for accident-analysis purposes at facilities that process large quantities of UF_6. It should be noted that "the values are neither acceptable exposures nor limits on exposures."[35]

The value for hydrofluoric acid is

$$\text{HF concentration} = 25 \text{ mg/m}^3 \cdot (30 \text{ min}/t)^{0.5}$$

where t is time in minutes of the duration of exposure. The value for uranium is 10 mg.

11.7.3   LES Claiborne Enrichment Center

The LES license application was the first NRC license application for a "one-step" combined construction-operating license. The one-step process greatly reduces the risk that regulatory requirements could change before a license is issued, thereby reducing the financial risk for the project. However, this process requires an adjudicatory-type hearing. Previously, one hearing was required before construction could begin, and another hearing was required before operation could begin. Neither required an adjudicatory-type hearing. Consequently, the designers of the LES enrichment plant not only had to demonstrate to the NRC that the designs were adequate from a safety standpoint, but they had to be concerned with several other audiences.

First, the NRC had to assess for itself whether the safety analyses report met its own regulatory guidelines and whether the facility could be built and operated safely. Similar assessments had to be made by the EPA and the Louisiana Department of Environmental Quality before they issued permits for the facility. The results of these assessments also were communicated to people in the surrounding communities. All three groups were considered when reporting the risks of the proposed facility.

Specific steps.   The strategy used to ensure that the risk assessment was performed cost-effectively was to try to ensure that the progression of work would avoid "eleventh hour" reanalyses that could prove costly and disruptive to the schedule. The only significant hazard in this facility is UF_6. As explained in Sec. 11.7.2, the two most important hazards associated with UF_6 are criticality and chemical hazards. Although the NRC had well-established guidelines for addressing criticality hazards, it had never finalized its guidelines for UF_6. Consequently, the first step in the LES plan to avoid last-minute challenges was to establish specific maximum values or quantities of hazardous materials that a person off-site could be exposed to during an accident.

Other steps in the process were as follows:

- Establish events, such as human error, equipment failure, and natural phenomena, that could realistically be expected to occur in this facility.

- Review the physical properties of UF_6 to establish accident scenarios that could result in large releases of UF_6.

- Review how the hydrogen fluoride and uranium could be transported off-site from the facility (in this case dispersion through the air was the most important mechanism).

- Review facility design and operations to establish the amounts and physical states of the UF_6 as it is handled at a gaseous uranium enrichment facility.

- Perform detailed calculations to analyze specific scenarios that result in large releases of uranium and hydrogen fluoride.

- Specify the quality assurance requirements for structures, systems, and components (SSC) appropriate to their safety function.

- If necessary, determine which redundant and diverse systems and components could be added to ensure that the risk from accidents is essentially zero.

The LES enrichment center is based on more than 30 years of gaseous centrifuge operational experience in Europe, where there has never been a significant release of UF_6. The process material (UF_6) in all areas of the enrichment plant is contained in closed systems that are designed using the engineering standards applied in high-vacuum technology. Secondary containment is provided at all process locations where UF_6 is heated to be a liquid or a vapor and the UF_6 vapor pressure is above atmospheric pressure. This is done using airtight autoclaves. Only piping and vessels operated under vacuum are designed without secondary containment. With these systems, any rupture would result first in an inward leak of air rather than an escape of

UF_6. The quantity of UF_6 outside the feed cylinders and take-off stations during facility operation is very small. For this plant, the instruments that ensure safe shutdown of the autoclave heaters were classified as quality level one and are designed, constructed, and operated using very stringent technical criteria and administrative controls and were subject to additional regulatory review. The balance of the facility plumbing and electrical systems was designed using commercial building codes and engineering standards and quality assurance requirements.

The steps used in this design process included

- Establishing how much UF_6 could be released in a particular accident scenario and knowing the distance to the fence line (which is the distance to the closest possible member of the public).

- Evaluating whether the amount of UF_6 released could exceed the exposure guidelines established in NUREG-1391.

- If the guidelines were exceeded, mitigation methods were established to ensure that either the event could not be initiated or the amounts of hydrogen fluoride and uranium released were reduced by containing or filtering the material released during the event.

Design solutions were identified for any scenarios that might result in unacceptable consequences, as illustrated in Fig. 11.1.

The license application was submitted to the NRC in the recommended format using the approach outlined in Fig. 11.1. All possible scenarios for releasing significant quantities of hydrogen fluoride and uranium were included in the accompanying safety analysis and environmental assessment. The specific accident scenarios that were considered are summarized below.

1. Criteria: Accident exposure limits at or beyond property

   a. NUREG-1391: 10 mg uranium

   $$25 \text{ mg/m}^3 \ (30 \text{ min}/t)^{0.5} \text{ HF concentration}$$

   t = release time in minutes

2. Natural phenomena

   a. *Earthquakes:* Design parameters (acceleration, amplitude, frequency) based on the estimated worst conditions in the last 500 years.
   b. *Winds:* Design parameters (velocity, rotation, pressure) based on the estimated worst conditions during the last 10,000 years.
   c. *Floods:* Water rise based on heavy precipitation.

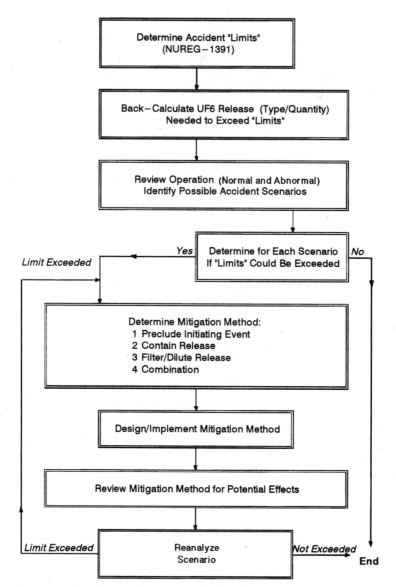

Figure 11.1 Uranium enrichment accident analysis approach.

3. Operating initiators

   a. Criticality: Double contingency principle.
   b. Transportation: Crashes with fuel fire.
   c. Fires: Electric generator fuel tank fire.
   d. UF_6 release

      (1) Liquid UF_6 is contained inside an autoclave. A serious injury and off-site exposure could result in the unlikely event that the autoclave failed to contain UF_6; therefore:

         (*a*) Diverse and redundant temperature, pressure controls
         (*b*) NQA-1 QA program for heater, door interlock, controls

      (2) Process lines and equipment—vacuum system. UF_6 is a solid at room temperature and atmospheric pressure. No potential for a serious injury.

4. Building design: Partial collapse of the building could damage multiple autoclaves and result in the maximum off-site release.

   a. The building structures were designated NQA-1 quality assurance level 2 because they could impact the autoclaves, which are safety class I.

As expected, the remaining (residual) risks to the public from this facility are found to be extremely low. The risk-assessment results also were discussed with LES public relations representatives and regulatory personnel responsible for communicating the risks of the facility to the public.

Issues raised by regulators. Most of the questions raised by regulators of the facility, primarily the NRC, were general in nature and focused on exploring the depth to which LES had gone to meet the regulatory requirements. Examples include the following:

- Details on the building and equipment response to an earthquake, strong winds (e.g., tornado), sudden pipe rupture, and failure of key components in the enrichment process systems
- Facility and effluent treatment systems emissions
- Site preparation and construction environmental effects
- Environmental monitoring programs
- Quality assurance and other management controls
- Nuclear criticality safety
- Decommissioning funding

- Emergency planning
- Physical security
- Nuclear material controls and safeguards

Although the license application identified policies and procedures required to ensure safety and adherence to regulations at the facility, the regulators agreed that the actual implementing procedures did not have to be developed until the start of construction and operation.

Most of the technical issues raised by regulators of the facility, primarily the NRC, centered on containment of the UF_6 when it is in liquid form. UF_6 expands when heated and can exert tremendous hydraulic forces on its container. UF_6 is transported in large cylinders, which are placed inside autoclaves while they are heated from a solid to the liquid and vapor phases. The autoclaves are designed to withstand the pressure that would be exerted if the cylinder or piping were to burst. The regulators focused on the heater instrumentation and control system logic for detecting and responding to process upsets.

Two requests were made for additional analysis on the consequences of specific accident scenarios. One required that the analysis of UF_6 dispersion after a significant accidental release be re-performed using a specific atmospheric modeling condition. That specific atmospheric condition (G stability) is observed in Claiborne Parish for a maximum of 10 minutes a day but is outside the envelope of conditions normally used in atmospheric modeling. The second requested analysis of an additional accident scenario where all nonseismically designed piping was assumed to fail simultaneously and catastrophically. This calculation demonstrated that the plant would not overexpose the public, therefore verifying the adequacy of the design basis to the NRC (500-year return period, nonseismic piping).

Concerned citizens. Typical of any new large industrial project proposed for a relatively small community, there were some members of the public against locating the facility in their community. Also as expected, several national antinuclear groups [e.g., Nuclear Information and Resource Service (NIRS)] tried to use misinformation to delay the project. Fortunately, because a thoughtful and well-planned community outreach program was implemented well before the project was even announced, the local community supported the facility.

The LES partners, which include affiliates of Northern States Power Company, Duke Power Company, Louisiana Power & Light, Fluor Daniel, and URENCO, have a great deal of experience in the design, construction, and operation of nuclear facilities. Consequently, they understand the need to communicate accurately the risks and benefits from the facilities. It also was extremely useful that the LES partner companies had exemplary track records of corporate citizenship and safety in operating nuclear facilities.

A local resident who had the ability to both understand and explain the project effectively was made a community relations representative soon after the project was announced. Later, an information office was opened so that community members could view detailed exhibits and photographs and obtain additional information. Most of the people who visited the office were interested in potential employment opportunities at the facility.

In addition, because no facilities like this one exist in the United States, several trips were sponsored for local residents to see the existing facilities in Gronau, Germany, and Almelo, The Netherlands. Other trips to other nuclear fuel cycle facilities, such as nuclear power plants and nuclear fuel fabrication facilities, were provided as well. In the 19 months between announcement of the project in June 1989 and submittal of the facility license application to the NRC, more than 80 meetings were held to explain the project to residents. Newsletters about the project are distributed to every household in Claiborne Parish, and LES demonstrates its community involvement with donations to enhance economic development and education, improve youth recreation opportunities, and assist in social services. As of this writing the plant is awaiting final license approval from the NRC.

11.8   References

1. R. W. Ormsby et al., *Guidelines for Chemical Process Quantitative Risk Analysis,* Center for Chemical Process Safety of the American Institute of Chemical Engineers, New York, 1989.
2. J. S. Arendt, D. K. Lorenzo, and A. F. Lusby, *Evaluating Process Safety in the Chemical Industry: A Manager's Guide to Quantitative Risk Assessment,* Chemical Manufacturers' Association, Washington, December 1989.
3. V. Covello, P. Sandman, and P. Slovic, *Risk Communication, Risk Statistics, and Risk Comparisons: A Manual for Plant Managers,* Chemical Manufacturers' Association, Washington, 1988.
4. *International Conference on Hazard Identification and Risk Analysis, Human Factors and Human Reliability in Process Safety,* Sponsored by Center for Chemical Process Safety and the American Institute of Chemical Engineers, Health and Safety Executive, United Kingdom, and the European Federation of Chemical Engineering, American Institute of Chemical Engineers, New York, January 1992.
5. R. L. Kotcher, "Turning a Permitting Challenge into an Opportunity," *Chemical Engineering,* pp. 157, 158, 162, March 1993.
6. T. O. Gibson, J. A. Senecal, J. F. Louvar, and D. A. Crowl, *Proceedings of the 27th Annual Loss Prevention Symposium,* American Institute of Chemical Engineers, Safety and Health Division, New York, March 1993.
7. M. E. Kraft, "Perceived Risk, Trust in Government, and Response to Repository Siting in the United States," *High Level Radioactive Waste Management, Proceedings of the Second Annual International Conference,* American Nuclear Society and American Society of Civil Engineers, New York, April 1991.

8. E. Peelle, "The Widening Gap Between Citizens and Experts: Can It Be Bridged?" Oak Ridge National Laboratory, Oak Ridge, Tenn., 1991, unpublished.
9. P. Slovic, M. Layman, and J. H. Flynn, "Risk Perception, Trust, and Nuclear Waste: Lessons from Yucca Mountain," *Environment,* 33(3):6–11, 28–30, 1991.
10. H. Kunreuther and R. Patrick, "Managing the Risks of Hazardous Waste," *Environment,* 33(3):13–15, 31–35, 1991.
11. *Probabilistic Safety Assessment International Topical Meeting Proceedings,* American Nuclear Society, New York, January 1993.
12. I. Rosenthal, "The Corporation and the Community: Credibility, Legitimacy, and Imposed Risk," *Process Safety Progress,* 12(4): 209–215, 1993.
13. S. Jasanoff, "Bridging the Two Cultures of Risk Analysis," *Risk Analysis,* 13(2):123–129, 1993.
14. T. S. Glickman and M. Gough, *Readings in Risk,* Resources for the Future, Washington, 1990.
15. D. von Winterfeldt and W. Edwards, *Decision Analysis and Behavioral Research,* Cambridge University Press, New York, 1992.
16. Outlook Editor, "Crossing Delany: Overhauling Food Safety," *U.S. News & World Report,* October 4, 1993.
17. G. Litsinger, "The Clinton Administration's Pesticide Policy: On Balance, a Nuisance," *Reason,* February 1994, p. 11.
18. N. Basta, "Experts Ponder New Ways to Assess Risk," *Chemical Engineering,* pp. 35, 37, 39, March 1992.
19. R. W. Prugh, "Quantify BLEVE Hazards," *Chemical Engineering Progress,* 87(2):66–61, February 1991.
20. J. Chowdhur, "OSHA Tightens Its Hold," *Chemical Engineering,* 99(5)37–42, May 1992.
21. Ralph Whitaker, "John Sawhill Gets Things Going," *EPRI Journal,* pp. 20–27, September 1991.
22. *Nuclear Waste: DOE Expenditures on the Yucca Mountain Project,* U.S. General Accounting Office, Washington, April 18, 1991.
23. G. King, "Public Communication and Participation Activities in Siting Controversial Facilities in the United States and Western Europe: An Examination of Lessons Learned," *High Level Radioactive Waste Management, Proceedings of the International Topical Meeting,* American Nuclear Society and the American Society of Civil Engineers, New York, April 1990 (also see other papers in this proceedings).
24. M. E. Kraft, "Perceived Risk, Trust in Government, and Repository Siting in the United States," *High Level Radioactive Waste Management, Proceedings of the Second Annual International Topical Meeting,* American Nuclear Society, New York, and American Society of Civil Engineers, Washington, April 1991.
25. J. Flynn, P. Slovic, C. K. Mertz, and W. Burns, "Development of a Structural Model to Analyze Public Opinion on a High-Level Radioactive Waste Facility," *High Level Radioactive Waste Management, Proceedings of the Second Annual International Topical Meeting,* American Nuclear Society and American Society of Civil Engineers, New York, April 1991.
26. P. Slovic, M. Layman, and J. H. Flynn, "Lessons from Yucca Mountain," *Environment,* 33(3):6, April 1991.
27. T. Moore, "The Hard Road to Nuclear Waste Disposal," *EPRI Journal,* pp. 4–17, July-August 1990.
28. *United States Department of Energy Environmental Restoration and Waste Management Five-Year Plan, Fiscal Years 1992–1996,* U.S. Department of Energy, Washington, June 1990.
29. J. D. Watkins, *Nuclear Weapons Complex Reconfiguration Study,* DOE/DP-0083, U.S. Department of Energy, Washington, January 1991.
30. J. A. Davis, "The Wasting of Nevada," *Sierra,* 73(4):30, July-August 1988.
31. Hearing before the Committee on Energy and Natural Resources, United States Senate, on the Department of Energy's Civilian Nuclear Waste Program, *Congressional Record,* March 31, 1992.
32. W. Poole, "Gambling with Tomorrow," *Sierra,* 77(5):50, September-October 1992.

33. F. J. Remick, "How to Spend Wisely," *Probabilistic Safety Assessment International Topical Meeting Proceedings,* American Nuclear Society, New York, January 1993.
34. "Nuclear Industry Wakes Up to Competition, But Is It Too Late," and "Nuclear Leaders Stress Unity in Making Nuclear Competitive," *Nucleonics Week,* p. 9, November 18, 1993.
35. S. McGuire, *Chemical Toxicity of Uranium Hexafluoride Compared to Acute Effects of Radiation,* NUREG-1391, U.S. Nuclear Regulatory Commission, Washington, February 1991.

Index

ABOUT THE EDITORS

ROBERT DESHOTELS is a principal process engineer at Fluor Daniel, Inc., where he has led process engineering and reliability engineering efforts for clients in the manufacturing, petroleum, nuclear, and electric power industries.

ROBERT D. ZIMMERMAN is a principal process engineer at Fluor Daniel, Inc., with more than 20 years of technical and management experience applying risk assessment to Department of Energy–supported fuel-cycle and waste-management projects.